Two Tales of Old Kodiak

Includes

Wreck of the *Rustler*

and

Confessions of a Seal Hunter

By Steve Descloux

With illustrations by Elise Dooley

Here are some stories of Kodiak's not-so-distant past - I hope you find them entertaining -
Best Wishes from
St Descl-

Todd Communications Anchorage, Alaska

Kodiak 2010

TWO TALES OF OLD KODIAK

ISBN: 1-57833-334-2

First Edition 10 9 8 7 6 5 4 3 2 1

Printed April 2006

Printed in the United States of America

Book design by Mike Larsen, Todd Communications

The text of this book is set in Georgia 12 point type

Todd Communications
203 W. 15th Ave. Suite 102
Anchorage, Alaska 99501
Tel. (907) 274-8633
Fax (907) 276-6858
e-mail: sales@toddcom.com
WWW.ALASKABOOKSANDCALENDARS.COM

To the Reader:

This effort began as a simple story about a boat wreck and necessarily evolved into a childhood memoir. It became clear to me early on that a view of 'Old Kodiak' and of the kinds of people who lived there would be necessary in order to understand how such a near tragedy came to be. Exactly what kind of place was Kodiak in the 'old days'? What lured people to this remote island? What made them stay? It is difficult to precisely convey the 'feel' of the town and the mood of the people at that time. Some Kodiak folks may remember it more quaintly, but viewed from my level of society it was as I have described, only more intensely so.

It should also be realized that we four boys who were involved in the *Rustler* incident were already well seasoned and toughened to most of Kodiak's harsh natural environment and routinely made survival a daily game in our play and wanderings. Weather and tides, the predominant natural rulers of all Kodiak Island activities, were not always cooperative with our expeditions and consequently physical discomfort and occasional outright misery became a fact of life for us. It is pretty certain that this conditioning helped us through the hours of cold and fear we endured after *Rustler* wrecked on the rocks.

What we couldn't have prepared for was how we would face our death, because for awhile we were grimly certain that we would be four sodden, surf-pounded little corpses before morning came. I would hope the reader might gain some insight from the details of our experience, of what it might be like to be a part of this sort of calamity. Some of the details were ridiculous and some terrifying but all were vividly seared into memory. It was not my intention to embarrass or scandalize anyone in the telling of the story therefore the name of the skipper and that of his crewman are fictitious.

Steve Descloux - April, 2005

Wreck of the *Rustler*

By Steve Descloux

Chapter **Page**

1. We Move North 9
2. Old Kodiak 14
3. Earthquake...................................... 20
4. Town Life in the Last Frontier 29
5. Kodiak Picnic 33
6. Of Fishing and Survival 45
7. Rustler 51
8. A Christmas Turkey 58
9. The Wreck 67
10. Guardian Angel 72
11. Aborted Escape.............................. 78
12. Freedom Ride 85
13. Rustler's Last Run 89
14. Help Arrives 94
15. Rescue 101
16. Short Ride Home 110
17. Rustler's Final Rest 116

CHAPTER 1
We Move North

In 1957, the year I turned four, my family lived in southwest Washington. My dad, whose real name was Michel but became known as Mitch, was partnered in a two-man gypo logging operation. We lived back in the hills of Dole Valley about thirty miles northeast of Vancouver in Southwest Washington. Our home was an old homestead that had been a part of a timber sale. Since the place had been logged off Dad called it our stump ranch. He took the summer off from logging with his partner Jim Brown, and flew to Alaska to spend a season commercial fishing for salmon with a Washington friend, Bill Wynkoop. Bill was originally from Anacortes. He was raised in an orphanage and had no family. Without anyone really saying so, we became his family. Starting at a young age, long before we knew him, he had traveled up and down the West Coast, trapping and fishing salmon in Alaska, fishing smelt in Washington, or buying Christmas trees in the Northwest and trucking them to sell in Southern California for a very good profit. Bill always had good success with his various endeavors. Once, after an especially good tree season, he actually chartered a cab to drive him from California, twelve or thirteen hundred miles to our place in Dole Valley and arrived as usual with a trunk-load of gifts for all. Another time he brought Ma a brand new console television set. It was a beautiful piece, and Ma was highly pleased, but Bill, being Bill, hadn't stopped to consider that we didn't have electricity back in the hills where we lived.

In Alaska he was known as *Wild* Bill. He was a big rangy German fellow with curly, thinning red hair, squint-wrinkled blue eyes, and ruddy, weathered features. Wild Bill fished salmon around Kodiak Island during the summers. He was a slam-bang boat operator and tended to be rough on the pilings and docks whenever he tied up to deliver his catch, but also a hard fishing skipper who always put in a good season. In later years, Bill helped pioneer the king crab industry with his wooden boat, a very stout old fifty-eight footer named *Sebanus*. Over the years he made virtually millions fishing king crab. Most of his money went into bankrolling the Kodiak bars, liquor stores, hotels and taxi-cabs with his free-spending nature. The bars all had a ship's bell hanging above the bar-top which was a signal to all that the drinks were on the man who rang it. Wild Bill, packing twenty or thirty thousand dollars cash around in a small, zippered Pacific Northern Airlines (PNA) bag, rang the bell plenty for the enthusiastic, cheering crowd. When he grew tired of the night life of Kodiak, he would often come and stay at our house. He and Dad spent weeks at a time in the off-seasons drinking, telling stories and rehashing old arguments.

When Dad went off to Alaska to fish with Bill, my brother Mike, second born son, about fifteen, couldn't stand being left behind in Washington while Dad was gone off to the 'promised land'. One night a week or two after the Old Man left, Mike packed a duffle bag, wrote a note for Ma, and stole away from home. He somehow hitch-hiked the two hundred miles to Seattle, found the headquarters of the cannery that Wild Bill was fishing for, and talked himself into a job as one of the crew on a salmon tender that was heading north to Port Williams on Shuyak Island, which lies off the north end of Afognak Island. The cannery operated a Salmon plant there in a quiet, spruce-timbered bay. It was early in the season and the place was bustling when Mike's tender pulled in and tied up to the barnacle-encrusted pilings supporting the dock. Dad and Bill happened to be in port, standing on the dock watching the proceedings with mild interest when, to their astonishment, Mike appeared over the rail at the top of the ladder. He had his war-bag hung on one skinny shoulder; a .22 rifle slung over the other and was grinning from ear to ear. Needless to say, Dad couldn't be mad and pleased at the same time. If he'd been mad instead, Mike would have been in for the licking of his life. Dad couldn't send him home so Wild Bill hired Mike on as a crewman for a quarter-share. They had a great season, a Huck Finn sort of working vacation with a big bonus payday at its regretful end. Mike had more money in his hands than he'd ever seen. And he'd had the time of his life earning it. He and Dad experienced the pristine nature of the islands and bays and open waters, chasing the wild schools, filling the boat time and again with brailer-loads of madly flapping, squirming, silvery salmon. Brailers so full and heavy the boat laid far over and the rigging strained when they winched it out of the moneybag. They met, and admired the friendly, hearty men and women who made this island wilderness their home. They saw sea mammals they'd only read about in books. They observed abundant game and fish, ducks and ptarmigan, fox and otter. And they got close-up looks at the giant bears. They were spellbound by the fresh ocean atmosphere and untouched wonder of the place.

Dad and Mike never even came back to the States. Dad sold his half of the logging business over the phone to his partner Jim, and Ma got a big check in the mail with a letter from the Old Man saying "to pack up the outfit, rent the place out, and fly on up to Kodiak. We're moving to Alaska. A place where the kids can grow up with real work, earning serious pay, instead of picking beans or strawberries and bucking hay for a few bucks a day in the States. The Alaskan people were all friendly and helpful, the land was vast and beautiful and there was room to breathe. The hunting and fishing weren't bad either." That was in 1957, two years before Alaska became a state.

So Ma made the journey with seven kids in tow, ranging in age about two years apart, Joe at sixteen (who, it might be said, never entirely forgave Mike for leaving him stranded with the family while the younger brother bailed out for Alaska), Linda, a dark haired high school freshman, Janice, a skinny, funny pre-teen with reddy-blonde hair and big blue eyes, David, tow-headed, solemn blue eyes and very quiet, Donna a gangly brown eyed seven year old, myself, often mistaken in Alaska for a little native boy, and Cliffie, who was a chubby baby of two. We flew non-stop to Alaska on PNA from Portland, Oregon. The big, silver Lockheed Constellation with its four shiny propellers and pretty, uniformed stewardesses, droned on with a numbing roar for over 7 hours, crossing the Gulf of Alaska in a straight line between the coast of Oregon and Anchorage. One of the four engines caught fire somewhere over the Pacific and was extinguished and shut down and we limped on into Anchorage on three. There we were bundled onto another big plane for Kodiak where we finally landed and disembarked to a small, one room terminal, crowded with all manner of strange people, all talking loudly to be heard over their own racket. There were men in smelly fishing clothes, their wives or girlfriends, men in suits, cab drivers, Navy sailors, and stocky brown Aleut (*see author's note (1)* men, and their women who wore bright scarves over their shiny black hair. All were packed into and around the little building, yelling over the din, laughing and joking with one another. Everyone seemed to know one another. Baggage carts were dragged over by the airline crew and left near the gravel parking lot for easy access. We used two big taxicabs getting our troupe and baggage the seven miles to the old Kodiak Hotel in the middle of town. There was a merry three-day reunion with Dad and Mike during our stay there, with new and interesting friends stopping in to say hello. I remember the strange linoleum floors in our rooms, (we'd had bare wood floors back home) and windows that afforded a great panorama overlooking busy, potholed streets below, lined with crowded buildings. The blue waters of St. Paul harbor and the backdrop of tawny mountains beckoned from beyond the town.

Dad had lined up a job at a sawmill on Afognak Island where he would end up filling several roles, sawyer, mechanic, cat-skinner, and logger or pretty much whatever was needed at the time. Having previously owned and run his own sawmills he knew about all there was to know about the operation. When all was finally arranged, we left town on a couple fishing boats which moved us, bag, baggage and winter groceries, to our new home at the sawmill camp. Even now whenever I smell coffee in a can, I vividly recall my first Alaska experience, sitting on the galley table on Coogan Fox's boat beside my sister Donna, taking turns barfing into an empty two pound Folgers can while we watched the watery blue horizon disappear sickeningly above, then below the little porthole by the galley sink as the boat rolled in the swells. Sky......sea......sky......sea...... sky......sea....

The mill camp (informally referred to as Annadel for the owner of the mill, Del Valley and his wife Ann), was situated in Afognak Straights less than a mile from the old Aleut village of Afognak, where Native folks had lived for untold years. We were amazed to find hot and cold running water in our house at the camp, and a nice big oil-fired cooking range which also heated the house. A great diesel generator supplied electricity to the camp during the day while the mill was operating, and was left running until about nine o'clock in the evening. This was especially important in winter during the longer nights. There was even an old brightly lighted Wurlitzer juke box in the living room of our house which was filled with 78 RPM records that we played at night while the lights were still on. Every night the generator was shut down at the same time. We usually had the gas lanterns either lit or filled, pumped up and ready to light. The bare, garish electric light bulbs would flicker suddenly, then dim down and die out. A sudden quiet would descend over camp and our home would settle into a mellow, shadowy, dim light which, after a little while, seemed adequately bright. The roar of the lanterns seemed to intensify the quiet. Lights-out meant it was nearly bedtime for us smaller kids. This was real modern living for us!

CHAPTER 2
Old Kodiak

We lived at the mill for about a year, learning new things, wearing off the cheechako title and generally falling in love with Alaska, and then moved into town. Dad had turned up a summer job as a boat mechanic at the San Juan cannery in Uganik Bay on the west side of Kodiak Island. He planned to do freelance engine work on fishing boats in town during the winters. After a few years at San Juan he was promoted to port engineer. He spent eight, five-month summers there, earning the respect of fishermen all over the island by the quality of his work. When Dad let a boat leave the dock it never came back with engine problems. We moved from the mill into Kodiak and set up house at the Pinch Apartments, a single story, four-unit structure with a board-walk down its length front and back. The apartments were located right on the Base-Town road overlooking the small boat harbor in the place where the big new Kodiak Inn was later built. The folks had to rent two of the apartments to fit us all in.

Kodiak was foreign and fascinating to the senses of a five year old boy who had never lived in a town of any kind. There were so many new marvels to take in, so many people, and all a-bustle. Cars, trucks and taxicabs rushed everywhere, raising clouds of gray dust. There were streetlights that lit up the night and shone their greenish light in through the window onto my bed in the apartment. Beach and cannery odors and the tarry stink of creosote oozing from the docks in the hot sun pervaded the air. Adding to the general din of downtown noises, intruded the periodic racket of seaplanes laboring down the channel and into the air, loaded with all manner of people and cargo, or a pile-driver sinking the foundation for a new cannery dock, echoing its whacking rhythm across the waters of St. Paul Harbor. Every day at twelve o'clock the noon whistle went off. It was actually a test of the emergency siren which stood on the hill above town near the cemetery. It was used as a fire alarm and potential disaster warning. The siren was a huge, rotating, yellow horn mounted on a high concrete base which, when switched on, wound up slowly from the deep starting notes which soon climbed in pitch and volume to a high yelling blast that could be heard from miles across the water at Cliff Point if the wind was right. It was always exciting to be walking on Mill Bay Road past the siren when it went off. It was best to cover your ears though, and walk fast before it reached its peak volume. Up close it was so loud it made one dizzy and caused the eardrums to buzz. When it went off at two in the morning to signal a fire it filled me with dread for those whose home was burning.

Soon after moving into Kodiak from Afognak, my brother Dave led me high up the side of Pillar Mountain, which looms immediately above the town. It was one of those warm, breathy days when the world seems to be at peace with itself. We sat back in the deep grasses on the steep side of the mountain and viewed the whole town spread out below with its blue harbors and busy channel. It lay strewn along the rocky beaches, bordering the narrow Near Island Channel. The blue expanse of the small-boat harbor glinted in the sun, squarely bracketed by the long black arms of the two breakwaters, diminishing the small, spidery float system stemming out from the town side beach. Tiny toy boats rested in the stalls and others lay anchored out near the entrance. Lush green islands with rock coastlines protected the town from storms blowing in off the vast Pacific and the Gulf. We could see the sky-blue domes of the Russian Church standing proudly atop the white sanctuary, bearing Heaven-ward the Orthodox crosses. Dave pointed out the Kodiak cemetery on the hill above the town, with its white crosses flowing over the contours of the green hillside. He told me those were white lilies growing there and from this distance I had to believe him. Down off to our right, a few canneries perched high on black wooden pilings above the beaches of St. Paul harbor. They were widely separated and each occupied a stretch of beach and extended out over the water. The docks and canneries were built atop closely-set pilings high above the beach, so that even the biggest spring tides wouldn't reach the dock level. Occasional gouts of white steam escaped from pipes that protruded from corrugated roofs, or from high up on a side wall. The steam floated away on the light breezes, disappearing in the sun. We saw boats soundlessly chugging back and forth, arriving from the fishing grounds or leaving the harbor, towing smooth, sparkling wake-trails behind them. More prominent even than the Russian Church, was the complex of huge fuel and oil storage tanks installed on high bluffs at each end of town. Union Oil on one end and Standard on the other, each with its own fuel dock built out from the beach directly below the tanks.

We often heard the term 'Old Kodiak' voiced by elderly Native friends as if it didn't exist anymore. They were the stalwarts of the island, remnants of an earlier time. I can still see my mother, half their age, at the kitchen table having tea with some of the older ladies and enjoying their friendly, animated conversation. They all wore gay, colored scarves over their hair and made great ritual of removing them when they came inside, then donning, tying and adjusting them just so as they said their good-byes. 'Old Kodiak' was already gone, existing only in their stories.

Kodiak was a warren of old wooden buildings and houses, jammed together and crowded along pot-holed gravel streets and roads, some of which were laid out along trails originally established by cattle. In the town's earlier days stock had ranged freely around the town and established convenient paths for man and beast. Kodiak was a busy, primary Alaskan port for decades after the territory was purchased from Russia. Winters were always hard. With most seasonal work finished, very little other work or money was available. The local people holed up as best they could, subsisting mainly on dried or salt salmon and fresh game, local beef and garden vegetables. When we moved to Kodiak, the town was supplied by ship, which docked about once a month. Having been raised on powdered milk and 'yukon eggs' (eggs shipped from the states were already a month old by the time they reached Kodiak), my first breakfast with fresh farm milk straight from the cow, and eggs right from the hen's butt when I was twelve was undertaken with some amount of finicky disgust. When they arrived, the supplies and 'fresh' food-stocks were bought up rapidly when money was available. Kodiak survived in a continuous tide of boom and bust. "*Chicken today, guts and feathers tomorrow.*" That was how my Dad described it. But the town always came back. What choice was there? Many folks evacuated the island during a long bust, but a small core of barnacles always managed to eke it out until the next windfall circumstances successfully intervened and put the town back on its feet again.

In the early nineteen-forties, with war thundering over Europe, it became clear that the United States might become involved and could possibly be invaded through Alaska. As a result a mighty flotilla of military arrived, making a beach landing near the tiny town. They brought trucks and bulldozers, cement mixers and civilian contract labor in droves. Many of these people became permanent citizens of Kodiak Island. The buildings of the town at that time were fairly spread out, being concentrated mainly along the Near Island Channel and thinning back across the flat toward Pillar Mountain and up the slope to the north. Some of the buildings were built by Baronov himself in the early days of Russian possession in the late 1700s. When the Army moved in, Kodiak found itself perched on the edge of an unprecedented boom, the results of which would last for decades and fix Kodiak solidly on the world map.

With the influx of tens of thousands of troops at the height of their stay, plus the contract workers and their families, the town inevitably and rapidly expanded. Now everyone was working long hard hours, year 'round. Shipping improved and groceries and supplies became more readily available. Money flowed like quicksilver into the coffers of merchants and bar owners alike. Soon new establishments sprang from the ground, filling in the gaps between the older buildings and swelling the town proper. A government housing project of more than 250 single-dwelling homes, later known as the Aleutian Homes, was laid out and installed just north of town. Here lived most of the families of the stateside civilian labor required to build the roads, reservior, bases, bunkers, gun emplacements and massive radio towers. They excavated and built artillery emplacements high on top of ragged cliffs, hundreds of feet above the beaches, each commanding a wide view of the ocean approaches to the island. Kodiak merchants continued to invest in the town, the liquor trade shifted into high gear, bars closing their doors only long enough to count the money, inventory the liquor and have the place swamped out. Commercial fishing went on pretty much as usual, but now steaming about the island under the scrutiny of artillery binoculars and avoiding areas declared by the military as Restricted.

Ten or twelve years later, in the Fifties, the Army having moved out, being replaced by a much smaller contingent of the Navy, Kodiak's population had shriveled considerably. But commercial fishing was on the upswing with the budding new king crab industry, shrimp and other fisheries being virginally developed. Seafood processing equipment, and the process itself, was in a continual state of re-invention. There was a new influx of Asian families, mostly from the Philippines, who came for the steady, mundane work of processing hundreds of tons of seafood each year. Work that was shunned by most local men, white and Aleut alike, unless they were down on their luck and needed a quick town job until the next fishing boat called for a crewman. The canneries were desperate for dependable employees and fortune led them to the Philippine Islands where millions were unemployed and those who were lucky enough to have a job earned 'guts and feathers' wages. For the Asians, the work in Alaskan seafood and the income was a huge step up from living conditions in their mother countries and they faithfully sent most of their money home to their parents, ensuring a better life for the extended family. Without these people, the canneries could never have produced the record shattering numbers Alaska bragged about to the world. The town seldom slept during the boom of this exploitation, which infused big dollars from the states and made Kodiak the number-one fishing capital of the nation for years in pounds caught, processed and shipped. By now few empty places remained for building new establishments in town unless an existing one burned down. The old buildings remained in service until 1964 when I was ten. That was the year the big Alaska earthquake and its catastrophic tsunamis stirred old downtown Kodiak like a kettle of reheated venison stew. After a gigantic cleanup, and several years of operating from small, temporary plywood structures, the town was laid out along straighter lines and the bar owners, merchants, and local industry began to rebuild Kodiak.

CHAPTER 3
Earthquake

It was about 5:30 in the afternoon on a cool, sunny day in March when the big quake rippled and rumbled across Alaska, wreaking havoc on us all. Less than an hour before it struck, my little brother Cliff, our buddies, Billy Gregory and Pete Fuller and myself had been playing out on the west breakwater of the harbor. We were about halfway out the long jetty, crawling in and out of the crannies and holes between the gigantic boulders, hiding from one another and looking for fishing lures or other treasures that someone may have dropped. Large Norwegian wharf rats skittered out of sight, squeaking at our intrusions as they fled. Gulls floated by at eye-level, chuckling at us and monitoring our activities for signs of a hand-out. Billy suddenly froze and looked at his watch with a worried frown and declared that he had to get home for dinner. His folks were strict about him being home on time. So we all dragged reluctantly home too.

At the time, we lived in a small duplex known as the Fannin Apartments, across from the bottom of Cope Street right next to the Base-Town road. The place was about two hundred feet back from the harbor and at maybe fifty feet elevation. After eating supper, Dave and I wandered down to the beach with full bellies to poke lazily around in the drift, looking for anything new from the last high tide. Dave was stepping over a small drift log and suddenly he teetered backward, arms flailing, then sat down hard on the sand. I sensed a deep rumbling from somewhere and then realized dizzily that the ground was moving under my feet. My first thought was that a huge ship had run aground nearby. I had never heard of earthquakes, and nothing in my young experience gave me a clue to what was happening. Dave, though, jumped to his feet and hollered *"Run! Head for the house!"* I was right behind him as he scrambled up over the inshore boulders of the breakwater and ran for the near-vertical footpath which led up the bluff to a road above. We tackled the familiar, steep trail at a pell-mell run and I felt the ground ripping and grinding under my feet as we climbed. As the terrifying subterranean rumble continued, my hair bristled and my feet flew. When we reached the road we turned around, gasping for breath, to look again from a height of perhaps forty feet above the harbor. Huffing and puffing, we gaped toward the harbor and saw the fishing boats careening around in their stalls, rocking violently in rough, chaotic water. Some of their masts actually clashed and tangled across the floats. The water was draining rapidly from the harbor and I saw three skiffs, tied up to a floatplane dock in the corner directly below us, that were sucked back so strongly their bow painters (ropes) were straining. As I watched, one of the ropes snapped and a skiff was carried swiftly away toward the harbor entrance. Suddenly, right before our eyes, the middle section of the west breakwater collapsed. Fractured rock and gray dust blew up and outward over the harbor with a deafening racket like the sound of a gigantic anchor chain being dropped onto the concrete floor of an empty aircraft hangar, the sound racketing back and forth over the town. I was suddenly glad that Billy had been punctual about his suppertime or we might have been still playing out there. There were fishing boats floating free, bumping along the breakwater, drifting toward the entrance in the powerful suck of the receding water. Even the channel was draining. We didn't linger very long to watch, but headed ourselves home again on the double. The ground was still rolling and groaning violently under us, electric poles and lines swayed wildly overhead and spruce trees were whipping madly about, slapping the ground. Just as we reached the corner of our house the quake stopped. The sudden silence and the solid stillness of the ground stopped us in our tracks. *"What the heck was that!?"* We went on up the steps and into the house where Ma and Joe, with his infant son Douglas, Donna, Cliff and Janice and her friend Mary Griggs were still staring at one another in a wild sense of shock. Dad was having a drink or two in the B&B bar across town when the quake hit and we all chuckled later to hear of the bartender, Holley Evans, frantically doing his best to save the booze as the bottles toppled from the shelves behind the bar and crashed to the floor during the quake. He finally gave up trying to fill his arms and started passing out bottles to the customers for 'safekeeping'.

At home we saw men and women running into the streets exclaiming this and that. I remember one lady who wandered up and down the middle of the road, wringing her hands and repeating shrilly over and over that we were all going to die. We heard a few voices shouting *"Get to high ground!"* This was good advice. Ma and Joe and Janice and Mary held a brief conference and it was decided that Cliff and I were to head for high ground immediately. We had to cross town to reach the bottom of Mill Bay Road, which ran uphill from town. We didn't hang around and ask questions but did as we were told and started right off. The Base-Town Road dipped a little as it approached Kraft's supermarket, then a recently-built, single story cinderblock building with tiled concrete floors. As we hurried down the slight dip we encountered sea water flowing steadily into town like an incredibly fast moving high-tide. We could see that it wasn't very deep. Cars and trucks were moving along the submerged streets, so we waded right in and kept to our course. We'd waded rivers before. Kraft's parking lot was nearly empty of cars, but we saw people like ourselves, slogging through the knee-deep oily water that was flowing slowly but steadily uptown. Pallets, lumber, empty drums and litter of all sorts drifted along with us as we made our way toward Mill Bay Road and higher ground. The noon whistle began growling loudly from the hill above town. It wound up slowly to the high, yelling blast we were so familiar with but somehow with a very urgent difference. Its noise covered all other sounds and brought a sense of impending doom over all activity. I saw some adults passing us nearby and they had worried frowns. The siren prolonged its baleful warning for about a minute, then fell off slightly and wound right back up again, repeating over and over and over- OOOOOOOOOOo ooooooOOOOOOOOOOOoooooooooo!, until after five or ten minutes it finally wound on down to a stuttering finish. I was glad it stopped. It drilled fear into my heart. Besides what more warning did anyone really need than the vicious shaking we'd all just felt. Cliff and I didn't know exactly where to go. Ma's main concern had been to get us out of harm's way immediately while the rest of them packed up some food and blankets in case things didn't settle down right away. They hadn't decided yet where they would go, but she knew we could fend for ourselves. There was no time to locate Dad, but before she left home Ma tacked a note to the door telling him where the family would be.

Just as Cliff and I slogged out of the water at the far end of town near the police station a taxi stopped alongside and someone called us by name. It was Janice and Mary in the back seat with baby Doug. The cabbie was on his way home to pick up his wife and two little boys and had stopped for Janice and Mary, then Cliff and me when they saw us. The cab crawled along in a continuous line of other cars up through the Aleutian Homes to the cab driver's house. We were out of view of town now. At every house on the street was a chaotic loading of cars, parents yelling for their kids, dogs barking and howling. It was all very unreal. An hour ago Dave and I had been playing on the beach in a quiet afternoon and now the whole town was in high gear, dogs and all. A deeply felt suspense pervaded over all. No one was laughing. Who knew what could come next. Working fast, the cabbie filled the trunk with what he seemed to think was needed then brought out his wife and two kids. They crowded into the front seat and Janice and Mary and Cliff and I (and Doug) occupied the back. Janice and Mary took turns either holding the baby or providing a lap for Cliff to sit on. I was jammed against the right rear door and occasionally spelled Janice and Mary by holding Doug.

We joined another long, slow procession of vehicles headed for the top of Pillar Mountain, coming at long last to a halt near the city reservior, far down from the crest. Apparently the line extended clear to the summit, the site of a White Alice, Distant Early Warning station where three broad, towering antennas presided, and where every spot level enough to park a car was now occupied. Our place in line was directly adjacent to the huge wooden water tank which sat about fifty feet back from the road. We couldn't see town from there but we were safe enough on the shoulder of the mountain. I didn't like thinking about what might happen to the tank, and us, if the earth started shaking again. We spent most of the night parked there, listening to the busy cab radio, feeding and changing the babies and talking quietly. The radio gave forth eyewitness accounts of people still in the vicinity of the town and on boats heading for the relative safety of deep water. One man was bravely holding forth from the second floor of the Donnely Building (the old Post Office) just a stone's throw above the Near Island Channel. He described the situation as best he could. It was a black night and the power was out. Most of what he reported described the sounds he was hearing as the tsunamis roared through one by one, gutting the channel of its docks, canneries, stores and homes. He told of the horrible splintering crashes and the groans of the cannery, the Donnely & Atcheson store, and the fuel dock being torn from their perches on wooden pilings directly below his fearful haven. The thundering of the giant waves when they came in made his voice shaky, *"I hear another wave coming up the channel and....."* He was uncertain about staying put but was also afraid to try getting out. We also heard strident calls from boat radios, patched through the Cab dispatch radio. *"Yeah, Rosario Straights! Rosario Straights!, Y' pick me up Mike?"*

We heard this dreadful, empty call often throughout the night, the strong signal making the needle jump emphatically on the tiny horizontal meter of the radio. No one ever answered the call. Many of the transmissions were scratchy and unintelligible, but all invoked a sense of dread in us for the lives of men on boats out there in that dark, uncertain night.

About three in the morning things seemed to have quieted down and we could sense that it was over. The Cabbie jockeyed the big car out of our place in line, turned around and drove the high ground over to Mission Road which follows the Kodiak coastline north from town out to Spruce Cape. He parked on a high bluff out near the Cape and we sat looking out over the black waters. All that could be seen was the running lights on a few boats moving around out there in the darkness. One boat came slowly drifting past, just below us, its cabin lights on, listing well over on its side with the mast light close to the water. We could tell that one side of the cabin was under. I could see shadowy debris bobbing in the water in the reflection of its dim cabin lights. As we watched the boat, it seemed for a second to be righting itself, then it soundlessly slipped under, the cabin lights diminishing as she sank, mast light winking out and total darkness closing off the vision. We had no idea whether anyone was aboard but we fervently hoped not. We slept intermittently and when I last awoke dawn had come. I couldn't make myself believe what I was seeing. My whole world had changed. Everywhere I looked floated the debris of Kodiak. Huge mixed rafts of shattered pilings, pallets and oil drums, half sunk boats, fully intact uninhabited boats, loose skiffs and lumber floated everywhere, from near at hand, below the bluffs where we stood, and stretching far out toward the north end of Woody Island. Whole buildings, with only the roofs showing, drifted on the quiet tide among the rafts of loose debris. It was dead calm and there was a flat, oily sheen on the water everywhere. The incredible scene was made even more eerie by a stillness that seemed to press in upon us as we stood beside the cab, gaping and shivering in the early morning air.

The cabbie had learned by radio that an emergency shelter had been set up at the high school and he dropped us there on his way to see if his home had survived. After thanking the driver and his wife for sharing his cab with us, Janice, Mary, Cliff and I and the baby, found our way to the gymnasium where the entire floor was taken up with spread blankets, people sleeping or milling around. Even the bleachers were full. The continuous din of subdued talk filled the echoing gym with the multitude of voices. There was an ongoing breakfast being served upstairs in the cafeteria. After creeping along in a seemingly endless line, we gratefully sat down to oatmeal mush and dry toast, and as we finished the meal Joe found us there. We'd had no idea where the rest of the family had gone last night, but trusted their good sense to get them out of harm's way. It turned out they'd hiked up to a house at the top of Carlsen hill, high above the Aleutian homes, where we'd once lived. The house was vacant and open, but they'd spent most of the night around a warm fire in the yard, mostly worrying about the rest of us. Dad had somehow made it home and found Ma's note and joined them on Carlson hill that evening.

Ma was with Joe when he found us at the cafeteria, and we left the chaos of the high school and headed home on foot to see if any thing was still standing. The main part of town was impassable and nearly unrecognizable. There was a yellow rope barricade already strung from building to building, surrounding the worst of the damage. U.S. Marine guards were stationed around the rope perimeter, armed with M-1 rifles and warned everyone away, preventing people from injury and also potential looters from rummaging through the debris. Smashed and broken buildings rested at odd angles and in unlikely places, some with exterior walls ripped off, indecently exposing their once private interiors. Furniture in one of these remained seemingly unmoved, paintings and pictures still hung askew on the walls. One building displayed a second floor bathroom, with the toilet oddly perched at the ragged edge of a missing wall, its drain pipe dangling nakedly beneath. Cars and trucks could be seen mangled underneath and among the wreckage. A dozen or more fishing boats, large and small, were scattered helter-skelter among the debris. Some were upright, like *Selief,* an eighty-six foot power-scow, grounded nearly a quarter-mile from the harbor, just below the public school house. Some of the boats were scattered among the debris, seemingly untouched. Others were laid over like dead whales, some with ragged black holes in their red hulls.

Our house was at the far end of town and we were forced to make our way up the flank of Pillar Mountain, skirting the rope barricade. We worked our way along the high streets, up long flights of steps, and through the yards of people fortunate enough to live above the reach of the tsunamis. They were all very neighborly about the trespass. Everyone was still in a state of shock and denial at the grim scene below. I fully expected to find our home in the same condition as the buildings of town, since it was located near the water although at some little elevation. But to our happy surprise it was completely intact. We were all alive and untouched.

For many months afterward the stories flew thick and fast. The Kodiak Mirror presses had been destroyed but for a while they continued to put the news out on mimeographed sheets, telling the tales and providing pertinent information for the town. The whole town chuckled about Fritz Deveau's remarkable resurrection. Apparently Fritz had been on a Good Friday spree all day uptown and was passed out drunk on his little fishing boat in the harbor when the quake rumbled through. His boat was tied up outside another boat, which was tied to the floats. He slept right through the utter calamity and chaos of the event. The skipper of the boat he was tied to, figuring no one was aboard, cut Fritz's lines loose and got his own boat headed out to sea. The little boat with the sleeping man on board had apparently drifted out on the strong ebb of water receding from the harbor and channel. He must have been in deep water when the tsunamis rolled in and his boat simply rose over them as they passed beneath.

Fritz woke up sometime the next day, shaky and hung over. He emerged from the cabin to stare around him unbelievingly. What was he doing drifting around out by Cape Chiniak? No doubt shaking his head and trying to remember all that he did the day before, he fired up the engine and headed back for town. Soon he began to encounter strings of debris, drawn out on the tide. Then he came upon oil slicks and more debris. He motored into the harbor with wide eyes and gaping mouth, staring around him at the wreckage and destruction everywhere. We heard that, for awhile at least, he swore off the sauce and started going to church again. Not all were so fortunate as Fritz and, though few people died in the disaster, many lost their homes and businesses and boats. The town of Kodiak was changed forever but the people were the same, picking up the pieces and immediately beginning to rebuild, some operating for years out of temporary plywood buildings.

CHAPTER 4
Town Life in the Last Frontier

Before the quake though, there were dozens of narrow, litter-strewn alleys between the bars, cafes and stores, where kids collected pop bottles for movie money or candy. A movie ticket at the Orpheum was thirty-five cents. A quart pop bottle was worth five cents at the small bottling plant right there in town known as The Creamery. Sixteen ounce bottles brought three cents and the twelve-ouncers, which were always the most plentiful, two cents. This enterprise not only got us into the movies but gave us a leg up on understanding story problems in grade school math. As kids do, we roamed and played pretty much at will around the town, up the steep sides of Pillar Mountain, or along the beaches and docks, with never a thought of harm from anyone. Kodiak had a curfew of ten p.m. for younger kids and it was enforced by the city police who brought home many a kid who may, or may not, have been up to mischief about town. The alleyways we knew so well from collecting pop bottles for movie money during the day, also served as emergency ditching corridors when the movies let out after curfew, and a cop car was spotted en-route home. If you could make it into the alley you were essentially home free. Our feet knew the way at a flat-out run through the dark, littered passages. Either the police never chased us, or they were so far behind we never heard their footsteps.

My folks never bought a home in Kodiak, but rented various

interesting houses around town. One of the homes, before the quake, was a white, two storied, five bedroom house situated diagonally across the intersection from the Russian Orthodox Church. The house, owned by the church was built using the same squared-log construction as Baronov's trading post. It was similarly finished on the outside with white shiplap siding and dark green trim. On the inside it had painted wainscoting topped by a narrow shelf, and flowered wall paper. It was known as the Malutin house and was steeped in early Kodiak history, having been originally used as the Russian priest's rectory. Mission Road was still a cow path when the house was constructed. When we moved in, there were five or six wooden coffins of various sizes stored by the church in the dim, roomy attic. Fine, gray volcanic dust lay inches thick in the back recesses of the open framing, having filtered in during the thick, three-day fallout from Mount Katmai in 1912. It was a big, creepy room, full of dark shadows and darker, threatening shapes back in the recesses. We rented directly from the pastor of the church who everyone knew as Father Stermer. I remember him as a towering, rotund man in a long black robe. He had a full beard of flowing black and white whiskers that lay like a hairy pillow over a good part of his ample chest. He always wore a funny little hat very straight on his round head and a large, gold, Orthodox crucifix that hung below his beard and gleamed beautifully against the black of his garment. Although no one seemed to give it much thought at the time, we were living in Kodiak at the end of one historical era and the beginning of another.

Sometimes we lived on the fringes of Kodiak and sometimes right in the town itself. In those days my dad was half fisherman and half boat mechanic. I think at least one of the reasons we lived near town so much was so he could be close to the harbor, where he performed as precision work on marine gas and diesel engines as could be accomplished while 'standing on his head in the bilge'. He was one of the most trusted boat mechanics in Kodiak for many years. His mechanical skill and the dependability of his repairs no doubt saved lives at sea. Dad wouldn't let a skipper have his boat back until he was personally satisfied with its engine performance, often after several sea-trial runs, fine tuning everything to get it running *exactly* right. My little brother Cliff and I knew many of the fishermen who kept their boats in the harbor because they often visited Dad at our house when they had engine trouble with their boat. My mother Helga was a full-blooded Swede with remarkably pretty blond hair, laughing blue eyes, and the gentlest of natures. She was equally good to everyone who visited our house. She always had a big pot of something savory on the stove and fresh bread or baking powder biscuits and wild berry jelly to go with it. No visitor ever left our home with an empty belly. I think one of the reasons Dad got a lot of his work was because of her famous cooking. Ma, thankfully for all, wasn't much inclined to drinking. Kodiak in those days was still very much a frontier town, isolated from even the slightly more civilized communities on mainland Alaska. It was a rough place where commercial fishing was the main livelihood, and the booze business ran the close second. Or, maybe it was the other way around. My dad, like most, worked hard in the one industry and drank hard in the other. Virtually all fishing business was conducted in the bars, and often these 'meetings' overflowed to our house. These occasions may have been loud, musical and boisterous, but these tough fishermen, Aleut or White, and their wives or lady-friends, nearly always behaved well and were genuine and courteous. My dad had earned these men's respect over the years with his generous and helping nature when money was scarce and their boats needed work, and though he was a small man, they also respected his lightening-like, pile-driver fists in various and not infrequent altercations with many of them. I never heard of any man that tangled with my dad once who came back looking for more. They all knew that he wouldn't put up with any unsociable behavior, drunk or sober, in our home and almost all behaved well when they visited our house.

Drinking seemed pretty normal to me because it was such an inherent part of our life growing up. Even as a kid I was wise to many of its traits. Although drinking was a rampant local pursuit around the whole island, most people were pretty careful with booze on boats if travel was planned. Responsibility for other's lives was a seriously accepted part of a man being the skipper of any vessel. Women and kids were especially regarded as special cargo, needing an eye kept on them for their safety. A skipper who was casual with these unwritten rules was viewed askance by any seasoned fisherman looking for a crew berth. Good hands considered him a Jonah, an accident waiting for a place to happen, and avoided his boat.

CHAPTER 5
Kodiak Picnic

There was a three day boat trip to the Uganik Bay cannery one year at the close of salmon season when I was about twelve. Cliff and I, and our two friends, George and Mike Eckenberg, were invited to go along on a trip by Carl Warner, the skipper of an Alaska Packers Association company salmon seiner. Carl was a friend of the folks and had been a visitor at our home many times. George and Mike's mother was a long time friend of the skipper and also a friend of my folks. Molly was a tiny, wiry Aleut woman with an impish sense of humor and clubbed black hair. She had lost her husband Lucky (Ersel) some years before when his boat, *Barracuda*, rolled over in the deep surf, right in front of their cabin at Tiger Spit on Raspberry Island. Molly had been on the boat when it capsized, and for some reason made it to the beach alive when no one else did. George and Mike, small boys, were waiting for them to anchor up and come ashore, and had witnessed the tragedy. They had stayed with us in town for a week or so after the accident and we four boys had bonded quickly as friends. Carl had looked out for them in the years since and helped out when he could, sometimes taking the boys out to his trapping cabins for a few days, or on short trips on his boat. He was making this Uganik trip to settle his account with New England Fish Company at the San Juan cannery, for fuel and groceries he'd purchased on credit from his competitors a few times during the season when he was fishing in that area. He thought it would be fun for us kids to ride along. We knew it would be a three-day picnic. We knew his boat. *Pheasant* was a cocky, well-kept little thirty six foot, wooden, bay-seiner, painted orange with black trim, the APA company colors. We were about as excited as four adventurous boys can be in anticipation of a three day boat journey, with plenty of new wildlife to see and halibut or cod to catch and eat. *And* we would finally get to visit the Uganik cannery. Carl asked Dad for the okay to take us along, who, after several agonizing questions about where we were going, and how long would we be gone, and who would be on board, finally told him *"Sure they can go, they'll have a ball, they might even learn somethin'."* At that moment we loved the Ol' man, but tried not to show any childish excitement, which we considered unmanly. Without actually saying so, Dad was entrusting Carl with the lives of his two youngest kids. Even at our young age we understood the unspoken part of the conversation. Carl was honor-bound to keep us safe and to bring us back in one piece.

On board *Pheasant,* the crew consisted of Bill Young, a middle-aged man with a balding head who looked to me like he'd worked over-time in the Breakers Bar stopping fists with his crooked nose, but who had the comical, infectious disposition of a rowdy teen. Next was Al Truitt, a stoutly-built, misplaced Tlinget Indian, originally from Southeast Alaska. Al was characteristically stoic and guttural when he spoke, but congenial enough and gruffly helpful to us kids on the boat. The third man was Dave Lindberg, a fairly new Alaskan from Hayfork, California and quite probably the hairiest man we'd ever seen. Dave was about twenty years old and, in those pre-Hippy days, had a beard that rivaled those of the Bible prophets and hair that had grown ragged and long through the summer salmon season. Dark, burly hair even sprouted from around his collar above his tee-shirt. He wore wobbly, black-framed glasses loosely on his nose and tended to be pretty quiet, like Al. We boys found him to be a highly interesting specimen. Dave was the green man on the boat with only the past salmon season under his belt. Carl and the others called him 'Crosspatch', apparently in some kind of derogatory jest, claiming he was growing all that hair to stuff a crosspatch mattress. Whatever that might have been was beyond our imagination, but Crosspatch he was and we immediately took liberties with his nickname.

The Skipper, Carl, was an occasional visitor at our home and so were Bill and Al. Cliff and I, and more importantly our parents, knew and trusted these men. If we hadn't, we would never have set foot on board their boat. Not even if it were tied to the floats in the harbor, except maybe to sell a newspaper. Dad had warned us about a few skippers and told us to stay off their boats. Carl was a compact, powerfully built man with short, wavy, salt-and-pepper hair that stood straight up on his head and made him look as if he were continually facing a stiff wind. He wore tiny, gold-framed spectacles that perched partway down his nose, the fine wire temples of which splayed outward around his beefy head and somehow remained hooked over his ears. He had a way of peering over the glasses directly into your eyes when he was talking to you, his gray-black eyebrows animating his speech. His dark eyes seemed to reflect capability, and concern, and friendliness. Like the others, Carl was weathered and robust, steady on his feet and as tough as they come. To a man they were all quick to correct us kids if we were doing something clownish or unsafe on the boat. The seriousness of the offense seemed to temper the gravity of the correction we suffered.

Mike received a direct lesson in safety soon after we'd passed through the channel leaving town. We were approaching Spruce Cape, where Carl would thread *Pheasant* through the reefs and rock-piles near shore, round the northern headlands, and adopt a westerly heading to line up on Split-Rock at the entrance to Ouzinkie Narrows. We boys had been cutting bottom-fish on the hatch, which we planned to use later that day as bait for halibut. There was a mess of fish guts and blood on the hatch and deck so Mike untied the deck bucket rope from the cleat on the portside mast stay, stepped with the galvanized pail to the railing and, holding the rope in one small fist, dropped it overboard to fill it. We older boys didn't think too much about it, we were scraping the heads and guts toward the scuppers with the deck brush and our boots, laughing and talking. We'd all used the deck bucket to get seawater for cleaning up our slippery messes or priming the manual pump mounted to the deck behind the wheelhouse on most boats. But we had never drawn water up while the boat was underway. It didn't occur to us that the boat moving through the water would create a very powerful reverse drag on the bucket when it filled.

Crosspatch suddenly appeared on deck among us and in one snatch had Mike upside down under his left arm, while his right hand caught the rope on the bucket and bent it over the rail to stop its escape. He'd reached Mike just as the bucket had filled and began to pull him aft. His quick move saved the bucket and maybe Mike too. Dave swatted Mike hard on the ass and set him on his feet and then proceeded to bawl out the four of us. Ol' Crosspatch made certain, in serious and audible tones, that we understood the danger. *"Whatinhell's goin' on out here? You guys tryin' to get yerselfs killed!?"* Then in somewhat milder speech he proceeded to show us how to throw the bucket forward, in the direction the boat was traveling, and upside down so that it would fill when the air bubble inside flipped it over and it began sinking. When it was full, if your timing was accurate, it had drifted back to your position at the rail where you had to snatch it up hand over hand, straight out of the water before the pull on the bucket started to work against you. Dave made us perform the maneuver several times until we'd sloshed enough water on ourselves in landing the bucket and proved we could get it right. Then he told us that *under no circumstances* were we to use the deck bucket unless one of the crew was on deck. And we didn't. It terrified us to think of being pulled overboard, or worse yet, losing the deck bucket. Those fishermen, unmarried roughnecks to a man, treated us more like men than boys and it swelled our young chests with feelings of maturity, and responsibility, and camaraderie.

In those days, for a deck bucket, most boats carried a standard galvanized milk pail with a sturdy steel handle. On a small boat the bucket did double-duty as everything imaginable from priming the deck pump or washing down the deck or fish-hold, adding coolant to the engine and serving as a very effective bailer when the skiff was swamped. The bucket's lowest position on board was its use as a crude and uncomfortable cousin to the chamber pot, usually required when traveling, or in rough weather when 'hanging it over the rail' wasn't advisable. In those days, before regulations were invented to discourage folks from using the ocean as a toilet, it was common practice when the urge struck, to draw a little water in the bucket from over the side, plunk it down on deck behind the cabin and take care of your business, sometimes hanging on with both hands to stay upright in rough weather, and usually suffering not only exposure to the elements, but ribald comments, air fanning, and nose holding from the rest of the crew. This may sound disgusting, but it was quite practical and downright necessary. It was never prudent to put more than two or three inches of water in the bottom of the bucket because things dropped into deep water tend to *splo-osh*. When you were finished, and had poured the contents overboard, it was considered bad manners if you didn't give the bucket a final rinse before re-securing it in its place.

To us boys, with our school year not yet started, and to Carl and the crew with their salmon season just finished, it was a fun-packed trip and a great time for all. We passed through places rare and beautiful to kids normally cooped up in the same ol' town. We lay over the bow mesmerized by the antics of the black and white porpoises playing in front of the boat, sometimes finning swiftly mere feet ahead of us, blowing their breath in our faces, and other times streaking like torpedoes across the bow. We saw pods of killer whales blowing as they moved along the sheltered, easy currents along the shoreline, hunting or traveling. We all made great effort to be the first to spot and identify seals, sea otters and sea-lions, and myriad seabirds of every description. Fat black puffins with brightly colored clown-faces fled in panic as the boat approached, traveling rapidly sometimes a quarter-mile across the water, attempting to get airborne and usually compromising by suddenly ducking under the water in desperation. Crosspatch explained that the birds were so full of little fish their short wings wouldn't lift them. We always laughed as the puffins flapped rapidly across the water, their wings as much in the water as in air and occasionally bouncing crazily off the waves, becoming briefly airborne. Deer or fox moved along the beaches, stopping to gaze unafraid at the boat as we churned on past, close ashore. The stiff westerly breezes ruffled the waters in ragged streaks of deep royal blue, sparkling in the sun, deepening the hue of the sky. We drew in lungfuls of heady, pure air, clean of the smell of town.

From Ouzinkie Narrows, *Pheasant* traveled westerly across inner Marmot Bay and into Whale Passage, a narrow gut about a mile long and maybe half that wide. This passage is situated between the high, timbered hump of Whale Island, and the hilly Kodiak mainland. Here the huge Cook Inlet tides pour back and forth every six hours like a swollen river, spinning the cold, green brine into sucking whirlpools and sudden, frothy tide rips around submerged rocks and shallows. The churning water made soft *slu-u-u-cking* sounds along *Pheasant's* hull as it tugged erratically at us with a sullen power that pulled eerily at the boat and put an uneasy tension in our stomachs. To the west, Whale Pass empties into wider Kupreanof Strait, stretching for several miles between steep mountains like a Norwegian fjord. As we traveled the length of this strait past the Port Bailey cannery, the blue-green blanket of spruce timbering the surrounding hills gradually petered out to a scattered few. The open areas among the sparse trees were covered with countless acres, square miles, of head-high grasses, salmonberry brush, fireweed and pushki, a broad leafed, tube stalked plant with skin blistering sap, all of which were still verdant in blending shades of green even though summer was at its end. We knew these hillsides were lush grazing pastures for Kodiak bears in the spring and summer. Their dark trails were easy to see crossing and climbing the slopes. Vast thickets of tag alder softened the steep ravines under a continuous canopy of leaves, each ravine containing a brawling, frothing creek working overtime to empty the high valleys of snowmelt. The tall fireweed was in full blush, mingling tinges of deep pink among the greens of the windswept slopes. Rounding Outlet Cape, Kupreanof opens to the southeast into Viekoda Bay and within it, Terror Bay. In good weather or a favorable swell one could cross the mouth of Viekoda and travel around the outer end of Uganik Island, then down into Uganik Bay. We were headed for the cannery which was situated up inside the sheltered East Arm of the bay, but this was a fun trip and there was no hurry so Carl took the longer route around the island, down the sheltered waters of Terror Bay.

In the early afternoon *Pheasant* idled into a small, breezy bight down inside Terror Bay. Crosspatch dumped the anchor overboard to the accompanying rattle of chain through the chock, Carl backed the boat to set the hook, and the engine was shut down. For a little while the sudden silence and the sunny beauty of the little bay seemed to require our equally silent attention. But not for long. There were fish to catch and soon we had our big, baited treble hooks jigging on the bottom, hand lines coiled in our small fists, focusing on our invisible prey. We spent sunny hours catching chicken halibut and flounders and the ugly bullheads, which we threw back. Bill Young was happy to fry some of the catch in a skillet on the galley stove, along with some spuds and eggs. Savory steam wafted from the cabin, making our bellies growl and our mouths water. The hatch cover and the dry web and corks of the seine, stacked neatly on the stern, provided seating as we all lay about like Roman senators, joking, laughing and eating until we couldn't hold any more. Even Al, the Tlinget, seemed to be enjoying the peaceful laziness of the day. I saw him actually chortling privately at our shenanigans a couple times, black eyes glinting from under the brim of his dingy halibut hat, his fierce-looking grin accentuating the crow's feet and other deep wrinkles in his brown face. We ate our catch with our fingers, like hungry savages, tossing the skin and spitting the bones over the side and wiping our hands on our pant legs, which already had fish blood and slime on them from catching and cleaning the fish. After some pleasant hours we pulled the anchor and *Pheasant* resumed her way toward Uganik. We boys sat on the flying bridge with whoever happened to be at the wheel, chattering like magpies, pointing out new sights, asking a million questions, and waving to other boats met in passing. We climbed the stays to ride high on the mast, the cool ocean breeze roaring in our ears, drinking in deeply the clean smells of the sea and the land. We lay on our backs on the seine pile and discussed in detail the fish we had caught and how the line had cut into our hands as they'd fought while we hauled them up hand over hand. We peered out of the grimy glass of the little porthole while we washed dishes in the tiny galley sink, and felt that life really couldn't be much finer than this. The steady breeze, hard in our faces, was sweet embellishment to the sturdy feel of the little boat as she churned her way down Terror Bay toward Uganik passage.

Coming into the East Arm of Uganik Bay the cannery became visible from a couple miles away, seeming very lonely and miniscule. It looked like a postage-stamp city pasted on the tide-line at the base of a high mountain. Up close it was all and more that we'd heard about in stories around the dinner table at home. My dad had worked five months a year for eight years there, first as a boat mechanic and then as Port Engineer, and our older brothers all had fishing tales to tell of the area. This made Cliff and me feel like we were right at home. We knew all about what was there, we were just seeing it for the first time.

The tide was low when we pulled in to the floats attached to one end of the dock. Rows of long black creosote pilings towered above us, supporting the timber-built docks and their processing and storage buildings high above the deep green water at a level roughly even with the low rock bluffs ashore. Behind the docks, scattered along the rocky, uneven ledge were the bunkhouses, the company store, office building, superintendent's house and other buildings, all perched on high wood foundations and all painted white, having rusting, corrugated tin roofs. The buildings were connected to one another by wooden steps, boardwalks and ramps which made travel by foot or forklift possible above the rough ground below. It was like a miniature town had been plunked down here in the middle of a wilderness. For us, the cannery offered a welcome stretch of the legs and plenty of interesting spaces to visit. We knew they sold candy at the store and we went there first to spend our meager, pooled funds on high priced chocolate bars. Thus fortified, we went exploring. At one end of the cannery was the fuel dock, wisely separated by an open stretch of water, and connected to the plant by a broad wooden causeway, also built on pilings over the rocky shore. Here men with big wood-framed hand trucks trundled blue and orange fuel drums along, the wheels thumping hollowly at each crack between the heavy planks. Fishermen carried armloads of groceries or gear along the broad walkway, no doubt grumbling that the skipper didn't move the boat around and tie up closer to the store. Four enormous, white fuel tanks rested horizontally in cradles on the bluff above the fuel dock with fat white pipes running parallel together down the steep bluff, routed away to various places like the delivery pumps on the fuel dock, and to smaller tanks for the oil cooking ranges in the mess hall or the big diesel generators that supplied power to the cannery twenty four hours a day, seven days a week, for months on end.

In the years of record high salmon runs, the boats fished almost round the clock, plugging away at the backbreaking labor of handling the sodden gear over and over as they sieved the waters of the fish-choked bays. The mere sight of tons upon tons of bright, silvery salmon madly slapping and flashing into the fish-hold made the work easier, and the days flew by. The cannery's salmon tenders, all bigger boats with large fish-holds, worked around the clock, running out to the fishing grounds where they anchored up and loaded as much of the catch from the company fleet as the boat would hold. They also delivered grocery orders and mail to each boat and chatted briefly with the skippers about fishing news. Then it was up-anchor and head for the cannery. The Salmon plants were often so glutted with fish they had to stop the fishing until they caught up.

The years having record *low* salmon runs were a little different. Competition was fierce among the boats to be the first to set around a show of fish. The boats would idle from point to point or slowly criss-crossed the bays, watching for a show of fish. The crews spent long, drowsy hours scrutinizing the water all around the bay for a jumper. A single, lazy humpy (pink salmon), flopping half-heartedly out of the water on its side a half-mile away could cause a championship ruckus. As many as twelve or fifteen boats might be involved, each maneuvering among the others at high throttle settings, jockeying to get into a position to cut loose the skiff and make a set, skippers and crews sometimes yelling or swearing at one another across the water. Quite often one skipper would 'cork' another boat that was already in the middle of making his set. The setting boat might have most of his seine out in a half-circle enclosing a school of salmon, his skiff towing the other end, both straining to come together and close up, when in roars the offending boat at high speed and cuts right in front of the setting boat or its skiff and pulls the pin on his own skiff to round-haul the fish right inside the other seine. There were variations of corking of course, but the end result was usually ugly. All sorts of bad words and feelings were vented on the skipper and crew who were desperate enough for fish to cork another boat. Sometimes guns were waved around, but more often fist-fights ensued, sometimes right on the boats at the time, or later in town after fishing season. Everyone was worn out from long hard hours and days and weeks of scratch fishing. Half a load of salmon at the end of a twenty-set day was often a cause for celebrating. As usual when there was no fish, prices went through the roof and it was a seller's market. The canneries were hungry for fish and offered little extras to the boats if they would deliver to them. A six-pack of cold beer or a gallon of ice-cream with every delivery tasted mighty fine to an overworked and dejected crew.

Carl, like many other men without a boat of his own, fished *Pheasant* on contract with Alaska Packers Association, one of San Juan's competitors. The canneries supplied the boat and commercial gear for the season and the skipper paid a percentage to the company out of his salmon settlement at the end of the season for using their equipment. Carl's boat delivered exclusively to APA. He charged most of his expenses like grub, fuel and oil for the boat, and clothes, raingear, hip-boots, cigarettes and candy for the crew on a boat account. For these essentials they were charged exorbitant prices at the cannery stores, every purchase carefully tallied on the boat's account. At the end of the season the cannery office tallied, by specie and price per pound, all the salmon *Pheasant* delivered, and then subtracted expenses plus the percentage charged for using the company equipment, sorted out the crew share, and wrote settlement checks if there was anything left over. The Uganik plant, originally named San Juan Fisheries, had a dozen or more of the little bay-seiners, most of them identical to the APA boats, but painted San Juan's company colors; green hull with gray topside. All the APA boats like *Pheasant*, had bird names such as *Tern* and *Mallard*. San Juan Fisheries, named their boats using the initials SJ, plus a number on each boat. One of these, the *SJ-11*, was bought for salvage and overhauled many years later by the same Dave Lindberg of our trip on *Pheasant*, who had by then become my brother-in-law. I crewed for him occasionally on that old boat as a grown man, in and around the same waters we boys had visited on *Pheasant*. By that time Dave had become a canny fisherman who knew how, when and where to catch the wild salmon. Not infrequently *SJ-11* was high boat for the season, delivering the most salmon caught in Uganik Bay to the cannery at San Juan. He married my oldest sister, Linda, and they still live in Uganik Bay year round, and although the family now has other boats, they still fish old *SJ-11* as part of their "Fleet".

The Uganik excursion, Cliff's and my first real boat trip, came wistfully to an end when *Pheasant* churned back into Kodiak after a colorful return passage, and tied up again at the transient float in the Near Island channel. We were home safe in time for starting school, and had richly expanded our views of the world around us. Our imaginations now fed experience into our blood and we looked around us with new eyes. The trip on *Pheasant* might convey some understanding of the concern that was usually exhibited and accepted by seasoned fishermen when women, kids or greenhorns were present on their boats. The tale about *Rustler* however, and her last short voyage, showed the other side of the coin. Undertaken on Christmas Day about two years after the Uganik trip, it was more of a nightmare than an excursion.

CHAPTER 6
Of Fishing and Survival

The American commercial fishing industry on Kodiak Island had its beginnings in the late 1880's when West Coast fish-canning companies from San Francisco and Astoria, Oregon sought out new grounds for exploitation. Having skimmed the cream from the salmon runs in the Columbia River, and entirely wiped them out of the Sacramento River with over-fishing and the destructive, muddy run-off from hydraulic gold mining, they began searching for a way to supply the newly developed technology of preserving food by soldering and cooking it inside steel cans. Exploration began with a small salt-fish operation, sent by sailing ship by an Astoria cannery in the early spring of 1889 to Chignik on the Alaska Peninsula. Word soon got out among the other West Coast canneries that there were easy pickings and an endless glut of salmon going to waste in the waters of Territorial Alaska. The very next year several fish companies sent cannery outfits north to Karluk, Larsen Bay and Alitak on Kodiak Island. These were complete outfits, the whole operation, including the hired Scandinavian and Italian fishing crews and their small boats, Chinese processing gangs, state-of-the-art processing machinery, lumber for the cannery buildings, plus grub, rudimentary medicines and other supplies to last the season. They were expected to sail north to the intended fishing grounds, build the cannery and set up all the equipment, then catch and process a ship-load of canned salmon by seasons end. It must have been an enormous undertaking for the crews and certainly underscores the old saying of those being the 'days of wooden ships and iron men'.

At Karluk Lagoon, by the early 1890's, there were dozens of newly constructed Salmon plants littering the inside shore of the long sand-spit separating the lagoon from the open ocean. The work was all done manually and the fish were easily caught inside the shallow lagoon where they massed by the hundreds of thousands at the mouth of the Karluk River. The gangs of fishermen from each cannery took turns using small boats to encircle twenty-five or thirty thousand salmon in each set with a giant seine, then drew the net into a tighter circle to crowd the fish together and seined them into their boats using a much smaller seine. They filled their boats quickly and repeatedly, delivering them to their cannery for processing by the Chinese gangs. It was a highly competitive endeavor, with all the canneries fighting to get their share of the catch. The season was short and they were frantic to make a good pack to ship south in the fall when the run was over. At the time, the only law enforcement in Alaskan waters was a roving Revenue Cutter carrying U.S. marshals, which appeared at odd intervals. There was so much fighting and trouble, sometimes involving gun-play, that the cannery superintendents finally held a meeting and worked out their own rules to stop the inevitable outbreaks of potential wars among themselves. The fighting delayed production. Filling their ships with cases of canned salmon was the prime directive given them by their employers in the States. (authors note (2)

Over the years regulations setting catch limits, better law enforcement capabilities and the independent nature of fishermen changed the industry in order to protect the salmon runs, the fishermen, and the canneries. When my family came to Alaska most of the canneries on Kodiak Island still maintained a small fleet of boats and hired contract skippers, but they also bought fish whenever they could from independent fishermen, vying for each skipper's loyalty to exclusive deliveries. The number of boats increased every year in a free-for-all fishery. Despite regulations and catch limits the growing pressure on the salmon stocks severely reduced the size of the return runs. A law proclaiming Limited Entry became a fact of life. Limited Entry set a finite number of commercial permits for fishing salmon. Many of these new permits were skippered by stateside fishermen who were unfamiliar with the local waters, extreme tides and unpredictable weather. Some of these men never got the chance to learn. The number of groundings, sinking boats and rollovers increased dramatically.

At the time we moved to Kodiak the fishing boats of the island were mostly simple wooden vessels with crude rigging and deck machinery. It should be realized that forty years ago safety at sea was *also* based on much cruder technology, and relied essentially on the experience and knowledge of the individual skippers and crews. 'Survival suits' basically consisted of wool long-johns and socks, worn under Frisco jeans and hickory or wool shirts. Life jackets were ridiculously bulky and actually dangerous to wear while working any type of fishing gear because the straps, buckles, and puffy floatation packets were easily snagged on halibut hooks, seine web or other gear that was often running under a hard strain through a block or around a winch drum. Salmon fishermen constantly lose the buttons on their shirts when working around seine web, and usually just cut the sleeves off above the wrists to prevent snags. The life jackets were generally stored in the seat box on the flying bridge or stuffed up in the forepeak of the bow, rarely seen except when digging out small gear or stowing groceries.

Life-rafts were unheard of on the small fishing boats. Most of the seiners used a skiff with an outboard or inboard motor to help tow the seine around the salmon schools while fishing. It was also used for quick trips like visiting another boat in the bay or running to the cannery, or even to town, for supplies or parts. It gave the crew a safe feeling to have their skiffs in tow when traveling, and they occasionally *did* serve as a lifeboat. Most boats had radios. They were huge, heavy boxes with lights, meters and big black knobs on the front. The radio pulled so much power it emitted a deep *"Hummmmm"* when the mic was keyed to talk, and drew the 12 volt lights down very dim. If you were trying to enjoy a book in your bunk in the evening when the skipper made his daily contact with the company, you were forced to time your reading with the answering party's response, when the light came bright again. These radios transmitted fairly well over open water and under favorable conditions, but if there were mountains or bad weather intervening between the talking boats radio reception was often scratchy and broken. Other boats in the area often relayed radio talk if they were in a better position and could communicate with both parties.

Few boats had navigation tools beyond marine charts, a gimbal-mounted compass, plotting rules and dividers. There was no loran signal for civilians in those early days, and only the bigger boats occasionally had a radar scanner rotating on its pedestal atop the house. Comparing it to today's standards, I shudder to think of the enormous risk the men took with their lives in pursuit of their calling on these tiny boats. And yet they knew what they were doing. They compensated for the risks by traveling with other boats whenever possible. They avoided running at night when practical or in weather that strained at the limits of their little boats, heading instead for a sheltered bay to anchor up and wait for daylight or sometimes days for the wind to lay down. The local skippers and crews knew the waters and the predictability of any given reach of water under various wind and tide conditions. They knew the run of the tides, and where all the reefs, tide-rips and rock piles were and, more importantly, where they weren't.

Common sense, caution, and first hand knowledge of their fishing environment kept men as safe as possible in the days when no emergency locator beacon would transmit their position to anyone, no Coast Guard rescue helicopters would come for them in time of trouble, no survival suits would float them and insulate their bodies from the freezing water, and no lifeboat would magically inflate for them when the boat was sinking out from under their feet in a howling snowstorm. At best, they made radio contact with another fishing boat in the vicinity and were either escorted, assisted, towed, or rescued. The last resort was the skiff. In these earlier days the Navy did what it could to rescue crews from boats in trouble, but it was the Coast Guard when they finally took over NavComSta, Kodiak, who made the difference. They had the equipment and their people were trained to do this highly coordinated, dangerous and unpredictable work. All fishermen appreciate the real effort of the men and women stationed at the C.G. Rescue Coordination Center, who frequently and literally risk their lives, usually under the worst possible conditions, for men and women they've never met and likely will never see again.

Many, and more, were the stories we kids heard firsthand around our kitchen table at home from those who survived close calls on boats caught in storms before the days of *call-the-Coast-Guard*. Or of wrecks on rock piles where men (and occasionally women) worked with grim fear and dread to save their boat and themselves, eventually limping back into the safety of the harbor in Kodiak. Some, who made it to shore after their boat sank or was smashed on the rocks managed to survive there, sometimes for weeks, before being rescued by another passing boat. Frequently some of these people stayed at our home until they recovered sufficiently from injuries to get a berth on another boat or go home to their village. Sometimes part of the crew didn't come back. Often these were people we knew. To me it wasn't really so surprising that these people drank them selves oblivious day after day while they were in port. It seemed as if they were cramming all they could into their lives while they were able. They knew that maybe next time they wouldn't be so lucky. They all knew, too, that they were going back out, so there was always the probability of a 'next time' in their fishing future. Something no one really wanted to think about.

It should be noted that not all fishermen and townspeople involved themselves in the mayhem that dominated downtown Kodiak in those days. There were many, Aleut and White people alike, who maintained a respectable, healthy family life, were deacons in their church, or otherwise maintained a sober attitude, reserving their bouts with alcohol for true celebrations. Their contribution to the community in retaining a core of respectability among its citizens will probably never be truly appreciated. I will say that they gave a young boy like me another side of life to compare with his own. Kids are impressionable. These people offered an important perspective to me in that tiny, cloistered community. But downtown, night and day, the band played on.

Downtown Kodiak was alive and jumping almost every day and night. The bars in the town were so situated that it was never very far to stagger from one to the next. Or crawl. It was common. Live music or juke boxes thumped out mostly country songs with a heavy bass through the open doors, much in discord with loud talk, raucous laughter, and shouting voices. Men and women, white and native, fishermen, trappers, construction workers, Navy sailors, local businessmen, popular recording artists, bums, movie stars, kids looking for their parents, news men, politicians and even foreign princes passed in and out of these rough establishments in a seemingly endless celebration. Some had their arms over one another's shoulders in comradely fashion for mutual propulsion and support, or occasionally someone flew backwards through the wide door of a barroom onto the sidewalk, brutally propelled by someone else's fist. On the street corners women punched their men, who often punched them back. Functional citizens took their wives out, ordering a nice candle-lit dinner and a few drinks just as if they were in a stateside establishment, but cautiously enjoying the clamorous regulars, sometimes even joining them, to be swept along by the crowd and forgetting where they left their cars. Cab drivers worked patiently around the clock getting people where they wanted to go. It all seemed pretty normal to boys too young to remember the quiet country life in the States, but the side of old Kodiak I knew really was a wild and rough and exciting place to live.

Illustration by Elise Dooley

CHAPTER 7
Rustler

In retrospect, given the tension of that environment, it really isn't all that surprising to me now that a normally dependable skipper like Carl Warner could let his sense of responsibility slip one day and consequently lose his boat, and worse, the respect and acceptance of many of his fellow fishermen. But so it developed, one cold and windy Christmas Day, when Mike and George and Cliff and I again happily found our selves invited by Carl for a two-day trip on his own boat, *Rustler*. This time we were going to Long Island, a timbered paradise of Sitka Spruce, only about an hour's run from town. To us Long Island was the very essence of freedom, being uninhabited and having miles of dim forest, open, windy hills and fresh, untracked beaches to explore. Untracked, snow-covered roads led through the quiet forest, threading among the bunkers and buildings abandoned by the military when they pulled out of Kodiak after World War II. We knew that the huge, white snowshoe hares congregated around and under the old bunkhouses and Quonsets, and would keep four boys and a couple .22 rifles seriously occupied for weeks if we'd been allowed.

Again the arrangements were made with Mom and Dad and permission given. So Cliff and I began frantically assembling the things we would need for Long Island, our warmest clothes, sleeping bags, an old bolt action .22 rifle that wasn't too pretty, but shot straight, plus as many boxes of shells as we could dig out of our absent older brothers shooting supplies. Carl was visiting with the folks over coffee at the kitchen table while Mike and George waited on the couch reading comic books with their coats and boots on. The skipper wanted to leave the harbor by early afternoon and we didn't want to delay him.

Christmas may seem like an odd time to be undertaking a weekend boat trip, but it had become a tradition in our family to have our humble home-celebration on Christmas Eve, most likely because Mom and Dad finally gave up trying to hold a house full of kids back from the ritual of exchanging our few gifts. That made Christmas itself, a day which we could all enjoy as a stress-free climax to the anticipation and secretive fun of the pre-holiday weeks. It wasn't that unusual either for some of our family to miss the holiday at home entirely. Sometimes the fishing was just too good to leave during the king crab season some twelve or fifteen hundred miles out westward in the Aleutians and would hold the crews on the fishing grounds, making it pay while they were on the crab. They spent weeks on end plugging their live-tanks with the giant crabs, fishing ten-by-ten pots with conventional rope rigging, and making big crew-shares at ten cents a pound on crab that averaged about eighteen pounds apiece. I recall my family eating a monster that weighed twenty five pounds. My dad and older brothers fished on the little boats pioneering the crab fishery in the Bering Sea and were often gone for months at a time.

We finally arrived with Carl at the harbor by cab and happily lugged our stuff down the ramp and along the wooden floats to the slip where *Rustler* rode slow-dancing in her lines. Raw gusts of cold wind swept down periodically from the northeast, creating little williwaws of dry snow, litter and small gravel that terrorized the streets of town, freighting over our heads to moan through the bony forest of boat rigging in the harbor, and ruffle visibly away across the waters of St. Paul harbor in long, dark grey streaks. The high breakwaters of giant black boulders protecting the small boat harbor provided no lee to the floats in this wind. The gusts rushed through, pushing the boats around within the confines of their stalls. Moorings slowly stretched tight, creaking and popping on the wooden pilings as the vessels strained against them, and then slowly relaxed as the gust petered out. Hulls moved heavily against tire fenders, making them cry with a sound like cold, packed snow under the boots on a frigid winter morning. The floats themselves moved, bumping around against their anchoring pilings, sometimes causing us to stagger a little. It wasn't really blowing all that hard, maybe gusting to thirty knots outside the breakwater. Wind was a normal part of life here and we were used to it. We knew that *Rustler* would easily take this weather in stride. She was built to fish gulf waters and had a deep, narrow hull of the design that rolled ponderously in heavy seas but recovered herself quickly.

We heaved our gear over the high rail onto the scarred wooden planks of the deck, and lugged it in through the galley, down the ladder to the engine room and forward about six feet past the oily stink of the silent diesel engine to the crew quarters. Here six spacious mahogany bunks were built, three to a side, into the vee of the deep, narrow bow. A single 12 volt light bulb, mounted overhead, glowed dimly above the triangle of deck between the bunks. The bulb cast more shadows than light into the rumpled bedding, magazines, pocket-books and clothing which littered the tiered bunks. Clearing a place on the lowest portside berth, we stowed our stuff out of the way and gladly left the dim, smelly confines below to crawl up the ladder back into the light and warmth of the wheelhouse. Carl told us to stay put for a little bit while he went uptown to take care of some last minute details and round up his crewman, Hector, and both their wives, who were also coming along. We gladly complied, we weren't budging now. We were finally ready to go, there were plenty of magazines of the wrong kind for us to peruse and also the ever present deck of cards to keep us occupied inside. When we grew tired of sedentary entertainment, there was the boat itself to explore.

Rustler was a stout old wooden vessel of about 50 feet, with a deep hull and narrow beam. She was painted white with black trim, and had a dark red copper-coat on her hull showing above the waterline. Her condition seemed a little worse for wear, but after all, it *was* a work boat. The long cabin began about eight feet aft of the bow and ran back twenty feet or so, being some eleven or twelve feet wide. The front of the house was built in a radius that would diffuse the brunt of tons of water against the house when the boat buried its bow under heavy-weather swells. The galley occupied the aft half of the house. From there a narrow passage-way led forward to the wheelhouse. On the right side of the passage-way, set into an alcove was a square hatch through the deck with a ladder leading below. Opposite the hatch a small mahogany door opened to the tiny captain's quarters with the high, wide bunk on the left. The galley was also fitted with rich, dark mahogany cupboards and brass pulls and hinges, with a generous, matching table aft, having storage benches built in on each side. We really appreciated the large, diesel burning cook range. The stove was mounted just inside the entry door and radiated a cozy heat that warmed the galley and, to a lesser degree, even the wheelhouse. With its short steel fence around the polished griddle top and adjustable crossbars to keep pots and pans from sliding around the stove in rough weather, it was a perfect place to thaw ourselves. Its heat was mighty welcome after the frigid wintry blast outside. The galley door, which was nearly aft on the starboard side, and the wheelhouse door, situated forward on the same side, were both crafted of heavy mahogany. Both were Dutch doors, mounted with large, brown-brass hinges, latches and door-knobs, each door having a small, single pane window. All the doors into the cabin had very high thresholds to prevent deck water from spilling into the cabin. The tiny head (toilet) was not much roomier than a tall, square closet. Its mystery of valves, plumbing and the manual pump used to flush the toilet was not in working order, which meant that if we needed to *go* we'd be forced to use the deck bucket. We boys didn't like that idea much, especially with women aboard. The head was entered from outside only, the door being placed midway between the galley and wheelhouse entries. The space was now used for the storage of boots, raingear, deck brushes, paint cans and the like.

Outside, amidships against the back of the house stood the tall wooden mast, its cable stays on each side veeing down from the top, bolted to wide plates built into the deck and railing. The top of the mast was accessed by wooden rungs clamped to and ascending the converging cables, each rung being shorter than the one below it. A single-bulb, twelve volt deck light was mounted about twelve or fourteen feet up the mast, aimed to shine down on the hatch. The long wooden boom, mounted on a pivot pin to the mast about six feet above the deck, was suspended at an angle by taut rope rigging and wood cased double-blocks (pulleys). Three or four feet aft of the mast, just in front of the hatch-coaming, stood the big deck winch with its twin drums that looked like giant thread spools. The deck winch was used in combination with rope and blocks to adjust the rigging, purse the seine when fishing salmon, lift and swing the salmon brailer aboard, haul crab pots, pull a stuck anchor and for a multitude of other inventive purposes. A solidly planked, thigh-high rail, capped with hardwood, ran down each side of the boat from the bow to just aft of the hatch, where it sloped down to about six inches above the deck, and curved gracefully around the stern. Large oval scuppers were spaced along the rails at deck level to allow water to drain quickly from the deck in heavy weather.

The power-skiff, used like a tugboat for seining salmon during the summer season, was sitting high and dry on *Rustler's* back deck, hanging over the stern rail about a foot. Its bow painter was tied into the eye of a longer, heavier line that ran taut above the hatch, between the bitts on the deck winch and around the winch's foremost drum. The winch was used to pull the skiff aboard over the stern with the help of a lifting-block hung on the boom. Once it was far enough aboard, tie-down lines on each side of the skiff's stern were fastened to permanent straps that had been spliced around the short rail on the boat where the scuppers were located. Then the skiff could be winched ahead until the stern tie-downs became tight, and the winch line secured with a few wraps and cross hitches over the bitts on the winch. That skiff wasn't going anywhere we were sure of that, we'd hung and played for awhile on the bow-line. It was rigid as an iron pipe. *Rustler* was fished mainly as a cape-seiner during salmon season because of her deep hull. Most of the bays were too shallow and her seine much too long and deep to catch salmon in the sheltered places, and so she intercepted the migrating schools as they traveled down the outside coastlines, on the outer-most capes of Kodiak Island or across Shelikof Straits on the mainland. These fishing grounds are wide open to the huge swells and hard, incessant winds blowing in off the Aleutians or the Gulf of Alaska, and were mostly fished by bigger boats. The cape-seiner skiffs needed to be powerful and brute-like, often fishing in seas that prevented the skiffman from seeing the boat except from their peaks as he towed his end of the long, heavy seine while making a set. Most of the power-skiffs in those days were tremendously heavy wooden beasts, powered by a four cylinder gas inboard engine with a large brass towing propeller, which was protected by a skeg and steel basket. It was common practice to haul the skiff up on deck when traveling as it eased the fuel consumption and made one less worry for the skipper if the weather should 'breeze up a little'.

The other main feature on *Rustler's* deck was the hand-powered bilge pump. Mounted on deck on the port side just aft of the house and plumbed through the deck with fat pipe to the bottom of the bilge, the pump was made of galvanized steel and vaguely resembled a large squatty pitcher. There was a tough rubber diaphragm in the bottom of the bowl that had a metal plate with square hole in its center. A long steel handle was fitted into the square hole, a bucket of salt water drawn aboard and poured into the bowl of the device, and the handle was then worked back and forth until water began welling out of the diaphragm. The bilge-water then overflowed through a four inch pipe, plumbed across the deck and overboard through the railing. On some boats the water simply poured onto the deck and found its way overboard through the scuppers. Once the pump began to suck, the real work started. We were familiar with the deck pump and how to operate it. Fishermen were always keen to show youngsters simple (and mundane) tasks aboard, and we'd long since mastered the short, quick strokes it took to pull the bilge water up the pipe until it began to well out from around the diaphragm, changing rhythm then to the slower, longer strokes which kept the water flowing out of the pump, yet didn't wear your arms out in the process. Almost all the fishing boats had these pumps as a backup for the engine driven pumps, which occasionally failed when they were needed most from a bad impeller or thrown drive belts.

We had been all over *Rustler* from stem to stern, from the crude flying bridge atop the house to the dark bilges below decks, and still Carl didn't come. We wondered impatiently what could be keeping him and the others. Daylight was fading and night fell fast in winter. Small hard pellets of snow ticked intermittently on the big square windows of the wheelhouse as we waited, and we worried that if it grew dark the trip might be postponed till morning.

CHAPTER 8
A Christmas Turkey

It was nearly dark when they finally came trundling down the floats with bulging grocery bags in their arms and good natured laughter, and bustled aboard and into the warm galley. We helped as much as we could in getting things squared away in the now-crowded cabin. Carl lived on board with his Aleut wife and their eight month old son. Hector and his wife were also Aleut people and were from one of the native villages on Kodiak Island. George and Mike knew them previously, but Cliff and I were just meeting them. They seemed like nice folks to us and we all got along fine as we made preparations to leave at last. The big marine diesel rumbled to life with a wakening roar which quickly subsided to a rattling idle as it warmed itself for the work ahead. The boat thrummed with new life and we four arranged ourselves along the rail in the stinging wind, waiting for the word to come that we were pulling out. We knew that Carl wouldn't let us actually help untie the boat when it came time to cast off, but we were ready to help him and Hector pull the thick lines aboard.

About twenty minutes later they stepped out of the wheelhouse and we commenced taking the lines in. Returning to the wheel, the skipper backed *Rustler* neatly out of her stall in a tight reverse starboard turn, nudged the reduction gear into forward, cracked the throttle open and we were finally on our way, the prop-wash boiling out frothily from beneath the stern, gleaming in the cold, greenish mercury-vapor lights lining the windy floats of the harbor.

Rustler heeled slightly to starboard as she cleared the breakwater while exiting the harbor and momentarily broadside to the wind, but almost immediately Carl steered port and pointed her bow down-channel toward Spruce Cape. Near Island parallels the length of the town shoreline across a natural channel of fairly uniform width, protecting the waterfront of the town from storms that blow in from the Gulf. Woody Island lies outside Near Island, separated by a half mile of water called Woody Island Channel. This channel was marked by channel buoys with blinking red or green lights which were hard to pick out on this night in an otherwise black void. Long Island, our destination, is about twelve miles in length and lies outside of Woody about a mile farther out. We didn't exactly know his intended course to our anchorage, or even what part of Long Island he had in mind, and it puzzled me at the time that we were leaving to the east. It became clearer to me in later years when I realized there were extensive reefs west of Near and Woody Islands, requiring a wide berth. Carl no doubt wanted to avoid that route in the dark. He meant to circle around the northeast end of Near Island after leaving the channel, back west down the Woody Island channel, around the rocky southwest end of Woody Island, then back east again in a big lazy S, to bring us to the northeast end of Long Island, where a snug, lee anchorage lay in a small bay near the end of the island. It wasn't the most direct route, but maybe Carl considered it the easiest and safest ride, given the wind, darkness and bigger seas offshore in unprotected waters.

All was fine and we boys finally got cold standing on the deck watching the lights of town slide past as *Rustler* churned her way down the choppy water of the channel. When Carl began the turn around the marker buoy off the end of Near Island, we made for the brightness and warmth of the galley to roast our freezing fingers and burning ears over the heat of the oil range. We made hot chocolate in heavy, bone china mugs and snacked on pilot bread smeared with peanut butter and jelly, and meandered back and forth between the galley and the dark wheelhouse where Carl steered, standing easy, with his feet slightly apart and remaining amazingly vertical while the deck tilted around his feet. His thick hands rested knowingly, one hand facing up, the other turned down on the spoke-handles of the big wooden wheel, fingers lightly curled in an easy grip. His face was merely a shadowy mask, highlighted by the glint of his gold spectacles in the dim glow of the compass light and reflecting ghostlike in the glass of the window before him. Back aft, Carl's wife had a small turkey on the galley table, which she was preparing to cook for Christmas dinner. She'd turned up the carburetor on the stove and the flame roared and guttered in the firepot, heating up the oven and emitting a fierce heat into the galley. We weren't overly interested in eating any more turkey, having had our fill of it the day before, but it took a long time to cook a turkey and at this point it was hardly a concern.

The sea increased to a moderate swell with an ugly chop in the Woody Island Channel as we turned our stern quarter to the wind. *Rustler's* bow rose and fell abruptly, corkscrewing dizzily in the choppy water and sending periodic sheets of spray outward into the wind, glowing red on the left and green on the right from the running lights on the sides of the cabin. The wind instantly snatched the spray away from the boat out into the darkness. We peered blindly through our vague reflections in the big windows out ahead of the boat and marveled at the skill of the man who could find his way through here without even having radar for eyes.

About halfway through this channel George and I were back in the wheelhouse, Mike and Cliff having gone to the crew quarters below to sort our gear and find places for us to sleep. After a while we noticed that Carl seemed to be having trouble keeping his balance. He was holding the big wooden wheel as much for support as for steering, his ample chest bumping the spokes as he swayed on straddled legs. It didn't take us long to realize that he was drunk. *Extremely drunk!* How he got that way so fast when he'd seemed perfectly sober when we left town, we couldn't understand, but it definitely worried us, and we both realized that he needed watching. George went aft to the galley and discovered that Carl's wife, and Hector and his wife were in about the same shape. The bright galley was now beginning to take on a loud party atmosphere. One look at Hector convinced us that no help would come from him. His eyes were dull, mouth slack, and his shiny black hair

Illustration by Elise Dooley

hung raggedly in front of his brown, weathered face. We boys probably could have steered the boat ourselves if it came to that, having taken the wheel for occasional short shifts on our few past adventures when the man on watch needed to relieve himself or go below for a quick mug up, but Carl was the captain and had more seamanship in half his pinky finger than we possessed as a group, even if he was falling-down-drunk.

Carl's wife, somehow still on her feet and, discovering that the turkey was too big for it's intended pan, had up-ended the naked bird in the deck bucket, which sat very unusually on the hot part of the stovetop, apparently being too tall to fit into the oven. The bucket was about three quarters full of water and was carefully bracketed by the crossbars and the little railings. Now and then it slopped some of its liquid onto the glowing stovetop to create small hissing clouds of steam from the scattered blisters of water dervishing about like visible panic with the roll of the boat. The bucket's rope handle was lying on the galley floor by the table. We were mortified! What the hell was she thinking? *"The deck bucket!?"* We gagged at the thought of eating any of that bird! We snorted incredulously at each other in disgust but being too polite to our elders, drunk or sober, didn't say anything about it to them.

Returning forward to take up our previous stations to keep an eye on Carl, George and I frowned steadily at one another in the dimness of the pitching wheelhouse, feigning anger to conceal our growing fear. Here we were thirty minutes from town, plowing along ahead of a mean, choppy sea on a pitch black night, with a bunch of drunks in charge. Very soon we started thinking of the trouble which certainly must lie ahead. Carl's speech was slurred and mumbling when he ventured to speak at all. His body lurched and swayed with the abrupt pitching of the boat, kept upright now by an iron grip on the spokes of the wheel. We two boys stood back to one side waiting, holding on, not talking. We knew something horrible was about to happen, and fear twisted our insides. We didn't have very long to wait. Suddenly, incredibly, a fat, black marker-buoy, encircled by a broad white stripe and topped with a blinking red light loomed out of the dark, rising wickedly in the foaming seas dead ahead of the bow. It loomed closer, dimly illuminated in the glow of the running lights on each side of the house. Bright, red-tinted spray shot up from the portside bow, and a jarring *"WHUMP!"* resounded and shook through the boat, accompanied by the crash of breaking dishes from the galley. The buoy disappeared under the bow, bouncing and thumping along the hull as *Rustler* drove right over it, heeling sharply to starboard until the big black can rolled clear of the hull. A cloud of steam boiled forward from the galley, fogging up the windows, and I remember hoping oddly through my terror, that the damned turkey had been pitched to the deck and rolled around enough to make it undesirable, and they would throw it overboard.

Carl turned his head slowly toward us with a blank, seemingly apologetic look over the rims of his gold spectacles, but offered no comment, then returned his dulled gaze forward, focusing intently through the glass, his eyebrows working. George and I, now really mad at Carl, glared fiercely at each other to mask our fear, then, maintaining eye-contact, we shook our heads slowly in resignation. We started aft to check the galley, meeting Mike and Cliff scrambling up the ladder from below and telling them in pretty audible and damning terms what had happened. We found the galley floor littered with several broken bone china plates which had somehow jumped from their deep nest in the cupboard above the sink. The turkey was still upright in the deck bucket on the stove. Most of the water had slopped onto the blistering stovetop throwing up the cloud of steam and stinking up the galley. We opened the top half of the Dutch door to get some fresh air inside and fastened its hook to secure it, then picked up the worst of the mess of broken plates, hurling the fragments with anger and defiance out the door, over the rail into the dark seas. It helped offset our near panic having something to do but the task didn't last long, and we were soon at loose ends again, the fear seeping back into us. Hector and his wife kept to themselves, muttering at the galley table, heads lolling in unison with the motion of the boat, subdued and apparently too drunk to move around or fully realize what was happening. Carl's wife had somehow materialized forward in their cabin and was lying on the bunk with the baby beside her. Carl was still at the helm, now intently forcing himself to focus, meeting each wave, using the wheel more for steering the boat, than just something to hold on to. We boys kept tabs on what was going on, and felt a little better knowing Carl was trying.

We hung around the galley for a little while, glaring at the contaminated, steaming turkey on the stove with loathing, quietly discussing possible things we'd like to do to it. We could drop-kick it like a football off the hatch, or toss it from high up in the rigging to smash it on the deck. We sniggered a little hysterically at our images of this mutiny. Finally we started back down to the crew quarters, Mike defiantly snatching a nearly full pack of Lucky Strikes and a lighter from the table in front of Hector as he followed. Below, we sat on the edges of the bunks, lit one of the cigarettes with Hector's Zippo passing it among us in silence, and began to wait. We weren't really smoking, just drawing a mouthful then blowing it out as we often did at our play ashore. One of us usually had a pack, they were easy to get. In our normal shore habitat we were often 'men' on various adventurous expeditions where we actually foraged our food in all day excursions to the salmon streams and beaches of Monashka Bay or Buskin River. We ate handfuls of dark, juicy salmonberries, green pushki stalks which were carefully selected and peeled, fiddlehead ferns and other green morsels we'd learned were safe to eat. Sometimes we built fires and cooked salmon or grayling we'd caught, or rabbits we'd shot. To kids pretending to be adults, cigarettes were a normal extension of our play. It was doubtful if anyone was going to catch us smoking right now, and we didn't really care if they did. What were they going to do? Tell our parents? We knew *Rustler* wasn't out of danger and still felt that this wasn't over. There was nothing we could do to stop it. So we waited. Staring vacantly at nuddie magazines or voicing anew our scornful disapproval of Carl and the others, and hoping against all odds that the skipper would get us into our anchorage, drop the hook, and things would settle down. All our previous confidence in him was gone. In his condition he was still far from being trusted to run the boat with any safe degree of competence.

We could tell from our anxious vigil below when *Rustler* began the wide turn circling the west end of Woody. The choppy swells the boat had been overtaking were now coming square on the port side and the boat stuttered roughly abeam in the hammering of steep short waves as she continued to make way blindly through the black void. At least the buoy hadn't seemed to damage the rudder or punched any holes in the hull. *Rustler* completed the long turn around Woody Island then bucked into the wind and waves on the port bow. We breathed a little then, feeling like maybe the worst of this situation was over, even though the boat was still fighting the choppy seas. We knew there was plenty of sea-room between Woody and Long Islands, but none of us felt like going topside again. Somehow, trying to see where we were going through the wheelhouse windows was very demoralizing. The incident with the buoy must have really sobered the skipper, or at least made him focus more intently on what he was doing. We didn't feel the boat making any unusual maneuvers and it seemed to be running a steady course, plowing steadily through the dark. We weren't convinced entirely of safety though, and remained below subdued and worried, and afraid.

Illustration by Elise Dooley

CHAPTER 9
The Wreck

When it came, it happened fast. One moment *Rustler* was droning steadily along at about eight knots, as she had been for the last thirty minutes, recently making a wide turn to starboard, presumably in toward our sheltered anchorage, next moment there was a loud BOOM, and the deck canted steeply under our feet, causing us to grab wildly about ourselves for something to hang on to as we were flung to the deck and against the bunks. The first impact deflected *Rustler* sharply to starboard where she sideswiped another rock with a heavy crash. The din inside the hull was deathly terrifying and unbearable as, still driving ahead, probably riding an incoming swell, her engine screaming and vibrating, she careened and scraped and bounced insanely over what seemed like a hundred feet of rock-pile and then, amazingly, after one final shudder when the heavy bow-stem took the last impact against the reef, bounced backward and floated free. Carl must have been thrown to the deck too, not able to reach the throttle and pull it back but had apparently regained his feet, as almost immediately the scream of engine noise stopped.

We boys picked ourselves up off the deck with livid panic jolting through our veins. The engine was still running, idling now, and we felt Rustler lift sickeningly on a swell to be carried sideways and slammed against the rocks with another jarring crash, a process that was repeated as we scrambled out of that dim hole, up through the hatch and out the galley door onto the deck without pausing to ask questions. As we hurried through the galley we were stunned to see Hector and his wife huddled way back underneath the galley table. She was screaming and moaning *"I don't wanna die, I don't wanna die! Oh God we're all gonna die!"* It came across like a line from an old TV drama, ridiculous and out of place. Again we exchanged pointed looks of disgust and sneers of distain. Seeing them like that gave us a tiny hold on our own terror, making us realize that we weren't quite *that* far gone. But we were about as close to panic as we could be without losing it, and the view from the deck did nothing to dilute our fear.

Out on deck, after being inside the warm shelter of the boat, the cold wind had an especially savage bite to it and drove bits of hard corn-like pellets of snow in bright yellow streaks through the wide cone of weak light from the single bulb mounted on the mast. Though it was dim, the light illuminated most of the deck and shone fifteen or twenty feet outboard on each side of the boat, sweeping out further abeam with the roll of the boat. At first it was hard to tell what we were looking at, but gradually we were able to make a rough assessment. We stood half crouched, clutching the rail as *Rustler* was lifted by another incoming swell, swept wickedly sideways and slammed against the rocks with a horrible crash and bounced off crazily, to strike another. We were again sickened by fear as *Rustler* took the punishment and the mast stays and rigging shook and rattled above us. Then she was sucked away from the rocks as the swell receded, bumping and grinding into more rocks, to float then at comparative ease, lolling about until another ground swell thumped against the outer rocks and boiled over, and through, the jagged reef and swept us, helpless, again into the rocks. The scene played over and over with frightening regularity. The foam of the breakers appeared dimly blue outside the reach of the deck light, but became tinged with orange as it approached, boiling toward the stern. I remember a fleeting thought about how pretty it was, and was reminded of my mother, knowing she would think so too, but didn't take time to comment. She would never see this, and I didn't want her to. We hung on, bracing for the next series of solid blows to the hull and wondering how long *Rustler* could keep us out of that cold black water. We were only on deck about five or six minutes but had a pretty good sum of the dangers surrounding us.

I knew we wouldn't have a chance in the water. That was easy to see. Not even if we had known how to swim. The skiff was still securely tied on deck, which was some solace, but it would take men with muscle to shove it over the stern. And looking at the cruel, churning cauldron that was doing its best to destroy our boat we knew that eight people and a baby jammed into the skiff would have little success in escaping it alive. Remembering the gruesome stories of others, I forced down rising images of our dead bodies littered along the rocky bluffs here, not more than five or six miles from home, rolling and flopping among the rocks, cold, sodden and lifeless. And of how our folks and families and school friends were going to feel when they got the news.

Whenever *Rustler* slammed her starboard side into the rock-pile it would have been an easy, if not terrifying jump from the railing to the rock. It stuck out of the water like a tiny black island, about twice *Rustler's* length, maybe three feet above the water. It was bare of any trace of growth or drift at this level of the tide. Behind it toward shore, although we couldn't see in the dark, we could guess, was more foaming water and a high rock bluff. We agreed that jumping to the rock wasn't a very good option and backed away from it in our huddled discussion. As the boat was pushed and dragged and bounced around, it became clear to us that she was trapped in what might be described as a giant, narrow tide-pool. *Rustler* was hemmed in on both sides by glistening black shale ridges that in some far distant time had been a part of the island. The headlands had been pounded by oceanic swells for eons and were now eroded into long, narrow rock spines, extending out from the bluffs ashore. They were common to most of Kodiak's rugged coastline, and all seem to run parallel to one another, following the line of a ridge that descends to the shore. The boat was trapped in a long depression between two of these rock ridges. There was no room to turn the boat around.

After taking in our dire straits, now certain we were probably going to be killed in some horrible, watery way before daylight, we became numb with dread, not easily accepting it. My chest was so tight I could scarcely draw a breath. Then Cliff suddenly wondered aloud if *Rustler* might be taking on water and seizing that idea as a means of escaping our tragic thoughts we headed inside to go below once more to the crew quarters and check the bilge for excess water. We filed back into the wonderful warmth and brightness of the galley where Hector and his wife were still on the floor under the table. She continually moaned dreadfully to herself every time the hull was jarred from an impact. Hector growled at her to *"Shadd-up! God Dammit! SHADDUP!"* from his sitting, fetal position on the deck, in the corner behind her. Once more we seemed to draw strength from our disdain of their useless condition. And once more we were surprised to find that the disgusting turkey simmered in the deck bucket on the stove. Through all the severe bouncing and jolting that had rocked the boat, the pail, with its tainted contents, was still upright and caged in place. It was really steaming now, probably from the frigid air that wafted over it through the open half of the door. The pale butt end and pimply drumsticks stuck up above the rim of the bucket, naked and uncooked. Again we sneered at it, gagged by the idea of cooking anything, let alone a Christmas turkey, in the deck bucket. Since *Rustler's* head wasn't working, we knew the bucket had been used for the lowest possible service and it was unlikely that the cook, in her altered condition, had even scrubbed it out. Our folks continually instilled in us a deep sense of respect for our elders so naturally we left the bird alone. I had Cliff and Mike stay there and get warm by the stove and keep an eye on the two under the table, while George and I checked below. Carl was in his quarters talking in low, serious tones with his wife, who was lying on her side on the bunk with the baby. He looked our way as we started down the ladder, his spectacles reflecting glassily from the shadow of his face, but we didn't stop to talk. We scrambled quickly down into the dimness below. The engine was rattling quietly at idle, and as we moved past it we could see that the thick plywood floorboards were wet. *Rustler* heeled abruptly to starboard again, lifted and hurled sideways by the incoming swell, and we instinctively braced for the crash. When it came water shot up around the floorboards, lifting one panel next to the lower starboard bunk to slosh up its side. Down here the impacts sounded with a fearsome, hollow *Boom*! and again the boat thumped and scraped among the rocks as it was dragged back in the receding swell.

Illustration by Elise Dooley

CHAPTER 10
Guardian Angel

Fresh terror gripped us as we realized the bilges were full. *Rustler* must be leaking pretty badly. It had only been about fifteen minutes since the crash and already the water was up to the floorboards. The boat wouldn't take much of this. As George and I stood there wondering what we could possibly do we were startled to see a pair of gray and red wool socks with feet in them appear from the shadows of the lower starboard bunk. The feet searched for the edge and swung over the side, reaching for the deck just as *Rustler* again smashed against the rock-pile. The instant the feet touched the deck, water again spurted from under the boards and sloshed up the side of the bunk, soaking the socks and bringing their owner awake to struggle shakily up out of the shadows and sit hunched over with his elbows on his knees, his face in his hands, oblivious to us. Under ordinary circumstances this may have been funny, but no thought of a smile came to me. None of this was funny. George and I stared at the bony figure huddled on the edge of the bunk, then at each other with wide, unbelieving eyes. He was clad in black Frisco jeans and a threadbare, wool Pendleton shirt worn over thermal-knit long underwear. A bony heel poked out of a small round hole in one of the wet socks. He must have finally sensed our presence because he lifted his grizzled head a little to look sideways at George and I, squinting at the dim overhead light, and groaned *"What the hell has that damned Warner got us into now?"*

We were so glad to find another person aboard, sober one, we weren't finicky about appearances and we excitedly asked him where the heck he'd come from. We'd been over the boat from stem to stern and spent a lot of time here below, laughing and talking. We were sure there had been no one else on the boat. Carl hadn't mentioned anyone. Nevertheless, the disheveled old man stuck out a pale, wavering, blue-veined hand, straightening up a little, *"Name's Max,"* he rasped, *"I been sleepin' off a drunk down here, what the hell's goin' on?"* We shook hands seriously with Max, told him our names and quickly apprised him of what had happened. He took it pretty calmly, seeming more disgusted than afraid; his haggard, unshaven face uplifted to us with its rheumy blue eyes glancing from one to the other as we quickly shared the telling of it. We knew he was horribly hung over. He probably hadn't been sober for a month or more. His hands and voice shook as if he had the palsy. One part of my brain registered the dim scene

Illustration by Elise Dooley

and struggled with the unreality of it. We were still holding on, George braced in the doorway of the wooden bulkhead separating the engine from the crew quarters, Max still sitting in the bunk, scooted back now so his feet were off the wet deck. He gripped the side rail weakly like an invalid, swaying and jerking with the punishing, fatal blows *Rustler* was absorbing. I held on to the middle portside bunk, bracing my legs, bilge-water spurting occasionally over my leather lace-up boots. It seemed like we'd been below a long while but it could only have been about eight or ten minutes. Max dug around somewhere behind him and produced a pair of deck slippers and a gray halibut jacket and crawled out of the bunk. He struggled into the coat and wiggled his wet feet into the worn Romeos, trying to hold on at the same time. The old man drew a deep breath that brought his bony frame nearly erect, held it for a few seconds, and blew it out through puffed cheeks, his shoulders dropping back to their normal stoop, and motioned George and me toward the ladder and topside.

Once more we fought our way up the ladder while the boat continued slam and lurch around. George and I went to the galley and Max went forward to talk to Carl, who was back in the wheelhouse, holding on to the wheel and staring out the windows. Cliff and Mike were still stationed near the stove and were fiercely glaring at Hector and his wife under the table. What had transpired wasn't clear but I think the boys had given them a chewing-out, telling them that they were scaring us kids worse by acting like they were. Max came aft to the galley and, after more introductions told us to come out on deck. We pulled our gloves on, our hoods and hat flaps down tight and stepped out onto the wild gyrating of the deck. Timing our steps, we moved around behind the house into the bitter wind. The grizzled old man followed us grimly, hair blowing around the top of his hatless head like white, inch-high flames, his open jacket flapping in the wind and bare white hands gripping holds along the way. It seemed hard to believe, but we'd grown so used to this pounding in the short time since the first crash that we were, for the most part, able to tune it out as Max gave us orders, yelling to make him self heard. *"I want you boys to get busy on that deck pump and take turns pumpin' until I can rig the belts on the Jabsco!"* (engine-driven pump) *"And keep on pumpin' until I tell you to quit!"* He started poking around in the shadows near the bottom of the mast. *"Where the hell is the deck bucket?"* he shouted. Cliff, true to his character, must have anticipated this question. He started for the galley door, *"I'll get it!"* he yelled back into the wind. We went after him, and as we reached the door Cliff was already stepping back outside over the high threshold, the hot bucket containing the wretched bird gripped in his gloved hands, steam engulfing his head and shoulders, and a determined, maniacal set to his young face. We stood back, a little awed as he made one stride to the railing and launched the steaming bird out of the bucket as far overboard as he could, baring his teeth in a snarl that ended in an impressive roar. The despised, pale carcass arced out in the square of yellow light that shone from the galley door, and turned a slow, single somersault, its scorched breast trailing steam. It sailed out about ten feet and made an insignificant splash; the sound swallowed by the constant din, and was claimed by the seething waters. Cliff pushed through us with the empty bucket, grinning, and we felt proud of him. There was something brave about his mutinous action with the turkey. Where we might have hesitated, Cliff strode right to the problem, taking his pent-up anxiety out on the disgusting bird; on the way it was being cooked, on the cook herself, on Carl, and on Hector and his wife. We all felt like Cliff did, and his stern intent when he stormed off to get the bucket inspired us with a kind of defiant courage. After retrieving the rope for the bucket from the floor of the galley, we turned it over to Max, who shakily but expertly tied it back onto the bail, and lurched carefully to the rail. George and I moved up behind him to hold onto his coat tails, bracing ourselves to drag him back in case he went overboard. Bracing his thighs against the rail, and timing his move to the instant the swell began to ebb, Max dropped the bucket upside down, leaning over as it fell to give the rope slack to follow, then after a second's hesitation for it to fill, drew it smoothly up and over the side in one fluid motion, full.

George had already fitted the iron pump handle into the diaphragm, and when Max emptied the bucket into the basin, he applied the handle like a veteran with quick, short, strokes to prime the big suction pipe, and we cheered quietly as the oily gray water, which had been sloshed and stirred in the bilges by the violent movements of the boat, welled up into the basin and began to flow out the pipe to pour over the side. We fell to with a will now that we had something to fight back with. I remember feeling stupid that I hadn't thought about getting the pump going right away myself, but then dismissed the thought, figuring it would have come to me eventually. Max half-crouched, shivering, coat-tails flapping, his frail bare hands gripping the steel bitts on the deck winch like the horns of an Old Testament Altar while the deck tilted and jarred under him, watching to make sure we were doing alright, then he left us to return forward. We pumped like hell, each trying our hardest to wear out the pump, trading off every few minutes. When it was our turn we worked the handle hard and fast, throwing our body-weight into it, as though it was our only chance at salvation. We knew it was important work and we stepped up to it gratefully.

Max said later that it took him a lot longer to get the pump going than he'd figured. There was a crude little door in the bulkhead at deck level between the engine and crew quarters where the front of the engine and the bilge pump was accessed. Kneeling in three or four inches of dashing water and working mostly by feel in the water sloshing around the bilge, being half in, half out of the doorway and hanging on with one hand while the other groped with cold clubby fingers, the old man fumbled to get the belts over the pulleys on the pump. Carl had shut down the engine so Max could work with the belts. I'm certain that the old man saved our lives by his clear thinking and, sick as he must have been, his quick, instinctive action. That he was still sick and suffering from an ugly hangover was easy to see from his shaking hands and haggard visage, but that old man worked on, and made it his business to try saving the boat. He had a calm, serious way about him that helped settle our initial panic. He wasn't scared and he knew what he was doing, making us doubly determined to act like men.

CHAPTER 11
Aborted Escape

Except for our hands and feet, we were getting too warm from our exertions at the pump on the pitching deck, and it seemed that *Rustler* wasn't taking such a pounding as she had been before. It was eerie with the engine off, the boat weltering around in the surge and suck of the ocean, thumping the rocks. Only natural sounds and our own thin voices came to our ears and we keenly felt the uncaring immensity of our dark surroundings. The wind gusts were louder too when they swept across the deck cuffing us about, stinging our face and neck with the corn snow. The gusts tortured low, unholy moans from the rigging. We felt some of the fear creeping back. Our good friend, Nature, was trying to kill us and we felt betrayed. We shook our fists angrily at the sea and the rocks and into the wind, glaring fiercely and hurling curses at them with much false bravado, and renewed our vigor at the pump handle. I have no doubt the four of us helped preserve the boat. It didn't occur to me at the time, but the more water that leaked inside *Rustler's* hull, the heavier she was when pounding on the rocks, plus she rode lower in the water. Her planking and timbers would have given sooner. Maybe we could have stayed aboard while her bottom was torn out. The deck and house would have held together for a time. It was not a thought to dwell on.

We pumped on and on with frozen fingers, trying to keep

them warm by rotating our stints at the pump through the galley. The two next in line for the pump remained on deck waiting their turn and the relieved man headed for the galley to thaw his fingers and face over the stove. Max had apparently turned the flame down as the top no longer glowed orange. When the relieved man stepped, huffing and puffing through the door it was time for the rested one to rejoin the fight on deck. We all took equal turns, the measure of a turn being that you pump as long as you could work the handle, probably not more than six or eight minutes, or until the pain from your freezing fingers and toes overcame the determination to stay at it. I was the oldest at thirteen and was getting a punishing workout. My arms and back ached and my lungs burned. Not only was it hard pulling and pushing that handle back and forth, we also constantly fought to keep our footing against the shocks of impact and the rolling deck. Cliff and Mike were so small that the pump handle was taller than they were, being designed for a grown man to grasp comfortably at about chest height. I don't know how they kept up with George and me, but they never faltered. Intense anxiety, the fear of sinking and dying, drove us all like a whip.

Finally the engine roared to life again, belching a cloud of sooty exhaust into the light from the mast, the wind snatching it instantly away, and we voiced a quiet cheer. Then seconds later a thick, gray-white arc of water shot out from the port side of the hull to plunge down deeply into the restless, frothy water that seethed around the boat. We cheered again, louder this time; feeling like *Rustler* was pissing on our enemy, and went at the pump handle again, helping the boat empty herself. Max appeared around the end of the house and stopped there, hunkered a little against the wind, his legs automatically adjusting to the tilting of the deck, one hand lightly grasping a cable of the starboard stay. *"Is she pumpin'?!"* he yelled over the wind, his voice jubilant, knowing it was. *"Damn right she's pumpin'!"* we hollered back, pointing overboard at the thick stream pouring out in a four foot arc that grew shorter and longer with the roll of the boat. Max threw his hand up about head high in acknowledgement; "*You guys stay on that pump anyway, alright?*" he yelled, and turned to retrace his steps forward, disappearing around the corner of the house.

After about ten minutes Max came back on deck to check on us, and to let us know that the water level was dropping faster in the bilge, and that Carl was going to try getting the boat out of the rock-pile. There was no room to turn the boat around so we would be making the attempt in reverse. Max wanted us to keep pumping when it wasn't necessary to be holding on. This news made us a little nervous. As odd as it might seem, we'd begun to accept our situation. After all, *Rustler* was still floating, not being pounded against the rocks so much as at first, and the threat of immediate danger was past. We didn't like the idea of adding new problems like the deep, rough water outside the rock-pile. Carl had a radio, but stubbornly refused Max's strong advice for him to call the Coast Guard whose life-saving helicopters and highly trained crews were not more than ten miles away. I think he was beginning to realize somewhat the scope of his blunder and what kinds of questions he would be required to answer if he called for rescue assistance. Maybe he needed more time to think. Maybe he felt that he had to get us out of this situation because he was the one who ran *Rustler* right into the middle of this rock-pile at eight knots. He was the skipper though and his decisions, on his boat, were accepted, even though we didn't like this one. Besides, no one was asking for our vote. To a man we would have had Carl make the call.

We fought down our anxiety as we felt the familiar clunk when the reduction gear engaged. Carl began lining up to back *Rustler* out through the cut in the rock-pile, where she'd careened her way in more than an hour before. We boys stayed on deck and still worked the pump when we could. We mainly hung on and watched wide-eyed astern as Carl reversed the big boat slowly toward the notch, fighting the wind, trying to position *Rustler* for the maneuver. He waited out a few big waves that boomed against the outside rocks and broke over them in exploding gouts of white foam and flooded like cream through the cut. We quailed inside as we hung grimly to our chosen holds, hating the knowledge that we were trying to escape through that foaming gap with its teeth-like rocks. Then there came a disordered pause in the surging of the water. *Rustler* now floated higher and rolled more nimbly in the heaving turbulence, her tiny mast light moving in shorter arcs and circles against the night above. Then a big grounder came looming out of the dark, building with a muted, audible rumble. The black rocks of the notch hissed as they disappeared under green water, the toppling crest glowing in the void. We instinctively knew this would be the one. It rose over the rocks as it thundered toward the stern of the boat, submerging the reef and making our hearts pound rapidly. Carl yanked the shift lever into reverse and shoved the throttle open. *Rustler* shook and vibrated, engine screaming, as he demanded all she could give. The in-rushing flood lifted her as she strained toward the notch, holding her own, then making way astern, picking up speed and backing upstream against the thunderous spill. Then she struck hard on the aft starboard side and the stern slewed sharply to port, slamming into the rocks, partly crossways to the soon to be back-flushing water. We were shaken to our toenails and our hair stood on end. All we could do was hang on and witness what we thought would be our certain, imminent death. But now being at least half sober, Carl was alert and before the rigging had stopped rattling from the impact, he'd shifted into forward, bumped the throttle up and pulled *Rustler* quickly out of peril and back into the deeper water in the middle of our narrow pen. He throttled the engine back and took the boat out of gear, and again we wallowed at the whim of the swells.

Meanwhile we boys hadn't been able to pump very much during all the commotion and when Carl idled down after the failed attempt, we scrambled back to our duty. We probably could have abandoned the effort since the engine-driven pump was still delivering it's constant, forceful stream overboard. But we had orders. Working that handle and watching the water welling up out of the pump and flowing over the side gave us something to think about beside thoughts of dying. It worried us to be kept from our task. George and I had seen the water sloshing over the deck-boards down in the crew quarters and it had almost panicked us. The one thing we were determined to do, after old Max got us going, was to keep Rustler from sinking. As we waited our turn we clung to the deck winch, or the coiled ropes which were lashed to their cleats on the mast and on the back of the house, or the ladder, or to whatever was convenient and not too close to the rail. We shared an occasional cigarette, passing it back and forth, voicing new, mutinous judgments against Carl. *"What the hell was he trying to do? Sink us?" "Shee-it!"* This kind of heated vituperation got our blood up and probably warmed us as much as working the pump did. The wind swept occasional williwaws of the stinging snow around the boat, burning our numb cheeks, and our wrists where the coat sleeves and gloves didn't meet. And *Rustler* still danced around the confines of the rock-pile, jostled by the swells, bumping the rocks, and heavily scraping her sides and bottom. There was no joking or laughter among us. We still labored under a cold, heavy dread. At least with the engine running we felt like there was still hope.

Soon after we'd returned to the deck pump and during my place at the cold, iron handle, the work suddenly went out of plying the lever, and the pump began gulping air and blowing it out with the water from around the diaphragm. That was the sure signal that we'd finished our task. It meant that the water level was down near the bottom of the big the suction line, low in the bilge. I continued to pump the lever until the diaphragm was hollowly belching only air, then lifted the handle out of the pump and stowed it in its place behind the steel ladder bolted to the back of the house. *Rustler's* bilge was dry, our job was done. We stood around for a few minutes, glad for a lengthy break, yet lingering on, hating for the work to end. The engine pump was now jetting half-hearted spurts overboard. It was easily keeping up with *Rustler's* leaks. That meant the leaks weren't that serious, a realization that put one more thing in our favor and eased our dread. With the pounding she'd taken in the first half hour in the rock-pile, it was a wonder to us her hull wasn't caved in.

The galley felt like an oven even though both halves of the door were wide open, each secured by its heavy brass hook to the side of the house. Hector and his wife had not moved from under the table but were silent now. We ignored them and went looking for Max, who was in the wheelhouse with Carl. They were talking quietly in low tones, swaying and dancing on the moving deck despite holding on. We caught the gist of it. We were going to wait awhile before trying the escape maneuver again. The tide was coming in, which fact had somehow escaped my panicked thinking, and the idea was to wait awhile until the water raised enough to float *Rustler* through the notch in the rock-pile. It made sense to us. We could already tell that the boat was floating freer around the seething pool, banging less frequently into the rocks. But now that her pump was keeping the bilge dry, we were essentially unemployed and waiting was hard.

We avoided going below, not liking the clammy dimness and the reek of diesel down there while *Rustler* moved sickeningly about. Hector and his wife had finally passed out in their corner under the table, so there wasn't a good place to sit. We were still highly disgusted with them anyway, feeling that their cowardly presence tainted the galley. I think we were a little scared of their behavior. Carl, who hadn't spoken to us since before *Rustler* ran over the buoy, not even to advise us about what we might be facing, was now back in his quarters standing with his thick, folded arms resting on the high bunk, talking quietly with his wife, the baby wiggling on the blankets between them. Max kept an eye on everything; the bilges, the time, tide and the charts, and on us boys. He'd quietly praised our work at the deck pump and spoke with us from time to time, never raising an eyebrow at the cigarette we sometimes shared. It felt best being outside although it was bitterly cold and windy on the back deck. Stinging fits of snow were hurled at the boat, defining the swaying arc of the deck light, adding to the slight accumulation on the boat. It was so dry the little pellets scurried around in small williwaws, spun by the effect of the wind on various obstructions on deck. There was lee protection on the starboard side of the house about half the time, whenever the boat gyrated around just right, so we huddled there by the open galley door near the heat, sometimes inside, sometimes out, ready to scramble if anything happened. We smoked more of the Lucky-Strikes, again sharing one at a time. We were still too scared to be hungry. The thought of food didn't enter our heads. We had a few near hysterical laughs about Cliff's heroic launch of that despised, half boiled, naked turkey. We deemed the action perfectly justifiable, Max needed the bucket. The thought of it again momentarily lifted our spirits. But that kind of laughing is too close to crying, and none of us wanted any of that. In our minds we each receded back into our own personal dread. We remained a team, as always, but more intensely now that we'd fought back together with the deck pump. Each was prepared to go the limit for the others and the hell with the rest of them. Except for Max and the baby.

CHAPTER 12
Freedom Ride

Rustler suffered at the whim of the swells for about another hour, the bouncing and scraping gradually diminishing as the tide increased the water depth beneath the hull. Sometimes we braced ourselves for an impact as she was lifted and carried sideways, only to experience a small bump, or, surprisingly, no impact at all, being pulled back at the last instant with the receding water. The rocky ridges that held us captive were now only visible when the swells broke over them. The bilge pump still spurted enough water overboard to keep its rubber impeller wet. All human activity was suspended. No one mentioned the turkey. I suppose it was forgotten or dismissed as unimportant during all the excitement. We four remained subdued, and staggered periodically between the back deck and the galley waiting for the next fearsome ride through the rock-pile, hoping *Rustler* would escape easily out into deeper water and hopefully even make it back to town. Finally we felt the familiar clunk when Carl engaged the reverse gear again. We scrambled to our previous stations behind the house, taking our positions this time more in hope than fear. Max worked his careful way around the back of the house to wrap an arm around the starboard mast stay, presumably to warn us about the coming ride. He spied us already clinging like barnacles and merely signed with his free hand for us to stay put, then went forward toward the wheelhouse, to position himself outside the door, watching aft, ready to shout directions to Carl.

It was a tense and familiar repeat maneuver, jockeying to stay in position while waiting for a big swell. We were glad to notice that with the rising tide, now even the smaller incoming waves were submerging the rock-pile. There was much less white water and spray in evidence now, and less confusion in the turbulence around the boat. Once again the big grounder we waited for appeared out of the darkness, raising itself in an awful, hissing black wall, rumbling forward to engulf the rock-pile astern and we heard Max's thin voice through the uproar, telling Carl to make his move. *Rustler* responded with a snarl, and began backing toward the notch again. We tightened our holds as the swell lifted *Rustler* and shoved her forward against her will. Carl pushed the throttle wide open, and with the engine screaming at her highest revs, *Rustler* slowly overcame the spill of foaming green water, shuddering and vibrating beneath us for a few seconds at a standstill, then creeping backward foot by foot until momentum was gained and she began moving into the notch. She picked up more speed, fighting the powerful current as she backed into the trough, but suddenly grounded with a jarring crash, and Carl quickly throttled back and disengaged the reduction gear before the swell petered out. *Rustler* was lying slightly stern down and listed over to port. It was a weird sensation to feel all motion stop while we clung to our holds on the tilted, stationary deck. The rush of the next wave began pouring in around the boat and we felt movement. Then she was lifted once more and started dragging back into the rock-pile. Carl slammed the boat into reverse again and poured on the coal. To our immense relief *Rustler* started moving, with wood-slivering scrapes and solid shocks, bumping and bouncing backward toward freedom. Above the heavy, distressing sounds of wood against jagged rock and the continual rush of wind and sea, screamed the big Jimmy diesel. The full power it force-fed to the brass propeller shook the whole boat. The rigging jumped and rattled above us. It wasn't an easy passage back out through the rock-pile as the hull took more punishment from the submerged reef. What probably only took thirty or forty seconds seemed like hours as we clung to our holds and willed the straining *Rustle*r onward with every nerve in our young bodies. Quite suddenly she slid into deep water, lifting gracefully over the incoming swells that broke against her rounded stern, backing out away from the rock-pile in a long starboard turn, riding the black seas like a queen. We yelled and cheered from our perches, heedless of the stinging wind and rough swell, or even the proximity of the bluffs close ashore.

Carl idled back, shifted into forward, then cracked open the throttle again and *Rustler* slowed to a rolling halt then begin to make headway. We were on our way! But the boat was turning back toward the rock-pile. Carl reversed back into the swells for a short way and tried it again. Same result. The boat seemed bent on running herself back into the rock-pile. Once more the skipper backed out away from the rocks, then drew the engine to an idle again and bumped it out of gear. *Rustler* rolled and corkscrewed in the dark swells, and again our high spirits were doused with fear. We quickly learned that the rudder must have been seriously damaged, askew, or maybe torn off. The boat wasn't responding to the helm as Carl tried to steer offshore away from the reef. Again Max rose to the emergency. We followed him back to the deck and learned as we watched. With his unsteady, old man movements he went right to the deck bucket, the bits of scorched turkey skin still stuck to the inside, slipped the retaining hitches off the mast cleat and moved carefully down the portside rail to the big tie-up cleat. The boat was rolling ponderously but Max leaned out over the rail to pass the end of the rope through the scupper, then quickly threw a couple hitches over the cleat with the end of the rope, and tossed the bucket over the side. He peered our way and hollered for somebody to *"Tell Carl to go ahead on 'er!"* George ran forward, and *Rustler* began to move tentatively forward once more. She started into her stubborn starboard turn again and Max yelled *"Tell him to open her up a little! More power!"* We relayed the order, all yelling at once, and the engine powered up, increasing our speed. The drag on the deck bucket strained hard at the rope, making it squeal and pop, tightening it on the cleat, and *Rustler* began to swing slowly to port. It was working! We were under way again, however crudely she was being steered. Here was a new use for the deck bucket!

CHAPTER 13
Rustler's Last Run

We learned later that *Rustler* had wrecked on an outside point of land very near the end of Long Island, and as we moved out away from the rock-pile the wind caught the boat and began blowing us offshore toward the open Gulf of Alaska. There was one last point of land jutting out toward the northeast end of the island, across from where we'd grounded. Working together, Carl and Max were trying to steer the boat there and run her aground, hoping to get us all safe ashore. The power-skiff, still riding on the stern, would be used to try for the beach. It was a close call for awhile whether they could swing *Rustler's* bow far enough inboard to accomplish this. We boys didn't know at the time what was going on except that we didn't seem to be heading for town. It took about twenty minutes for the boat to plow her way across the wide bay, taking the weather on the starboard stern, corkscrewing in the seas, with Max alternately pulling the deck bucket out of the water if Carl needed to bear to starboard, and dropping it back overboard for a turn back to port. We boys remained outside in the raw windy weather on deck and kept our eyes on Max, ready to spring to his aid if he faltered or slipped. Carl came back to the end of the house periodically to coordinate *Rustler's* progress with the old man, who shivered violently at the rail. They shouted commands and directions back and forth over the hiss of the seas and the moan of the wind through the rigging. We boys felt helpless again, at the mercy of whatever was to befall *Rustler*, wondering uncertainly what we might have to face next. And dreading it, whatever it was.

We felt the boat slowing, the engine idling down again and dropping out of gear. *Rustler* pitched easily fore and aft in the swells rolling beneath her hull. Carl came out of the wheelhouse and he and Max stood swaying at the rail, peering up ahead of the bow at a wide swath of waves rushing toward what must have been the beach. It was too dark to see very far, strain though we might, but we could hear a new sound of continuous, close-breaking surf out ahead of the boat. Carl and Max, after a short, serious sounding discussion, went back into action. Max returned to crouch at the port rail again, ready with the deck bucket, and Carl made his way back into the wheelhouse. He reversed *Rustler* once more, the crippled rudder turning her predictably back to starboard, bringing her almost full circle, pitching and rolling insanely through the close-ordered march of the seas. We had to scramble back to our places behind the house and reclaim our previous, familiar hand holds as Carl backed *Rustler* hard astern, forcing the turn and at first the seas pounded her stern like a giant, soft hammer with much thumping and spray, shifting the power-skiff in it's tie-downs. The salt spray dashing over all on deck felt warm when it hit our numb faces, and we didn't pay it much attention. Max was getting the worst of it and he wasn't crying. As *Rustler* began to come around we wallowed through the troughs and over the swells, rolling violently far over and snapping back wickedly, the rigging jumping and rattling above our heads. We hung on for dear life and watched the swells comb over the port rail and swill around the deck and over our boots, the skiff being yanked back and forth within the confines of its tethers right next to Max, who was kneeling now on the wild deck, his pants-legs awash. He gripped the rail and the cleat and rode it out with a grim, determined set to his features and never wavered. I was beyond fear and panic. All feeling was on hold, balled up in a knot in my guts. The best I could do was ride the terror of the moment, waiting for it to be over, and pray that we didn't roll over and sink this close to safety. But that old Slab didn't roll over. She pulled herself around in a tight, unrelenting arc until Carl threw the reduction gear into forward, applied about a quarter throttle and headed into the wind, away from the beach, Max steering again with the deck bucket. In this final maneuver they hoped to run offshore a ways then swing back around and run the boat in as straight as possible toward shore, grounding the keel on the sandy bottom.

Carl and Max both had to know that *Rustler* would never make it in close to the beach. The hull draft was too deep, meaning the keel would ground in ten or twelve feet of water. There weren't really any alternatives, the rudder was gone. The boat was leaking pretty badly. The beach sounded fine to us. We boys returned to our crash positions and once more began the wait for the impact with the bottom. *Rustler* came in under low throttle, riding the following seas easily, until she found bottom with a sodden *"whump!"* that shuddered through the deck, shook the rigging and stopped all forward movement instantly. We boys rode it out easily, our arms wrapped tightly around various parts of the boat aft of the cabin. Carl throttled back slightly but kept the boat in forward gear and, as she lifted with the next swell, *Rustler* moved ahead to thump softly again to a halt. Fortunately the bottom here was sand, not rocks, and for awhile we inched closer toward the beach in this fashion until no further progress could be made and Carl drew the throttle back and pulled the reduction gear into neutral. Looking for black rocks and sand on a pitch black night, we still couldn't see the shoreline though we knew it was there. It was a great relief to be near the beach, but we all knew it would be no fun trying to get ashore. We boys finally moved stiffly back into the galley, following Max and shielding our eyes against the brightness inside, but soaking up the benevolent heat radiating from the stove. We stayed by the stove, painfully thawing our freezing hands and warming our chilled bodies. Max, also dripping wet and shivering, went to the wheelhouse to talk again with Carl.

We now found ourselves faced with more waiting. The tide was still rising and *Rustler* scuffed and thumped the soft bottom in the endless incoming swells, being forced incrementally toward shore. We wondered again how *Rustler's* bottom held together. As each swell lifted and dropped her, occasionally thumping her keel hard on the sand, we noticed that she was beginning to pivot around to starboard. Little by little, as the waves worked on her, *Rustler* swung broadside to them and they broke hard against the port side rail, dashing more spray across the deck and repeatedly heeling the boat abruptly on the narrow keel until she'd gyrated completely around and the bow once more separated the seas. Then everything calmed down to the regular, soft thumping we'd come to accept as normal. *Rustler* still pitched up and down but rode much better in this head-on position and only hit bottom hard with the larger swells. Max was still talking earnestly with Carl. One of us, maybe George, went forward and listened to their talk. Max was trying again to convince Carl to call the Coast Guard. This was good news and we began to hope again for rescue.

It took another half hour or so but finally Carl gave in and sent out the distress call on the radio. The first we knew of it was the wonderful, crackling, electric radio voice answering his call. We heard it clearly from the galley. *"This is Coast Guard Rescue Coordination Center Kodiak back to the Rustler, what is your position?"* We crowded up the passage-way and grouped together at the entry to the wheelhouse to listen intently of our impending rescue. And so it went, back and forth, they seeming to ask a million questions, and Carl returning information seriously into the microphone while staring blankly through the window before him. Max stood to the right of the wheel, interjecting an occasional comment to the skipper. We boys kept a tight rein on our hopes, knowing that we were still in a tight fix and that it wasn't going to be any summer picnic getting to the beach. We had no idea how that would be accomplished and the notion offered nothing to boost our courage. None of us could swim and had never been in water deeper than we could wade or crawl out of. Getting into the water voluntarily was definitely not an option we desired. Besides, maybe the Coast Guard wouldn't even be able to find us. It was extremely dark and windy, and still snowing in fits. I never felt so alone and afraid, waiting for God knows what; waiting to be saved, ready to die if need be, to help Cliff, or George, or Mike. We were still scared, but swallowed it down because we all felt the same and sniveling wouldn't help. Real men didn't cry over shit like this.

CHAPTER 14
Help Arrives

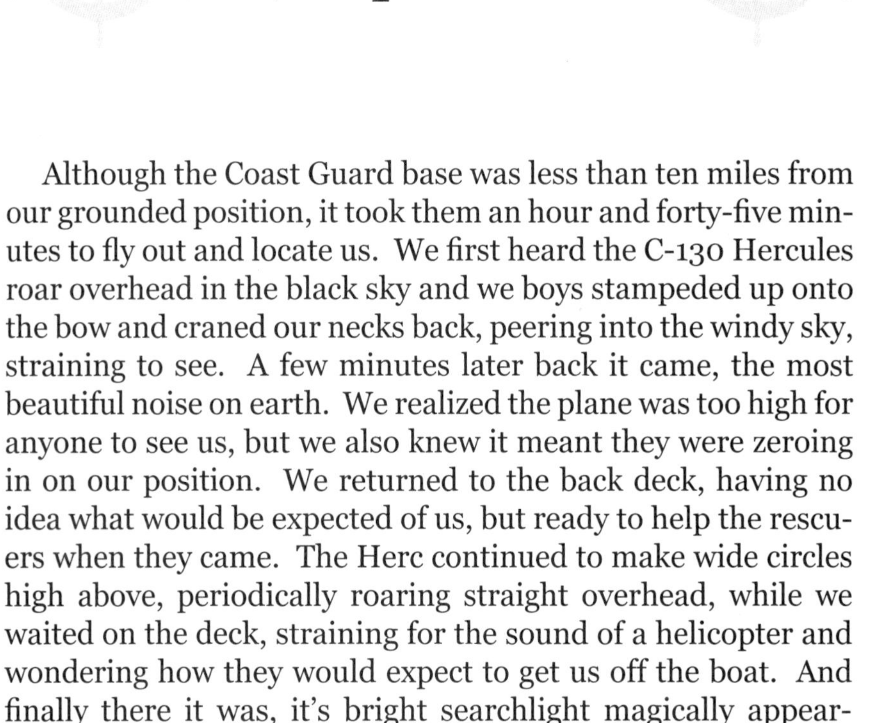

Although the Coast Guard base was less than ten miles from our grounded position, it took them an hour and forty-five minutes to fly out and locate us. We first heard the C-130 Hercules roar overhead in the black sky and we boys stampeded up onto the bow and craned our necks back, peering into the windy sky, straining to see. A few minutes later back it came, the most beautiful noise on earth. We realized the plane was too high for anyone to see us, but we also knew it meant they were zeroing in on our position. We returned to the back deck, having no idea what would be expected of us, but ready to help the rescuers when they came. The Herc continued to make wide circles high above, periodically roaring straight overhead, while we waited on the deck, straining for the sound of a helicopter and wondering how they would expect to get us off the boat. And finally there it was, it's bright searchlight magically appearing high in the black sky about a half mile to the west, a giant spot of blue-white light shining down in a bright cone, moving slowly along the rocky beach. The breakers rolled through the big arena of the spotlight as it slowly followed the beach-line toward the boat, the white crest of each wave glowing phosphorescently against the luminous, emerald back of its twin ahead of it. Oddly no sound came from the chopper as it crept along above the beach looking for our boat. The wind was noisy and blowing toward the source of the sound, carrying it away. There was no way they would miss the boat, the searchlight covered more surf than beach. Help was definitely here! We knew then that we would probably live to see tomorrow.

At last, over the din of the breakers, the gusty, biting wind and *Rustler's* idling engine, we could detect the high speed, fan-like buzzing of the big rotors growing in volume as the huge machine loomed out of the dark about two hundred feet off the water and flew right over the boat, deafening us with its rackety roar, heading out into the darkness toward the Gulf. A second helicopter suddenly appeared above the beach a few hundred feet down from our position, its light hurting our eyes as it hovered there, then began lowering itself to settle carefully on a clean patch of black sand. The rotors and engine maintained a high, noisy rpm for a short time, then switched off and wound down gradually, the high whine of the turbine engine decreasing in pitch and volume with the slowing rotor blades. The other chopper returned from out in the dark where it had gone and hovered briefly over our boat. The white light shone down, brighter than any sun, creating black shadows of the rigging which played over the deck as the boat pitched on the swells. Squinting painfully but gratefully into the brilliance of the light, we all waved our arms and yelled impatiently at them to hurry up and land so we could get on with this. We knew of course that they couldn't hear us, but we were teetering on the edge of an anxious hysteria and felt better for venting a little pressure. We were almost jocular for a minute or so, with shoulder punching and a bit of guarded laughing. The helicopter hovered around the vicinity of the boat for several minutes then moved off slowly toward the beach, looking that area over and presumably making a plan. It then flew back down the beach and began to settle for a landing just beyond its silent twin. This pilot left the engine running and the searchlight on, aimed straight ahead of the aircraft, lighting up the beach for a few hundred yards and providing us a shadowy view of the marching swells and the beach-line.

It was about three hundred feet between the boat and the beach. Three hundred feet of close, breaking swells. When our eyes began to recover their usefulness after staring at the bright lights of the helicopter, someone noticed the shadow of a man with a weak flashlight near the shoreline. The indirect light from the helicopter caused a dim, orange silhouette, outlining the moving figure. The shadow began wading out into the surf. We could just make him out, more visible when the waves broke around him. At first we couldn't figure out what he was trying to do. He moved this way, then over that way. Finally he started back toward the beach, the flashlight making a tiny orange spot on the water in front of him. He seemed to be the only one who had a light, no others shone from the beach and we couldn't make out any other men ashore there. Being Christmas night we thought maybe they were flying with a skeleton crew. After a few minutes, the shadow-man moved back out into the breaking waves and worked his way through waist-high surf toward the boat. It became clear to us now that the man in the orange suit was fighting his way out to a pair of ragged black rocks, the one on his left being bigger, jutting up about two feet above the waves that bloomed and boiled around it. The rocks were less than halfway between the boat and the beach, closer to shore. The water was easily chest deep on the rescuer and I wondered how he managed to keep his feet when the swells broke around him. The way the little flashlight was waving and dipping, we knew he was having a tough time of it, probably swimming half the time, and we praised his determination with open admiration and thought he must be a little bit crazy. He finally crawled like a half-drowned cat up onto the bigger rock and knelt there with his knees spaced wide for grip and balance and rested for a few minutes, the waves breaking against the rock and sheeting him with spray. He waved his feeble light at the boat and shouted something at us, but we couldn't hear what he said, only the wind-snatched sound of his voice. Max was on deck now too, peering with us at the man crouched on the rock, listening intently over the noisy rush of natural sounds and the loud buzzing of the helicopter on the beach. The Coast Guardsman held the dim light on himself and plucked at the shoulder of his orange flight suit and yelled again. "*--ie---aa-et....!*" Again the wind snatched away the words. "*Life jackets*!" George yelled, "*he wants life jackets*!" None of us remembered seeing any on board and, without checking, we signaled a negative back to the man on the rock.

I knew one thing for certain. I wasn't voting for going into that cold, breaking water, life vest or not, but about then Carl came aft and told Max, that the rescuers had radioed him to tie a line on the skiff and push it into the water. This was about the same plan he and Max had in mind for getting us all to the beach. Only now there was already someone on the other end to help. The idea was to tie a coil of line onto the stern of the skiff with enough scope to reach from the rocks to the boat, put the coil in the stern, then let the skiff blow ashore, fastened to *Rustler* with another line on its bow. The Guardsmen would grab the end of the shore line, then we could pull the skiff back out to the boat using the deck winch. We would have a lifeline between the boat and the beach. Or, more specifically, to the big rock where hopefully someone would help would get us ashore. A few of us at a time were to ride the skiff through the swells to the man on the rock, who would guide it to his position with the rope. This was *way* better than jumping overboard with a life jacket on.

Carl turned to us for the first time, his eyebrows arched high, spectacles midway down his nose, and his eyes serious. *"There's some coils of line up on the wheelhouse, y'think you boys can get one of them down?"* We knew where the line was stowed and started for the ladder, glad again for something we could do. What followed might have been comical and fun under other circumstances. For us it was deadly serious work and we went at it cautiously. We scrambled up the ladder like a line of quail and started across to where several big coils were strung together on a rope strap. Scuttling across the top of the swaying house was like trying to maneuver on a high platform in a slow-motion earthquake and we stayed low as we moved. The rope strap securing the coils was tied off at each end to the low pipe railing that encompassed the sides and aft end of the top deck of the house. The knot in the strap was tight and

I worked at it frantically with frozen, ungloved fingers, letting a vicious anger loose on the Gordian strands, along with quite a string of the worst cusswords I knew, until the knot was free. After extracting the first big coil of yellow line I retied the strap the best I could to re-secure the remaining coils while Cliff and Mike and George dragged the single, freed coil to the back of the house, crouch-angling across the high, teeter-tottering house, where they clung to the aft rail and muscled the tight, heavy bundle up and over until it fell to the deck below. We all scrambled back down to the safety of the deck, not liking the exaggerated craziness of the boat's motion up there. Max tied one end of the crab-line into the bow painter of the skiff, his hands working stiffly but expertly, while Carl carried the coil to the deck winch, paying out the line and laid it down to one side. He spanned out a few fathoms of slack and tied it off with a couple cross-wraps and hitches over the bitts (stout steel posts) of the winch. The skiff was rigged.

I leaped at the chance to help get the stern of the skiff untied, then joined Max and Carl as they put their backs against each side of the bow, their hands under the square chine, straining backward with their legs. I lifted and pushed with both hands on the bow stem and we slid the heavy boat back about a foot. Again, working in time with the pitching deck, it moved some more. And again. We repeated the effort about a half dozen times. It took some real work, staggering to keep our feet on the lurching, deck. Cliff and Mike and George got a hand in wherever they could and we inched the cumbersome skiff backwards on the deck, until it was almost ready to teeter. *Rustler* still grounded hard occasionally, causing the rigging to jump and rattle over our heads. Carl warned us to get forward and stay clear of the bow line and, when *Rustler's* stern dropped into a trough, he and Max gave the bow a final hard shove and we watched the skiff rumble neatly down over the stern rail, snatched away by the next swell rolling out from under the boat. The skiff was swept back eight or ten feet, then water sprayed from the painter when it yanked around tight against the winch where Carl had tied it off. Once the skiff was in the water Max moved up and slipped the securing hitches from the bitts and paid out the yellow crab-line, letting the wind and waves carry the skiff ashore, the line running snakelike around the bitts.

The two rocks where the drenched rescuer crouched were almost exactly in the right place. The skiff drifted backward, rocking crazily in the close swells, each wave tossing the pointed bow high in the air, rolling under the flat bottom and dropping it uncaringly into the next deep trough, the stern being thrown up then, high above the wave tops. I could tell right away that this wasn't going to be easy no matter how much help we had, and my heartbeats quickened again with the now-familiar fear. A few swells broke over the dipping bow, dumping water into the skiff and I fervently hoped our lifeboat wasn't going to swamp before we even got to use it. The wind and waves did the work of powering the skiff in toward shore until it was about a dozen feet off to the right of the man in the orange suit, closer to the smaller rock. He rose briefly upright on his knees on top of the rock and crossed his forearms over his head, fists closed, signaling us to tie it off. The orange of his insulated coveralls shone wetly in lucent outline around the dark silhouette of his form. Max immediately snubbed the line on the winch and flipped a couple tight hitches over the bitts and, without hesitating, the rescuer slid backward off the rock down into the water that boiled and surged around it.

He was joined by the head and shoulders of a second orange figure who had apparently made his way out the rock unnoticed by us while the skiff was drifting inshore. They now had to retrieve the shore line Max had tied to the stern. They had a trying time breasting the surf, working their way over to the skiff to retrieve the line, half wading, half swimming, getting knocked back and fighting the swells. Coming anywhere near the plunging, pounding skiff in that hell of wind and marching swells in the dark was predictably and highly dangerous. Yet again, the two men didn't hesitate. The skiff was stationary, being tied to the boat but rocked more violently now, jerking on its tether and sawing up and down at every swell as the men fought for a favorable position near the stern. The newcomer held onto the back of the first rescuer's suit and shoved when he lunged for the skiff. He caught the port gunwale while the stern was down in the trough and dragged himself partway over into the skiff. Then the bow fell into the next trough and the stern shot into the air high above his partner, who was washed back by the swell. The fellow in the skiff searched quickly with the weak flashlight and scrabbled for the line, getting a rough ride over three or four swells, legs hanging over in the water, then heaved himself back over the side. He went into the water while the stern was at the top of a cresting wave and, still hanging on to the gunwale, rode the stern into the next trough where he shoved himself away from the skiff and was carried back by the following wave. The two men regrouped and worked together separating the coils and somehow managed to get back to the big rock with their end of it.

Now Carl slipped the skiff's bow line off the bitts on the deck winch and wound several wraps around the drum. Max engaged the power-take-off lever at the back of the house and the drum began to turn. The wraps of line remained stationary as the smooth, thread-spool drum revolved inside them until Carl put a little tension on the line so it would tighten on the drum and began pulling the skiff in. He tried not to hurry, but let the skiff come through the swells as fast as possible without causing them to break hard against the bow. We boys exchanged hopeful glances, this was working! It gave a little vitamin boost to our courage. When the skiff was winched up close again to *Rustler's* stern, Carl tied it off, letting it hang three or four feet back so it wouldn't hammer and chafe against the boat. It dropped steeply into the troughs at the same time the boat stern rose over the crests. One second the bow of the skiff was a foot or more higher than the stern of the boat, next second it fell three or four feet below the deck. Watching the violence of the skiff's regular pounding almost made me sick and I wondered how we were going to climb into it.

CHAPTER 15
Rescue

We heard the radio blaring a call from the open door of the wheelhouse and Carl turned and started forward, pausing to peer back at Max, *"You got 'er okay pardner?"* he hollered. Max returned his gaze with a tired, miserable, straight smile and a couple nods, his thin reply lost in the din. When Carl disappeared forward, surprisingly steady now on his feet, Max came to me and informed me quietly that he wanted me to go first in the skiff. I remember thinking, *"So here it is. My time to go"*. What we know today as adrenaline I felt as plain old panic pulsing through my veins like electric shocks and I fought hard to control it. I couldn't risk my voice in answer, for fear of exposing my rising cowardice. All I could do was glare at the deck between us and give him a couple short nods of my head. I was unwilling to look the old man in the eyes because I knew he'd see my terror. I was the oldest. To me that meant I had to set the example for my brothers. It was mine to do I told myself. No matter how scared I might be, I was going to have to do this. I accepted it. Then Max told me that I would be carrying Carl's baby ashore with me, and I suddenly forgot my personal panic and began to worry about how in the hell I was going to hang on to a little baby while jumping into the skiff, and getting him safely ashore. Plus I had to be the first on to try it. I whined to myself and found myself wishing, even *willing* now to go alone, but once again a sense of responsibility muted my personal fears. I had a job to do.

Minding the bow line that ran the length of the deck and sawed up and down in mid-air, jerking taut and slacking, we boys and Max moved back to the stern to study the plunging skiff, noticing the twelve or more inches of water sloshing around the bottom, and trying to get a sense of it's timing as it fought its painter a yard from the boat. It seemed to hang for an instant at the top of each rise before falling down into the deep troughs, yanking the slack out of the rope. It was too far to jump to the skiff, hanging back as it was, so Max went to the deck winch and eased the skiff up closer to *Rustler's* rearing stern until it hung about a foot back. It was closer alright, but now it slammed roughly into the boat at the top of every swell. I could see though that it would be possible to time the jump so that it came just after the skiff's bow banged *Rustler's* Ironbark rub-rail and started following it down into the trough. It should only be about a three foot drop from the stern down onto the small triangle deck built as a seat or work platform into the bow of the skiff. It might easily be a *six* foot drop because of the fall of the boats into the trough. I probably wouldn't be very graceful, but I thought I could do it.

Max didn't wait around. *"Okay now, Steve you get in the skiff, and I'll bring the baby out."* In my intense focus of the moment I didn't even think to say good luck or goodbye to my brother and friends, forgetting for a moment that they had to make the same crossing and were probably feeling as sick about it as I was. I moved carefully as in a bad dream to the center of *Rustler's* stern and straddled the low rail and crouched there just to the side of the snapping bow line, one foot on the deck and the other on the thick rub-rail which wrapped around the stern, gripping the wide top-rail with both hands. *Rustler* plunged and rose through several swells with me riding the stern rail like a greenhorn cowboy through the dizzying arcs, keeping one eye on the bow line, the other on the skiff. Then, timing the maneuver, I made a low vault over the stern and dropped to the little raised deck in the bow of the skiff. In landing my knees buckled into a hard crouch and my hands grabbed the tapering gunwales so I wouldn't be thrown overboard. It worked, but as the bow painter snapped tight, yanked upward when *Rustler's* stern rose sharply over the next swell, I was thrown backward off the platform and landed staggering, somehow on my feet, in the water that was dashing around in the bottom of the skiff. Everything good seemed to come at a cost, I was in the skiff but now my boots were filling with liquid ice. I collected myself for few seconds trying to regain my balance then crawled back up onto the little triangle deck. It was going to be hard to remain there and not be thrown off again, and I knew I dared not stand up to reach for the baby. The bow jerked violently at each change of direction, first yanked up from the trough of a swell then jerked roughly back from the next one's peak. I jammed my knees up tight against the insides of the bow, one against each side, sat back on my heels and for a second or two gripped the gunwales a foot or so back from the point of the bow but after witnessing the crashing impact of the bow-stem on the back end of the boat, going on repeatedly right in front of my face, I moved my hands back. *"Keep your hands off the bow!"* I yelled to Cliff and Mike and George. *"It'll smash your fingers!"* That was the only advice or encouragement I remember passing on to them before Max showed up with a sleeping bag wadded up in his arms and knelt down on the deck above me, the boys holding his coat-tails to steady him. Max's hair was a halo of guttering yellow flames in the backglow of the deck light, his face a black shadow. *"The baby's in here,"* he hollered, *"try to keep him dry!"* I held my arms up, terrified by images of the little guy slipping out of the bag and going overboard or falling between the boats. We waited out a couple swells making a few test tries to get our timing, then with an *"Okay!"* Max leaned down as the stern rose and I was carried upward, my arms searched for and found what felt like a baby through the thick, baggy material, Max let go and I was yanked downward again, clutching the kid to my chest and bracing myself with my knees, muttering quick thanks to God toward the black sky.

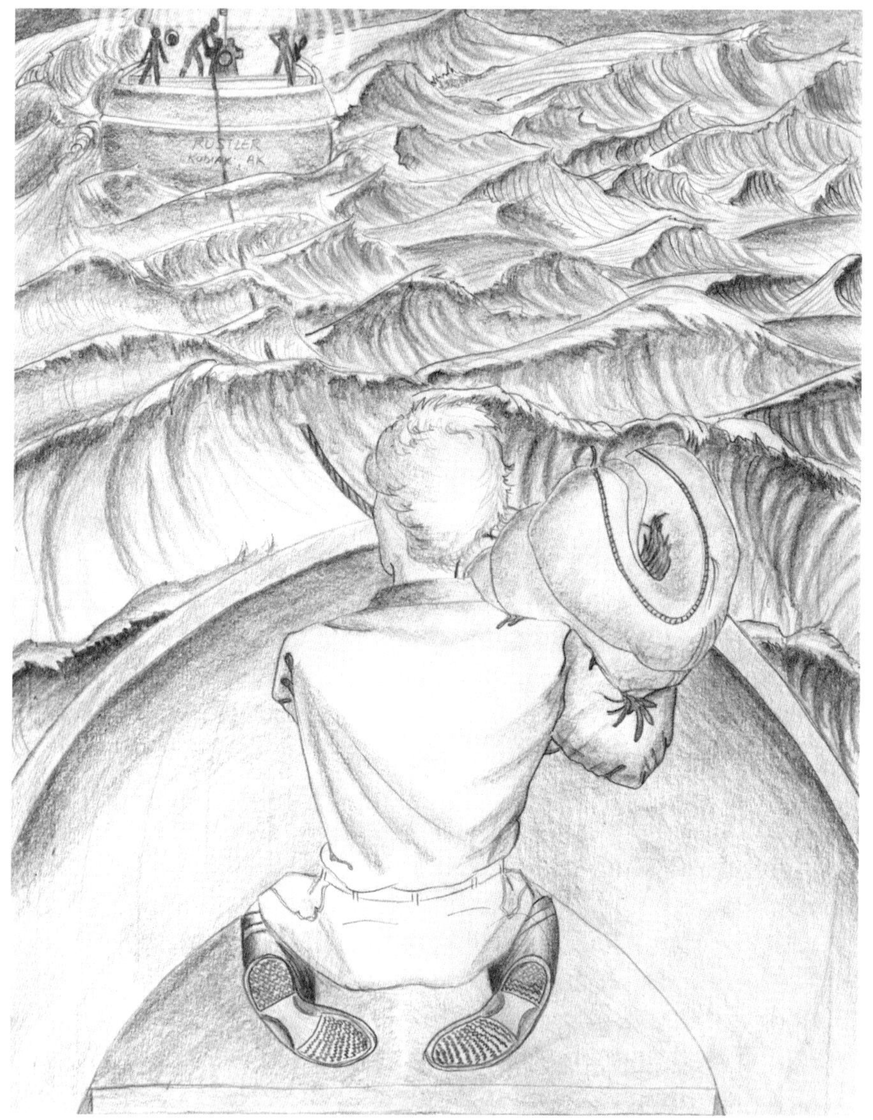

Illustration by Elise Dooley

The violence of the boats crashing together suddenly ceased and I saw Max at the deck winch paying out the bow line through a few wraps around the bitts. The way the line snaked around the posts multiplied its friction, so Max controlled the rate of travel by allowing slack or putting tension on the rope. Even a relaxed tug would tighten the wraps enough to stop the skiff immediately. My lifeboat now rocked violently up and down, moving out of the lee of the boat, and the wind began to whip spray into my face. Again it was odd that the spray, which I knew to be icy cold, felt so warm on my face. It was cold though running down the neck of my shirt. For a short while I eyed *Rustler* as she slowly receded into the darkness, the lonely deck light, ridiculously dim yet providing a cone of backlight to the shadow figures on the deck. Mike and Cliff and George had taken seats on the side of the hatch. They were riding the seas almost nonchalantly, like veterans, watching me float away, hoping for my safety as I was theirs. George pointed at the skiff and said something and Cliff and Mike nodded. They were studying my progress and making a plan for their own ride in. I felt a little better for them and turned my back to the spray, still holding the baby somewhere in the sleeping bag, and staggered my way to the stern searching blindly with numbed, soaking feet for the ribs in the bottom of the skiff and bracing along the boxy engine cover to keep from being thrown down. Reaching the stern I leaned my waist against the raised deck partition, facing aft. As my eyes adjusted better to the dark I could make out the orange-suits waiting for us and growing closer as the wind blew the skiff ashore. Max kept just enough tension on the painter to keep the bow into the swells. Laying the bundle with the baby onto the raised deck as gently as possible I worked with the sleeping bag, groping blindly with freezing fingers to find the top, locating the baby inside, and pulling him up higher. I folded the bag in half underneath him and wrapped it back around his little body, keeping his head down inside a few inches. I opened the top again and peered closely at him. His solemn face and dark eyes, wraithlike and barely visible in the dark, stared back at me without making a sound. He didn't seem afraid and had felt quite warm to the touch when I'd handled him, so I knew he was alright.

When we'd drifted back almost to the man on the rock he played the weak flashlight beam over us briefly and yelled *"How many?"* I hollered back, *"Just me and the baby!"* He peered beyond me out toward the boat and raised his crossed arms. The skiff jerked to a stop and bucked madly in place, sending more regular gouts of spray blown back by the wind and showering us from the bow. More cold rivulets ran down the back of my neck. I tried to ignore the freezing water and focus attention on my rescuer. Using more hand signals, he and Max guided the skiff in very close to the rocks. Spray from each swell now shot up between the jagged black rock and the plunging stern of the skiff. Here again the sea was trying to thwart our rescue right on the brink of safety. I prayed that the bow line held. If it snapped the skiff would be on the rocks in an instant. The man on the rock beckoned for the baby with his arms and it was a hazardous matter to climb up into the seine-well and kneel at the stern waiting for the right moment to pass the baby over to the rescuer in the sopping orange suit. Once again the baby would be handled across a gap of almost certain death if he fell. Inwardly I cowered at the thought, but tuned it out to focus on our timing. The instant the skiff hesitated at the top of a swell I lifted the sleeping bag up through the blast of spray and set it into the outstretched arms of the rescuer. The skiff fell away from him and I quickly grabbed the stern to hang on. The man turned and passed the bundle carefully down off the rock behind him to the second rescuer, who had positioned himself chest deep in the water against the back side of the rock. I couldn't see him but I could see part of the sleeping bag held high above his head.

Again relief flooded through me. Now responsibility for the baby was in competent hands and I felt confident about making the beach on my own. We boys had been caught by high tide more than once while exploring or fishing the beaches and reefs around Kodiak, and had waded around rocky points sometimes to our necks in surging water, clinging to the rocks and working our way along to gain the beach on the other side so we could get home without waiting hours for low tide. Even now in the dark, especially with help nearby, I knew I could make it to the beach. The man on the rock looked at me. *"Ready?"* he shouted, grinning at me, water dribbling off his nose and chin and down his neck into the collar of his suit.

"Just step across, I'll catch you" All I could do was get up and crouch in readiness and when the moment was right, the stern lifted me up to the rock, and I jumped, rather than stepped, and felt powerful arms grapple me in. The salt spray dashed over us, soaking my coat and running in more icy streams down my neck. The man on the rock yelled into my ear that I was going to have to carry the baby ashore as it would take both of them to get people off the skiff and over the rock. He pointed straight in nearly a hundred feet toward the beach. A hundred feet of marching waves and breaking surf boiled and glistened in the oblique light from the helicopter down the beach. He put a hand on my shoulder and looked me in the eye. *"It's not too deep. You should make it fine."* Peering back into his face, I thought, *"Right! Easy for you to say, you're over six feet tall",* but his confidence in me bolstered my determination to give it my best try. I nodded to him, shivering and he helped me slide down off the back side of the rock into the surging, icy brine.

I got a panicky feeling when the water reached my armpits just before my feet found the bottom. *"OY!-OY!-OY!-OY!"*..... My breath came in uncontrollable gasps. Black, freezing water gushed suddenly around the sides of the rock and piled up over my neck and I clung like a terrified octopus to the rock, and to the pants leg of the man on the rock. *"You'll need to hurry and get out of this water!"* the fellow holding the baby yelled as if I didn't already know. He moved over closer to me and held out the sleeping bag. I took the baby from him and held him to me, crossing my arms over his little legs and leaning him upright against my right cheek. The added weight planted my numb feet a little better on bottom and I stepped away from the rock with a swell rising at my back.

Time became a slow-motion dream. All I could manage at one hundred percent effort was to get one foot solidly on the bottom in front of the other and keep moving. At first the swells were lifting me off my feet for a few seconds. The sleeping bag was covered in light canvas and I found that it tended to float me a little which was of some comfort, but I felt myself running in place, fighting to stay upright in the water, the floatation effect tending to push me backward off my feet. That was the trade-off for keeping my head out of the water. It made me mad and made me fight harder, helping my progress. Not one bit of this whole affair had been easy. The bottom provided good footing though, being mainly gravelly sand, so when my boots touched down after the crest of a wave passed me I was quick to move with the swell while I could. It wasn't exactly wading. Each foot of ground was fraught with resistance on all sides. The best I could manage was an off-balance slog through cold, heaving molasses. I was so busy concentrating on staying upright through each swell that I didn't have time to be afraid. I shivered wretchedly. My jaws ached from being clenched to prevent my teeth from chattering and my body moved in spastic jerks. An occasional glance toward the beach rewarded me with a feeling of growing relief. It was getting closer. My relief was spliced with worry for Cliff and Mike and George, and I wondered how they were going to deal with this. After what seemed like an hour of fighting the water, I found that the swells were now only coming up to my waist. I lowered the baby to ease my aching arms and back. The lower part of the sleeping bag was dragging in the water and the whole bag was wet on the outside with salt spray, but the baby never struggled or whimpered and I knew he must be okay. Soon the swells were spilling around the backs of my thighs, foaming around me and pushing me toward shore. Then it was down around my knees and I suddenly felt very heavy. Everything but the top part of the bag and the baby was soaking wet. Finally I was walking with dragging feet out of the sea onto the black, sandy beach. For the first time since Carl ran over the buoy in Woody Island Channel, I *knew* I was going to live to see tomorrow. Just a couple hours ago I figured I was as good as dead-and-drowned and now, somehow, I was alive again. Miserable for certain, but alive and on my feet, even though I couldn't feel them. Inside sopping gloves my fingers were so cold it felt like someone had worked them over with a claw hammer. I gritted my teeth hard against the pain, and allowed myself to whimper a little now that I was alone. *"Now as long as the plane doesn't crash on the way back to town, we can all go home and get warmed up"* I whined aloud as I moved down the beach toward the blinding searchlight of the buzzing helicopter.

CHAPTER 16
Short Ride Home

The aircraft itself was nearly invisible behind the dazzling brilliance except for the leading arc of the angry, spinning rotor slicing through the reflected light above the aircraft's nose. I trudged past the other 'copter. It crouched silently on the dark beach like a white, behemoth insect, just outside the ray of light. The gusting wind kept the quiet rotors nodding but didn't seem to be rocking the aircraft any. There was no activity near it. I had been instructed to go to the aircraft with the searchlight and my wooden feet were moving carefully along, feeling the way, taking me there. The bulky sleeping bag with the baby in it blocked all view of the area just ahead of me. It had grown very heavy from being soaked and my back ached in new places from its weight. The brilliant searchlight obliterated all other sense of proximity above and to my sides. My pupils were dialed painfully to pinpoints and I could only sense the deep, inhospitable void surrounding me because I knew it was there. The din of the surf was drowned out by the fan-like roar of the rotors. Every obstruction on the beach ahead of me, no matter how small, became a black shadow within a bright-white, gleaming corona, the long shadows stretching toward me. Seaweed glistened and flapped soundlessly in the salty spindrift. A few small drift logs loomed on the sand before me. I approached the roaring rotors hesitantly; the stiff blast they produced cancelled the real wind and tore at me, pushing me backward a few steps. I wondered how the heck I was supposed to get to the safety inside it. The racing air seemed to be screaming off a snowfield it was so cold on my skin and clothes. As I moved around to the starboard side of the helicopter, the red lighted interior became visible through the open side door. I couldn't see myself standing out there all night so I started toward the door, crouching slightly in needless fear of the rotors buzzing eight or ten feet over my head, and spied a man coming from the cockpit. He took my arm, never offering to carry the baby, and led me to the wide sliding door then helped me up into the aircraft and I felt heat coming from somewhere. The man yelled something noiselessly and motioned to a plastic-covered, cushioned, bench seat which ran the full length of the cabin opposite the door and wrapped around the rear bulkhead. I sank down gratefully and rested the baby on my lap. My hands and feet ached from the cold and I felt a little guilty sitting in the clean cabin with water running from my clothes. Puddles from my entry lay like pools of watery blood on the painted metal floor, their transparencies fooled by the red light. I checked the baby, pulling the bag down away from his face. His dark Indian eyes stared solemnly back at me, then his head swiveled around to look here and there, quietly taking in these unusual surroundings. The noise was deafening and cold air drafted over me through the open door, re-chilling my clammy pants and wet hair. I laid the baby on the seat then pulled off my wet gloves and forced my hands inside my shirt under my armpits and felt for the vague warmth through the deep ache of my fingers. Now began more waiting. Nothing happened for a long time. I began to worry that something bad may have happened to Cliff or Mike or George. I shivered and waited. The man who had helped me had disappeared forward and I was alone in the aft cabin with the baby. I was miserable enough, but the baby and I were safe. I worried about the boys, willing the time to pass.

Finally, after what seemed three eternities, Mike showed up outside the door, his clothes and hair still dribbling water.

He was also escorted by the man who came from the cockpit and helped up into the cabin. It was nearly impossible to hear over the roar of the engine and rotors, but I got it from him that Cliff and George were coming together on the next trip. Mike sat next to me and began his own rituals of trying to warm up, sitting on his hands for awhile, then hugging himself, shaking and shivering. At one point we looked at each other ruefully, shaking our heads. We'd made it! Not long after Mike arrived, Cliff and George appeared like drowned rats, shivering violently in the icy rotor blast, and made their way stiffly up into the aircraft. We'd all made it ashore. They acknowledged our weak hails and took seats next to us. I could only guess at the story they would tell of their trip from the boat and the watery slog to the beach. The tide was still coming in and I knew the water was getting deeper out by the rock. We all shivered uncontrollably from the cold blasts of air that found their way into the cabin. We waited, impatient to be off, but no one came. We had no idea what was going on but, as we learned later, Hector and his wife came next, needing extra help to get to the beach and were directed to the other helicopter. Next Max and Carl's wife made the harrowing trip in. Carl had elected to stay with the boat. It was the skipper's right. If he abandoned Rustler, anyone could board her and claim salvage rights. It was doubtful that it would happen, but Carl thought there might be a chance to save the boat. I'm sure he knew as well that he would have a lot of questions to answer to the Coast Guard about what happened, and probably needed some time to think.

Max suddenly appeared at the wide door of our aircraft and beckoned to me for the baby. I moved stiffly to the door and passed the bundle down to him. *"Everybody's loaded"* he shouted, *"I'll take the baby to his mama and come back."* He stumped off into the dark, hunched over in the icy blast. I returned to my seat feeling much colder now that the wet, warm sleeping bag and baby were gone from my lap. Presently things started happening. Max came back with one of the men who'd helped us on the rock. Even he was shivering and obviously miserable as he helped the old man climb up into the helicopter. Max looked completely done in. He was gray with cold and shook violently as he tried to squeeze some of the water out of his sleeves over the edge of the door. The man in the orange suit laid an arm over the old man's thin shoulders and hollered something to Max, gesturing to the seats. I'm sure Max was feeling guilty about trailing water into the cabin, but the rescuer waved it off and shook his head. He turned and slid the big door closed cutting off the icy gusts and the intense roar of the rotors. It wasn't exactly quiet inside even with the door closed, but the heat began to make itself felt. To us it was like heaven. We all smiled at one another when we heard the engine winding up for take off. Soon we felt ourselves lifting off and the aircraft dipped its nose and arced away in a banking turn. We were heading for safety at last.

The ten-minute flight back, the landing at the Coast Guard Base and ensuing ride home were anti-climatic. The big H-60 was pushed around a little by the wind as it descended, feeling for the ground and landing solid after a couple soft bumps of the tires. We were down! The pilot cut the engine and the screaming turbine began winding down instantly. After a minute or so the door slid open and there were Guardsmen in dry clothes waiting to help us down to the solid concrete of the ramp. We emerged stiffly, chilled again by the freezing gusts on our wet clothes. The other H-60 was sitting nearby, its rotors also still turning down. Our sense of hearing was restored. Bright hangar lights illuminated the scene. The windswept, black sky loomed overhead. Nature seemed crouched around us, held at bay by the light. I loved the outdoors and here it had tried to kill me. It had also taught me some things about my self and drove home two important facts. Your life suddenly becomes precious when threatened, and human life is very tenuous and fragile.

It was somewhere around 11:30 pm and we were back, alive and safe. We had assured the Coast Guard medics that we were all unhurt and, except for being very wet, cold, tired and hungry, we were fine. I don't know who made the decision but as we milled around together in a kind of daze, not speaking much around all these strangers, two Ace-Mecca taxicabs pulled onto the tarmac near the aircraft. Some one had called us a cab. All we wanted was to go home and get dried out and warmed up.

The cab ride home was quiet. Hector and his wife, Max and Carl's wife and the baby, now swaddled in a dry wool blanket, all rode in one cab. Mike and George, and Cliff and I rode in the other. We were all so tired we didn't talk much except to chuckle again about Cliff and the turkey, and Max coming out of his bunk like some sort of Lazarus, looking like a prime candidate for a halfway house, and him taking charge, to give us hope and save the boat. We shook our heads and wondered about him. Who was he? Just another old washed-up fisherman on the skids in Kodiak. Probably a wino; he had the look. He was a handsome, soft spoken old guy, not exactly fitting our notion of a hero. But that he was. I'm sure that by now Max has been long in his grave and I have always regretted that I never even thanked him for saving us. I'm sure that all Max wanted the last time I saw him as he climbed into the other cab, was some dry clothes and a couple good stiff drinks.

Cliff and I lived closer to town than Mike and George so our cabbie let us off before taking them on out to Spruce Cape. We thanked the driver, said so long to our wet friends and trudged for our door and home. To me it seemed like long months since we had so happily exited that door to an anticipated adventure on Long Island. It was only a few minutes after midnight when Cliff and I came inside the house. Less than twelve hours had gone by since we'd left. The house was quiet except for the welcome rumble of the oil furnace. Everyone was in bed, but of course Ma got up when she heard us come in. You can imagine the horror she must have felt when we told her in brief what had happened. Ma hugged us to herself, wet clothes and all, then ordered us to the shower to warm up and by the time we were in our pajamas, she had some hot food on the table for us. The heat from the shower and the forced air furnace, combined with our full bellies, pushed us over the edge into drowsiness, and after she gave us each a fierce kiss on the forehead, Ma tucked us into bed like babies, and we both drifted off toward weary slumber. One of my last thoughts before sleep came was the one I had envisioned earlier from the deck of the rock-bound *Rustler*, when I had imagined our young corpses rolling and pounding in the frothy surf among the black rocks and seaweed of the Long Island bluffs. The horror I had felt for Ma and Dad and everyone else when they would hear about it the next day. I recoiled from the ugliness of the false vision and forced myself to dwell instead on nothing beyond the reality of being home, cocooned snug and warm in my own bed.

CHAPTER 17
Rustler's Final Rest

Carl stayed with *Rustler* throughout that night as she thumped her keel on the sand, being forced incrementally ashore with the lift of the tide and steady, onshore wind. In the following days he found someone willing to pull her off the beach at high water and tow her up into the protection of Woman's Bay, straight across from the Coast Guard Cutter Dock. There they floated her in, high up the beach at full tide and tied her to huge boulders and an old piling from a bygone Navy dock that still jutted from the rocky beach. And there she rested for many years, a large ragged hole in the hull below the water-line on the port side, laid over like a dead whale far to starboard, the tide filling her at every flood. In the years after, I went up and inspected the wreck a few times, but always got a grim, shadowy sort of feeling when I was close to her and never went back on board. Barnacles and mussels were now feeding from her carcass. *Rustler* was dead. Her massive keel, heavy timbers and stout ribs and planking had been pounded and slammed on solid rock by great hydraulic forces for hours, protecting and shielding us from the maw of that hellish night. I mourned her loss. To me, her death meant our life. I often thought that *Rustler* would have provided a nobler memory had she slipped quietly beneath the waves as she was towed to Woman's Bay rather than being abandoned to become an unsightly derelict, rotting away on the beach. The road to Cape Chiniak ran right past *Rustler's* last grounding. Silently saluting her from the car while passing by was close enough for me.

The wreck of the *Rustler* was a very close call. If it hadn't been for Max our survival would not have gone as well. Yet, as tough and terrifying as it was for me, I can think of twenty and more other fishing boats, sinking or going on the rocks, that were a hundred times worse; men, and sometimes women and kids going down with the boat, or drifting around for days in storm battered rafts, or clinging to foamy rock piles in survival suits, praying for a helicopter or boat to come for them. Often it occurs that there is little to work with in fending off nature's moods on the ocean. Survival suits and inflatable life rafts are puny armor against a winter storm. These essential survival tools usually just buy a few miserable hours for the victims until an Emergency Locator Beacon brings rescue. Even so, these items are far better than the old long-johns and wool shirts men used to wear to insulate against the cold. Abandoning a sinking ship into a wooden skiff in a screaming gale would have been roughly equivalent to a reluctant climb up the gallows steps.

Today the combination of survival suits, inflatable rafts and emergency locator beacons saves lives consistently but when just one part of the system fails to perform it often boils down to your brains and your bare hands and a strong will to get home alive. Sometimes that isn't enough but I believe that one of the toughest parts to overcome in a human being is the will to live, especially if that will is built-in. Experience is one thing that will influence the outcome of survival. Training and practice are another. One never knows how they will react under calamitous circumstances until they occur. The first reaction is usually denial of the reality of what has happened, and an intense desire to protect life and limb by running away or hiding. The human body is frail and fragile but under high stress the mind can make us do things to keep the body alive we might otherwise think impossible. Fear can be a positive motivator. Panic is a killer. There are men and women everywhere who have their own horror stories to tell, and I'm sure they'll agree that survival is dependant on managing an optimistic and proactive frame of mind and that sometimes it takes enormous effort to focus on the moment when death or harm is breathing down your neck.

Although I later fished, and traveled on boats in Kodiak waters, I never again found myself in the dire straits of shipwreck. There have been rough trips, uncertain times and mechanical breakdowns while underway on boats, but none to compare with the trip on *Rustler*. For a time I held some bad feelings against the skipper for getting us into a very ugly situation, but over time I have seen people make bad decisions in all kinds of situations and even made a few myself, and eventually came to realize that it's basically due to being human. Carl made one bad blunder and it probably still disturbs his conscience today. I forgave him early on. He was, and is, a fine man and one who would ordinarily never put anyone in harm's way.

I never talked very much to my friends or family about the near disaster on that trip, but rather buried it in memory. For my part there seemed to be a stigma attached to the occurrence. It was as though it were somehow my own fault for allowing my self and brother to get into such a predicament. It certainly didn't seem like anything to brag about, going out on a boat trip with a bunch of drunks, but it did teach me something about human nature. I experienced at a young age what men (and boys being men) are capable of. There had been no similar situations in my own short past to compare with those terrible long hours, but over time I came to realize that we boys had behaved with spirit and guts. I have come to remember our part in saving *Rustler* with some amount of pride. We were tested hard at a tender age and measured up to the situation. The lesson we learned was more than just what to do, or how to do it but that, when the chips were down and all the cards were on the table, we had the moxie to see it through, win, lose or draw.

The End

Steve Descloux July, 2005

Author's notes:

(1) I have made exclusive use of the name Aleut in describing the native people of Kodiak Island as that was considered the proper name for these people at that time and it seemed to fit better into the context of the story. I mean no disrespect to my proud Alutiiq friends who once actually considered themselves Aleut. But anthropologists since the early 1980s have made a distinction between Aleut and Alutiiq. The differences lie primarily in language and culture, but also in geographic location. Kodiak Island's indigenous people are of Alutiiq descent, whose ancestors also inhabited areas of Prince William Sound and the south coasts of the Alaska and the Kenai Peninsulas. In comparison, The Aleut people have distinctively occupied the western end of the Alaska Peninsula and the islands of the Aleutian Chain.

(ref. The Alutiiq Ethnographic Bibliography - compiled by Rachel Mason - www.ankn.uaf.edu/aeb.html#introa - Chap. II, Sec. A)

(2) The amazing details of this era were documented in a fine memoir, 'The Trail Led North' by Mont Hawthorne in collaboration with his niece, Martha Ferguson McKeown, who is the author. His story, written during the 1940s while Hawthorne was in his mid-eighties, is a well told piece of incidental Alaska history.

Preface:

Readers beware. This story may to be offensive to some. I would hope that it merely be accepted in the spirit of what it is; a true account from memory, start to finish, about a boy's adventures and experiences on a small-scale commercial Harbor Seal hunt. If you are ultra-sensitive about this subject I do not recommend that you read this story.

I will apologize in advance to those who *do* read on and still regard the endeavor of commercial sealing as barbaric savagery, and who are gruesomely offended by explicit description of the work itself. It is not my intention to offend, but rather to make the details of the experience available to those who are interested in such things, and to preserve for my own children and grandchildren a few of the stories of their predecessor's lives. I don't apologize for hunting seals. The reader must be mature or forgiving enough to realize that in 1970, trapping and seal hunting was a very acceptable, honorable and even admired occupation of rural Alaskans. I will say that, as inured to the killing of animals as I was, growing up in a family that ate almost exclusively wild meat and fish in their daily diet, it took some soul searching to actually get myself worked up to kill my first seal pup. This became especially poignant to me because I had to do it with a club. Thinking back on that brute-like initiation I realize that I didn't really face the issue one hundred percent. I had neither the maturity nor the education to really think about it. I shelved it deep in the back of my mind like the fear of God until I was standing over my first baby seal with club in hand. By then it was too *late* for me to think about it. Before that actual moment, the notion of bludgeoning a cute, helpless little animal on the head and cutting its hide off wasn't allowed much time to bother my psyche. Furs were quite popular and many were bought from the trappers by the local citizens and tourists before the fur buyers even got a chance to see them. It was simple economics. With the excitement that only a fifteen-year-old boy can feel in the certainty that he is about to embark upon his first real adult employment, the only thoughts at the forefront of *my* thinking were the coming adventures of traveling more than a hundred miles by small boat down the wild east side of Kodiak Island, working in places I'd only heard about in stories around the kitchen table and seen on marine charts, *and* getting paid for it. I didn't even know if I was up to the challenge. To my way of thinking I was going trapping, which was considered a man's job. I didn't know enough about the gory details to consider that it could bother me. Maybe I didn't want to know.

In the States however, and indeed around the world, public opinion, specifically about seal hunting, was being altered by very aggressive, well planned protests and film-media coverage, mainly thrust under our noses by the budding Greenpeace organization. These protests were not favorably received by the majority of Alaskan people, who really don't like *anyone* telling us what to do. These crazy protesters were threatening our very livelihoods and essentially calling us a bunch of blood-thirsty, insensitive savages as well. You know how kids are, name calling begets bad feelings and *more* name calling, sides are formed and a fight generally ensues. The same thing happened here and, ultimately the general public was horrified and shamed by grisly, bloody images of brutish men killing fuzzy, white, innocent-eyed seal pups and stripping them of their hides. These very graphic films and photographs were, I believe, mostly filmed in the Canadian Arctic. As a result, a law called the Marine Mammal Protection Act, introduced by Senator Magnusen, was passed by the U.S. Congress in 1972 which curtailed the taking of any more sea mammals by white people in the United States. The trappers lost the war on that one, being a very misrepresented, maligned and therefore, unpopular minority. Change can be tough to live with if it abruptly dictates that you will not henceforth have access to one of the traditional resources you are dependant upon, the very resources upon which the economy of the State of Alaska was originally founded.

Alaska's Native peoples, the original hunters of these creatures, having no more say-so about it than the trappers, were graciously allowed by the Magnusen Act to continue taking sea mammals, but denied the commercial value of the skins attainable by selling to fur buyers. Instead, now they must work the natural materials into some form of art or clothing, at which they are marvelously and ingeniously adept. Their works could then be sold to tourists or collectors at rates which far exceed standard fur prices, giving them more bang for their buck. This arrangement definitely benefits many, but other Alaska Natives, probably a majority, were stripped of the economic alternative of commercial hunting and trapping. Some Native people, as with any other culture, have little or no artistic talent or interest, but may be exceptionally good hunters. The restriction on selling commercial sea mammal skins eliminated the option of making a good living from their abundant local resources. These original people, living a tough life as they do in very remote areas have even less economic opportunity than white people who choose to live in the bush. Stopping the harvesting of seals by the white hunters scored a solid win for the protest groups, and was certainly a soothing balm for the national 'moral' conscience. For the individuals who depended on the fur business to put spuds on the table it was a little different matter, a good part of their yearly income was gone.

For some years following the Magnusen Act there was substantial increase in herd populations, but now, thirty years later, the once teeming herds are gravely diminishing. Although it's as plain as pilot bread to anyone with half a brain, no one seems to know exactly why. I learned it from Mr. Spessard in tenth grade biology. Commercial seal hunts in Alaska were controlled by strict quotas and closely monitored by the Fish and Game Department. The thinning of the herds had little or no adverse effect on the health or population of the animals. Quite the contrary, hunting pressure eliminated many animals which had weak survival instincts, and actually sharpened these instincts in the stronger animals, improving the gene pool for the future herd generations. In nature only the strong live to maturity. The law-protected, welfare state of the sea mammals now appears to have weakened their very survivability.

The story is as true as my fifty year old memory can make it. I have not embellished the experience, incredible as that may seem, but may have waxed a bit romantic in describing it. The filter of memory is good at dimming actual pain and suffering. It wasn't very romantic, but rather grueling work and privation. It was a time of emergent growth for me, an important step toward maturity. Every detail impacted my memory deeply. In the telling of the story, as I relived it, the minute details welled up from hidden places and flooded my mind with colors and smells and emotions. I trust you will find them interesting.

Steve Descloux March, 2005

Confessions of a Seal Hunter

By Steve Descloux

Chapter **Page**

1. A Different Set of Values................ 129
2. Elise 136
3. The Skiff.. 143
4. Departure....................................... 150
5. Ugak Island 160
6. First Hunt....................................... 166
7. The Run to Tugidak 174
8. The Life of a Seal Hunter 182
9. Feral Boy 189
10. South-end Cabin........................... 197
11. The Biggest Herd 207
12. Hallucinations & Killer Whales 212
13. The Weather Breezes Up 217
14. Engine Problems 224
15. Magical Return.............................. 230

Pronunciation Guide

Some of the places and names used in the stories may seem almost unpronounceable. Offered here you will find them as I learned to say them. (place emphasis on capitals)

Afognak	a-FOG-nak
Aiaktalik	eye-AK-ta-lik
Aleut	AL-yute
Aleutian	a-LOO-shun
Alitak	AL-i-tak
Aliulik	ali-OO-lik
Alutiiq	a-LOO-tick
Chignik	CHIG-nik
Chiniak	CHIN-iak
Geese	GEE-see (hard G)
Kaguyak	ka-GOO-iak (hard G)
Kaiuganak	kie-YOO-ga-nak
Karluk	KAR-luk
Katmai	KAT-mie
Kiavak	KIE-avak
Kiluda	ki-LU-da
Kizhuyak	ki-ZHU-iak
Kodiak	KO-diak
Kupreanof	kupri-ON-off
Monashka	mon-OSH-ka
Ouzinkie	yoo-ZINK-ie
Pasagshak	pa-SAG-shak
Shelikof	SHEL-ikof
Shuyak	SHU-iak
Sitkalidak	sitka-LEE-dak
Sitkinak	SIT-ki-nak
Tugidak	tuh-GEE-dak (hard G)
Ugak	U-gak
Uganik	u-GAN-ik
Viekoda	vie-KO-da

CHAPTER 1
A Different Set of Values

From the time I was five years old in 1958 my family lived in what was still the frontier town of Kodiak, situated in the North Pacific and far removed from the cushy, frantic modernism of the States. What we considered ordinary living would probably been considered quite uncultured and backward to most of an American society so fervently engaged in pursuit of the American Dream, bulging with as many frills as could be bought or mortgaged. We were a poor family, more concerned with mere survival, and although we lived in actual houses in town, our life *was* almost like a permanent camping trip. Even as a kid I often wondered at the kind of people that would forsake the comfort and convenience of life in the States to seek out the far reaches of civilized living, especially in a backward place like Kodiak, to eke out the boom-and-bust kind of existence which outdoor living generally demands. They must certainly possess the basic requisite qualities of grit, independence, self sufficiency, ingenuity and frugality. A high tolerance for general insufficiency, pain and suffering would be helpful.

Over the years my family adopted many of these unlikely *Chechakos* and helped 'break them in' to Alaska's very different set of unwritten rules to live by, some of which if ignored, could get you killed. One common thread these people seemed to share was an immediate, expansive love for the rare beauty and wilderness and freedom of this Kodiak Island. With the exception of the town and its short road system, and six Aleutiiq villages, these islands are as honest-to-God wild as they were ten thousand years ago. There, instant calamity can occur if you are not careful, and often does even if you *are* careful. Giant bears prowl anywhere they please, the all-critical weather and tides dictate your every plan and can prevail against you and threaten life itself. Even today, as modern and well supplied as any city in the nation, Kodiak remains a tough place to live. That means you have to be tough (or stuck) to remain there.

Thousands have come to these islands to try their hand at living this frontier dream. Some died trying, and many returned home to the States after suffering through a season or two, finding the *dream* to be more of a nightmare. There are a few who managed to survive long enough to learn the local intricacies of living with Kodiak's rough, bawdy nature and made the place their permanent home. These few seem to find that the hard reality of making your own existence in these far-flung places results in what might be called a rather macho satisfaction in their ability and mental toughness in coping long-term with the myriad difficulties of life on the Island. This is true of all rural Alaskans. It seems to bring about deep and subtle, almost indefinable contentment with life, which, for most true Kodiakans, goes missing if they move back the States or sometimes only as far as the mainland. A persistent little ache for the place haunts them. The minute they set foot back in Kodiak (they always come back) the contentment returns. They're home. It is difficult, if not impossible, to describe this feeling to one who doesn't share it. Many have tried. The famed Robert Service, peerless Bard of the North, probably came as close as anyone in his ballads of the Klondike. He best captured the understated toughness and grit and the appreciation for the vast solitudes of the north country.

This 'macho satisfaction' in one's own abilities is true of the women too, who would really care to live nowhere else on earth--although it *is* nice to fly out to the States once in awhile.

Don't get the idea that frontier women are a bunch of rough and tough gals. It has always amazed me how a woman can work right alongside a man, say on a salmon boat, covered in fish gurry, pulling like hell on lines and web with every muscle, put in a full day of seining while enduring the maddening, biting no-see-ums and white-socks, cook for the crew (men cook too) or stand wheel-watch, mend web, fuel the skiff, fix the kicker (outboard), or any of the other million little things working on a boat requires, yet maintain a woman's perspective, concerns and general femininity. Of course sometimes they get cranky and peckish, but so do men who are cooped up on a tiny boat living for weeks or months in each others faces. With all due respect I must say that the women of this caliber that I have worked beside often outshine many men. When you hire on as a deckhand on a small fishing boat you make up a third or quarter of the workforce. If you can't pull your weight on deck your mates have to carry you, and man or woman, you are a drag on the operation. You will likely be looking for another berth when the boat hits town after one trip. Only those women, who possess supreme confidence in themselves and are mentally and physically tough enough, and have a real love for the clean open reaches of Kodiak's many bays and waters continue to make their living thus in this predominately *man's* world. The mysterious, rugged interior mountains and beckoning high valleys, the lack of general populace and the very visible wildlife and sea mammals become a requisite part of their lives. It's a very tough existence, physically and financially, but one that is infinitely rewarding. My hat is off to these true Alaskan women.

Public opinion has been altered over the years to now regard women in the workplace a common sight. Today women work at almost every profession previously only thought of as man's work. Thirty years ago it was uncommon to find a woman working on a fishing boat unless she was the skipper's wife or girlfriend. If a woman took a deckhand job, often as not she was viewed askance by 'public opinion' as to her character and virtue. Credit must go to those who stuck it out regardless of what the public thought. They paid this price to live as they pleased, not necessarily to promote the cause of women's rights or feminism. Their efforts, however, did much to help alter public opinion on the subject. They essentially proved they could handle the job as well as a man and get along as a real part of the crew. Many of them now own and operate their own fishing boats, some with all women crews, including my niece, Shawna whose two teenage daughters make up her crew.

Kodiak in 1970 was still emerging from the mountainous, smoldering refuse heaps of the remains of shattered buildings left by the massive earthquake and tsunamis in the spring of 1964 that scrambled the main part of the city like a bowl of eggs. The commercial fishing industry was in high gear with new fisheries and processing technology being rapidly developed by big Seattle and International money, and old fisheries techniques and equipment in a state of continuous improvement by the fishermen themselves. A long-planned hydro-electric plant project was in full swing up inside Kizhuyak Bay, drawing water power from Terror Lake. The entire Kodiak Naval Base (NAVCOMSTA-Kodiak) was preparing to shut down operations and abandon the island. The U.S. Coast Guard would be manning the entire base in a very wise move on the part of the Military and Department of Transportation. The town was beginning to catch up with the States in the way of modern services and buildings. Kodiak High School had been expanded with a big vocational complex, and Native students from villages on Kodiak Island and on the Alaska Peninsula and the Aleutian Chain swelled the ranks of the student body. The town-folk invited them into their homes much like exchange students for several years until the dorms were built, and the streets and stores were filled with new faces. It was very crowded. During my first two years at KHS we attended school in shifts, morning shift and afternoon shift. It must have been *'hell with all the frills'* for the teachers and staff.

I had been raised by parents who were very non-racial.

My dad especially having adamantly admonished us from a tender age to treat all people with respect never mind what color they are. You accept a man as a man. Period. At least until he proves himself to be a coyote. As a long admirer of Indian and Native ingenuity, toughness and hunting techniques, it was very easy for me to make friends among the new kids from the villages. Our family had many Aleut friends from around the island and they often stayed at our house when they were stuck in town waiting on weather or boat parts. My little brother and I soaked up their stories about village life, trapping and hunting, or tough trips on their boats, which sometimes ended with disastrous or tragic consequences. We learned from their experiences and longed for the days when we could get out there and have a few adventures of our own.

We grew up in a frontier culture (there really is no other term for it) with hunting and fishing being very much a part of staying fed. Trapping was a natural extension of this environment, and although there weren't a lot of people employed at it, there was a substantial core of local men who made it a part of their seasonal livelihood. Animal fur was still very much in demand and even though prices weren't always tops, a winter and spring trapping season would at least pay the cannery bills from the previous salmon season, and maybe even grubstake the start of the up-coming season. It was a hard way to make a living, but most the island's barnacle-like inhabitants preferred the bush and fishing over a town job.

My older brother, Dave was a trapper, mainly in Uganik Bay and up on the North end of Afognak Island, and Cliff, my youngest brother, spent at least one season at Blue Fox Bay on Shuyak Island trapping with our brother-in-law, Joe Terabasso who lived up there with my oldest sister, Linda and their kids. Another, later, brother-in-law, Dave Lindberg, trapped extensively on Afognak Island. Our views on trapping were simple enough. Economics. But we were always taught to respect the animals we hunted and killed. Basic unwritten code my dad preached over and over was to "Make a clean shot so the animal don't suffer and so you won't ruin any meat; don't kill any more meat than you need, and; use every scrap of meat, fat and gristle that wasn't blood-shot from the bullet". I knew my feelings about killing animals for meat. Cliff and I had hunted with our one BB gun, a Daisy Pump, from the time I'd received it as a Christmas present from my brother Dave when I was nine. We were so little we had to put the butt on the ground and use both hands and our weight to cock the powerful spring. I must admit that in the fascination of learning to hunt and shoot at animated targets like songbirds, which were pretty easy to sneak upon, and the big scavenger birds such as crows and magpies that required a real Daniel Boone to get within effective range, we overlooked the fact that we were killing merely for the self-satisfaction we got from succeeding at it. When after a few years we moved up to the .22 rifle and began to hunt 'big game' like rabbits, we began to lose our taste for killing little birds for no reason at all. We actually felt guilty at the memories of our past sins. Killing for plain enjoyment probably qualified us for hell. We never hunted rabbits or ducks with the BB gun because we knew that it wasn't powerful enough for a quick kill. We didn't intentionally make our prey suffer. But rabbits were meat, thus fair game for the hungry hunter and his .22 rifle. We usually brought them home, but sometimes we built ourselves a fire on the spot and 'cooked' the still warm critter in the flames, not knowing enough to let the fire burn down to a hot bed of coals. We sprinkled on liberal amounts of the salt and pepper we always carried, mixed in a little plastic bag, and ate the stringy, half cooked meat right off the stick, squatting by the fire and licking the salty blood from our fingers like little savages. This was a meal of *Providence* and certainly every bit as justifiable as picking the local berries and wild greens and Pushki stalks we had learned to eat (1). We wouldn't have starved if we hadn't killed the rabbit, but this hunter play-acting was a critical part of our experience in learning to survive in the Kodiak environment. I had by then consciously adopted the Native American understanding (or justification) of the matter. Animals were put on earth by the Great Creator (I call him God) for our direct use and benefit.

Many years later while living for a time in the States I watched as my boss called up his big, prime, three year old Hereford bull. The animal came trotting ponderously up from the crick toward Carl and stopped a short distance away from him like a pet expecting a treat. Instead the bull was pole-axed between the eyes by a single, tiny .22 caliber bullet from fifty feet away and quickly slaughtered in the small field next to the sawmill during our lunch break. The thirty minutes it took the mobile slaughter truck operator to put that beautiful, trusting beast into his truck, (shot, bled, gutted, hoisted vertical by the hocks on a gambrel with meat hooks, skinned, beheaded, and split in half with an electric power saw) was more disturbing to me than any wild animal I ever shot, cleaned and butchered myself for meat. It really wasn't much different I suppose, but it struck me as so very clinical and impersonal. I am certain that Carl must have felt some pangs of remorse, even though a practical man. He loved animals, and had grown this animal for his family's personal food. He'd hand-fed the bull himself from a yearling and must have had feelings toward the beast. My wife and I lived clear across town from the mill and often in the quiet of an evening we heard him calling his cows in to be fed. His clear yell, "SAWBOSS!-SAWBOSS!-SAWBOSS!" rang out and echoed all over the little town.

I believe that in any conscientious hunter there abides a respectful affection and admiration for the beauty and intelligence of the prey. So the original people believed, and usually made offerings of thanks to the animal for giving up its life to provide them with food and skins. Most of that kind of traditional and spiritual hunting culture has long since been lost to the convenience and efficiency of white-man ways and modern equipment.

CHAPTER 2
Elise

Early in the spring, in my junior year of high school, my brother-in-law Tom Dooley was delivered his first fishing boat. He'd had it built by a company in Seattle and shipped to Kodiak by SeaLand, using funds somehow saved from his previous summer's salmon crew share. In the few years since his Navy discharge at NAVCOMSTA Kodiak, where he had been a member of the elite runway crash crew, Tom chose to stay in Kodiak. He had fished salmon with the old German, 'Wild Bill' Wynkoop (wine-koop) on the ancient, steel-hulled Washington Fish & Oyster Company boat, *WAFCO 20*, which Bill had operated when he fished for that company decades before. They used the '*Twenty*' as living quarters, personal tender and for towing the heavy 32 foot, open wooden jitney, the *Jaqualine D*, the boat they actually fished. Tom's first salmon season was spent as a green deckhand, and then the next season Wild Bill made him the skiff man, probably after noting the uncommon size and strength of his crewman. Their fishing skiff, probably a 16 footer, was of the stout, plank build common to Kodiak, known as an 'Opiem' after the man, Ed Opiem, who built them near the village of Ouzinkie on Spruce Island. Tom's first season as skiff man was spent towing the seine behind a pair of oars. Wild Bill was too cheap to realize that an outboard motor would maximize their efforts and improve their speed in closing and pursing the seine, especially when it was blowing. After a brutal fishing season Tom worked on Bill all the next winter, and by spring had convinced him to buy a brand new outboard motor which Tom himself would pay for out of his crew share at the end of the season. The next summer, with the amazing, effortless power of the brand new eighteen horsepower Evinrude they put in a very good season. Tom was becoming less an Alabama country-boy and more an Alaskan fisherman. He was deeply hooked.

Tom's new 'moneymaker' could hardly be called a boat, being not much more than an unpainted bare hull. It was essentially a big, open, plywood skiff some 24 feet long, having a rather high pointed bow and a motor-well boxed-in just forward of the stern. Even so, I was pretty impressed when I came home from school one afternoon and there the boat lay in the yard. Tom had recently asked me if I would care to go on the spring seal hunt with him. *Would I care to...*?!! That didn't even need an answer! I was as fired up as he was to start working on the boat. Tom had a town job on weekdays. He was the motorcycle mechanic for Jack Mann, the local Honda dealer, and I was still going to high school, meaning we could only work on the boat on evenings and weekends.

Tom had been planning the set-up of the new boat for months and knew how he wanted to put it together. We started the project by supporting the big skiff up off the ground using pallets. Tom was always fairly direct in his approach to work. He simply backed up to one end of the big skiff and latched on with his long arms and giant hands, then straightened his legs to lift it as high as he could while, working fast, I stacked pallets underneath from the side. Then he eased his new boat gently onto the pallets and we repeated the maneuver end for end until we got the desired height and stability. Next we rigged a Visquine and two-by-four shelter over the boat, allowing for a little working room along the sides, and strung an extension cord from the nearby pump house for power and lights.

Tom was a good carpenter. He built a strong, diminutive plywood dog-house just back from the bow, which proved to be a little cramped for his XL size. The 'cabin' wasn't much bigger than about five by six feet and maybe four feet high from the bottom of the boat. The sides tapered forward to follow the inward curve of the bow, leaving a narrow strip of ledge to cap the gunwale on each side for foot-access forward. The front and rear cabin bulkheads he fitted to their respective ribs across the flat bottom and tight along the sides to extend up and make the height of the cabin. Access into the little dry cubby made by the tiny covered bow was through a cut-out in the forward bulkhead inside the cabin. This is where the anchor, chain and lines would be stowed. The ribs inside of the cabin were decked over with plywood, and a two by six frame was fastened to the deck on each side to define the bunks and keep our thick, cushiony foam mattresses in place. Tom wanted to preserve maximum room aft of the little cabin for the fish-hold, which must pack as much salmon as possible, and so purposely shortchanged himself when it came to his personal bunk room. Tom stood about six-foot-six and would have to suffer sleeping semi-fetal or on his back with his knees in the air. I, on the other hand, could stretch out just fine in my bunk with room left over for my gear. Or so I thought. Storage space on any boat took priority over personal comfort. Even more so for a lowly crewman. On this tiny boat it was doubly true. Tom ultimately decided that the extra room at the foot of my bunk would be the perfect place for the coffee pot, lantern and cooking outfit.

He had also fashioned a strong plywood double door, the bottom half acting as a bulkhead to keep fish from spilling into the cabin. As small as I was, I had to stoop to enter the cabin. Tom had to duck-walk or crawl. There were no portholes or windows for light or visibility. There was no need as the steering was to be done outside at the back of the house.

He then boxed in a deep compartment on each side of the motor-well, using thick marine plywood to create voids for the future salmon seine. One void would hold the heavy leadline, the other, the bulky corkline. The aft couple feet of the well was already covered and would serve to hold the web. Tom had purchased two pumps for the boat. One was a long, gray plastic 2 inch hand pump of the variety one sees used by bush pilots to pump out their leaky pontoons. The other one he'd splurged on, a dinky little plastic, electric pump with a cheap-looking, 1 inch red accordion tube for an overboard outlet. Although Tom chuckled and agreed, he probably didn't appreciate it when I told him it looked like a kid's toy. I'm reasonably certain that he had a hard time justifying the extra cost. Every item on his boat was selected by careful priority and planning, on a shoestring beget, and after all, this was a 'siwash' seiner, everything was done by hand. But the Eighty-Five had an alternator to keep the big battery charged and by now Tom knew first hand that a pump can save your bacon. We mounted both pumps with the suctions just forward of the seine-well on the starboard side where the heavy pile of the leadline would create a permanent list, causing any water in the boat to collect there. Both seine-wells had a drain to allow water to gravitate to the pumps. A stout, 4X4 tow post was installed, braced strongly into the frames of the boat on both sides and at the back, made high enough to clear all towing obstructions.

Next we gave the boat its first coat of paint, a Navy grey color, copiously applied inside and out, and Tom carefully lettered the name of the boat in black on the bow and stern. He christened her *Elise* after his and Janice's tow-headed two year old daughter. After applying dark red coppercoat to her flat bottom and to the six inches above the chine, the painting was complete and she suddenly looked like a real boat. Next came a multitude of finer details like cleats, hand-rails on top of the cabin and the new radio and its long, white, fiberglass whip antenna. There was no mast, boom or hydraulics on the boat. This would be a 'siwash' outfit. The small seine would be brought aboard by hand. Tom had carefully planned the placement of every item long in advance. He was like a kid with box full of new toys. He was taking his future into his own hands and enjoying doing it, staking everything he and my sister Janice could save or borrow on his belief that he could catch enough salmon to make it pay. I personally thought that he was starting a little early. I figured it must surely take many years to learn enough on a boat to run your own operation. Most of the fishing skippers I knew were 'old'. But he had several seasons under his belt with Wild Bill, and Wynkoop knew how, and where to catch salmon. Having fished and trapped on Kodiak and Afognak Islands for decades, Bill knew the waters. Tom was no *Chechako* that was for sure, and he learned fast. And remembered what he'd learned.

Finally, after removing all but one layer of pallets to lower the boat, we tackled the job of installing the outboard, a massive, eighty-five-horse Evinrude. Again Tom served as the forklift, muscling the heavy, awkward motor out of his truck and standing it up on its skeg with me like an ant pulling and tugging and lifting wherever I could get a hand in, grunting audibly now and then to make sure he knew I was helping. Then, while I struggled to balance and stabilize it, he ducked in just below the powerhead and strained upright with it on his shoulder, staggered to the stern of the boat and rested it carefully back on the ground on the skeg. After recycling several lung-fills of air, Tom recovered sufficiently to finish the job by taking hold of the beast again and hoisted it up to the stern of the boat. With me chattering directions (he couldn't see in front of the motor) and lifting on the skeg we somehow got it over the stern and into the motor-well. Then with a little more grunting and jiggling, the clamps finally slid with a heavy thump down onto the transom. We centered up the motor and tightened the clamps and added a safety line to prevent losing the motor overboard in the event it was somehow ripped from the transom. It happens...say when you run the boat full bore afoul of a submerged rock or reef that is obviously in the wrong place, or run over a log in the middle of the night while traveling. We mounted the steering wheel and motor controls on a small, angled console built onto the back of the cabin and strung the cables aft to the motor, making sure nothing we did would create a snag for lines or seine web. After installing the huge battery, on the port side to help offset the weight of the leadline, and hooking up the starting system, we began to feel like the boat was pretty much as ready as we could make it. I longed for the day we would put it in the water and make the test run, but as it turned out I was in school that day and missed out on *Elise's* maiden voyage.

After knocking off from our labors on the boat every evening, and after a big supper of Janice's fine home cooking we spent a few hours on other preparations. For weeks we worked on our new Herter's skinning knives with Carborundum stones, honing the long, curved blades to surgically fine edges by feathering the bevel back the full width of the blade, which Tom said would be quick to re-sharpen while hunting. We also put razor edges on our large, folding 'ringing' knives, and hand-rubbed hot boot grease into all the leather sheaths and into our leather hunting boots. Our Alaska trapping licenses were in our wallets, we checked and double-checked all our camp gear like the heavy, white, 8X10 cabin tent, the Coleman lantern (single burner to conserve fuel, with plenty of mantles and a spare generator), two-burner Coleman stove and a gas jug for their Blazo fuel. We had a five gallon water jug, which would be refillable at any of the myriad, clear, icy streams pouring off the mountains into every bay. Our very limited cooking gear consisted of a skillet, one large saucepan, a frying spatula, one big spoon and a couple big stainless-steel kitchen knives. There was a plate, bowl, cup, fork and spoon apiece, and Tom's pride and joy, the gray, one-gallon, ceramic coated, percolator coffee pot, complete with the innards. Fishermen and seal hunters were always wet and cold, and to them hot coffee, slurped from heavy white china mugs, was the 'Balm of Gilead', girding men up in the thick of the fight to return them to the fray strong, alert and refreshed. Coffee, for Tom, was probably as important as food. The pot had a very wide base and so would be quite stable in rough weather. Other than buying groceries, mix oil for the outboards, Blazo fuel for the Colemans, and two drums of fuel for the outboards and motorcycles, we were as ready as we could be.

Tom planned to use the motorcycles, an older Honda Trail-

90 and one of Kodiak's first new Honda 90 three-wheelers, to hunt the long sand beaches of Tugidak Island which is basically a giant sand dune about 15 miles long, some miles off the South end of Kodiak Island. Spotted hair seals migrated to Tugidak by the tens of thousands in the spring to birth their pups, dispersing themselves on beaches around the island in small herds that might be as few as twenty or as many as five hundred or a thousand animals. No one could expect to do a very big hunt on Tugidak on foot.

CHAPTER 3
The Skiff

Tom and Joe Terabasso were currently still partnering on a dwindling winter Harbor Seal hunt on the weekends out around Pasagshak Bay and Narrow Cape which were accessible by car. In early spring the hides were still prime on adult seals. They hunted from Tom's 13-foot Boston Whaler, a small, unsinkable fiberglass runabout. They used small caliber, scope-mounted rifles, making head shots only, as that is the only part of a seal visible when he is in the water. A bullet hole anywhere else in the beautiful hide seriously degrades the price. It's very hard to shoot from a rocking skiff but they were consistently successful, losing some percentage which sank before they could retrieve them. When you shoot a seal in deep water and it has just drawn a breath, the air will trap in the lungs from the way the head lays down, closing off the windpipe. If the seal has just *exhaled* when it was killed, chances are good that it will sink. The advancing spring weather finally turned too snotty for them to continue hunting as, coming in one day to beach the skiff near the mouth of Pasagshak River where the truck was parked, they got thrown crosswise in the breakers and the skiff flipped over, dumping them and their gear into the surf.

Who invented the maneuver I don't know, but at that time among the 'skiff community' the popular method of getting yourself and your skiff safely onto the beach through a heavy surf was to first cruise the length of the beach, picking the best landing place, hold the skiff just outside the breaking surf until the biggest swell approached, waiting for the stern to lift and keeping the bow to the beach, then twist the throttle open just enough to stay on top, and ride the wave as far as you dared before it broke, quickly shutting off and raising the motor to prevent it's hitting the beach and making sure to hold on when you ran out of water and the rapid deceleration began. If you timed it right, the skiff would surf smoothly in and produce a loud sigh as it slid up the beach to a stop on the sand above the breaking waves. The sound was a little different if the beach was rocky. If you missed your timing, and everyone *has* at one time or other, you knew right away it was going to be interesting.

Tom and Joe lost their rifles and some other gear when the skiff flipped, but retrieved the boat and motor, oars, fuel tanks and the anchor, plus the seals they'd taken that day. While stripping and wringing out their clothes, shivering naked on the beach, they talked it over and decided to pack it in for the season. The old timers always said there came a point in time when you have to stop fighting the weather and hole up for awhile until it blows over or eases up. People who can't or won't make this call often die as a result.

In the wake of the decision to abandon the hunt Tom, had the skiff to consider and decided to leave it anchored far up the river in the flats as they had been doing while they were not hunting. It would be alright there for a few weeks or until the weather turned favorable for a trip around Cape Chiniak and back to town. The Whaler would never fill with water and swamp like wooden skiffs. It was designed to be self-bailing as long as the drain plug was left open. In fact, the only time the plug was ever installed was when there was a load in the skiff sufficient to submerge the drain. (Personal experience later taught me that if snow weighs the skiff down, or ice plugs the drain, the whaler *will* fill up with water). The skiff would tend itself if left unmolested by humans. At that time Kodiak was a place where people could generally be trusted not to vandalize or steal or shoot holes in personal property left unattended far from town. It was a small community and people usually looked out for one another.

The day came when, the work on *Elise* being finished, and the seal pupping season already some weeks advanced, Tom told me it was time to bring the skiff around from Pasagshak. Not having a trailer, we still could have loaded the Whaler into the back of his pickup and hauled it to town, but he didn't want to beat the skiff up over thirty-five miles of washboard gravel roads. The weather was mild and sunny, perfect for a quick trip. Cool, light breezes of fresh spring-like air stirred the senses with promise of new growth and warmer days. We made the trip to Pashagshak in *Elise* and, being empty of all but fuel and ourselves, she flew across the water at close to thirty knots with a powerful, steady roar, the 'Eighty-Five' trailing a long white wake, neatly dividing the sea far astern. The speed-induced wind numbed our faces, tore tears from our eyes and roared in our ears. We were both nearly giddy with pleasure in the obvious success of our efforts. In a very short time we were rounding the point into Pasagshak Bay and heading for the mouth of the river. Tom had timed our arrival to coincide with high tide and *Elise* was able to idle up the river right to the spot where the skiff lay at anchor.

Now, I don't know whether Tom knew it or not but I had never exactly operated a kicker. I'd *seen* it done often enough, and knew pretty much how to start it. Just pump up the bulb on the fuel line, crack open the throttle and pull the choke knob out, then put one foot against the transom and yank on the starter cord furiously until the motor fired up. I also knew how to engage the forward and reverse lever. But Tom unknowingly saved me the embarrassment of admitting my deficiency by explaining that this was an older kicker (it may have been the very Eighteen Evinrude he'd bought from Wild Bill) and it needed to be started a certain way when it was cold. He explained the procedure and let me yank on the cord to get it going and we made sure it warmed up and ran fine. Tom looked at me pointedly and with mild concern, "You figger you can run the skiff okay Steve?" (his southern accent rendered my name as 'Staeve') I didn't have to think about it, I already had, knowing he would be running out in front of me with *Elise*, and that the skiff wouldn't sink on me even if it filled up with water. It seemed safe enough to me. I gave him my best version of a scornful grin and with bravado I didn't exactly feel, told him, "A'*course* I can". So we pulled the skiff anchor and took in the shore line and tied them onto the bow cleat to keep the anchor from bouncing around. Then Tom headed *Elise* down the narrow tide-swollen river toward the bay, with me following at slow speed, cautiously figuring out how to control the outboard and steer the skiff as I went. We exited the river into the blue, breeze-ruffled bay and Tom ran out a few hundred yards, slowed down, and then took the boat out of gear, waiting for me to catch up. I approached *Elise* cautiously and lay off several yards while he gave me further instructions like, "Just stay in the middle of my wake and keep on comin'", and "if you have a problem with the kicker don't worry, I'll be watchin' behind me."

So I made myself as comfortable as possible sitting on the right side of the low, inner transom while gripping the outboard throttle and tiller with my left hand. The 13 foot Whaler is built very low to the water and, sitting on the transom as I was, I could reach down without leaning over, and dabble my fingers in the water. Tom had removed the shiny chrome hand-rails to strip the skiff for work. It all felt very foreign to me at first, a boat doesn't respond the same as a car, but it wasn't exactly Chinese algebra and by the time we'd rounded the point coming out of the bay I was already getting fairly comfortable with it. Indeed, it surprised me to find that it wasn't all as hard as I'd imagined. But I didn't have time to get cocky. The wind picked up outside of the bay and it suddenly became pretty sloppy with a close, three foot chop marching against us. Spray from the bow of the skiff, as it bounced over the waves, dashed back into the boat and began getting me wet. I slowed down a bit to avoid the spray and stop the bow from pounding, but after a few minutes I could see that Tom was pulling way ahead. He hadn't slowed down at *all.* He was probably running 'sea trials' with his new boat and forgot all about me. "*Shit!*" I hissed to myself, using a glare of anger to quell my rising concern, and twisted the throttle open again. The skiff responded instantly and lunged ahead to speed over the swells, careening recklessly along, with me trying to keep a tight rein on the steering. The little Whaler went pounding wildly over the sea, dashing spray in the air at the jarring impact of every wave. My grim face was streaming water into my collar from the bullet-like salt spray, and I was scaring myself right along, but I refused to back off the throttle until I finally saw that I was beginning to over-take *Elise.* Then I slowed down just enough to stay within a hundred feet of the stern. The skiff behaved much better at this speed, and I noticed that I was only taking occasional spray now in the smoother water of *Elise's* wake. I had just scared myself not a little and was bending ornery thoughts toward Tom for not realizing that I wasn't right behind him when, probably hearing the skiff, he turned around and flashed me a wide grin! "H-e-y-y-y-y!", I could see him say. I faked a devil-may-care grin right back of course. Couldn't very well let him know I was practically whimpering in my booties just a few minutes ago, but I thought about it as we pounded along toward Cape Chiniak a few miles away, and came to the conclusion that the only gauge I was going to have in this endeavor, on whatever personal danger I might be in, would be the degree of concern expressed by my skipper and mentor. I looked at Tom, standing at the helm of his own new fishing boat, his body remaining amazingly vertical and motionless while the boat gyrated beneath his feet, blazing a white streak across the swells, each wave punctuated by twin gouts of white spray shooting out to port and starboard. I didn't see any sign of concern in his demeanor. It looked to me like he was having fun! Okay, I told myself, this little chop is pretty normal stuff to a fisherman. Hell, this must be flat calm compared to the weather they usually travel in. I began to relax, and enjoyed cautiously experimenting with taking the waves at different angles and speeding up to run alongside the boat awhile and exchange more grins with Tom. By the time we got to the Kodiak boat harbor I had apparently been sufficiently trained to run the skiff. I was soaked, shivering and cold through and through but wouldn't have traded that ride for anything. Tom seemed satisfied that I would be alright running his skiff. This first solo trip levered my self confidence up a notch or two. I had always felt like such a late bloomer, a townie, which I was, but hated the truth of it. Many of my high school friends had been fishing on boats since they were little kids or at least for several years. Here *I* was just learning to run a stupid skiff. But I was keyed up to get going and stopped belittling myself. I had a lot of catching up to do, that was all. I had a lot to learn.

At the boat ramp in the harbor we loaded the Whaler upside down into the back of his short-bed Chevy, and hauled it home to make a few modifications on it. As mentioned before, Tom's way of moving anything from one point to another was basically to pick it up and carry it. Whoever was helping him had to keep up the best he could. He was a very big guy, still lean and rangy as a young man, and his strength seemed to know no bounds. First we muscled the Whaler out of the truck and carefully turned it upside down on the ground. Then, since I was too small and weak to fully carry one end, it was my job to lift the bow as high as I could while he crawled in underneath and got the skiff up on his back like a canoe, then, with me supporting a fraction of the weight and balancing it from the stern, he staggered over to the work area and we got it back on the ground. The bare hulled, 13 foot Boston whaler, being constructed of fiberglass, foam and a few strips of wood, was very lightweight for its size but still weighed over 400 pounds. Working with Tom taught me that moving big, heavy items by hand was do-able. With him around we didn't need machinery. First we applied several layers of fiberglass strips onto the three hull points of the Whaler's distinctive bottom to provide extra wear protection when beaching the skiff, and when that had cured we flipped it over and went to work on the tow post. He had designed and built a short, four-by-four post, necessary for the upcoming salmon season, and we bolted and fiber-glassed it onto the inner deck of the skiff about two feet in front of the inner transom. The post was set into the front edge of the attractive, mahogany seat and had wooden four-by-four braces to the sides and back. It needed to be attached very stoutly as it must withstand the incredible towing forces placed on it while seining. When the resin on the tow-post had cured, the skiff was ready to go.

Illustration by Elise Dooley

CHAPTER 4
Departure

Only a few days after school let out (having made the grade, I would be a senior next year) and with spring weather goading all Kodiak fishermen into the frantic preparations for the coming salmon season which they'd had all winter to do, Tom and I started loading the boat. *Elise* was moved from her slip in the harbor and tied up close to the access ramp which led down from the dock, at street level. We worked at the higher parts of the tides when the ramp had floated up and didn't make such a steep descent and climb for the many, many trips it took to transfer all the gear and grub from the truck to the boat. Every fisherman knows this drill. They make trip after trip, carrying all manner of awkward, heavy supplies, groceries and gear. The bigger boats couldn't usually find dock room anywhere and their crews often had to walk the floats long distances to their boats. My excitement in our imminent departure was somewhat diminished by work as we somehow stowed several truckloads of our camp gear and grub, two drums to be filled at the fuel dock before pulling out, several large, nested, plastic garbage cans to salt and stow our hides in, one of which now held part of our groceries, 500 pounds of salt, an ice chest filled with meat and perishables, the two motorcycles, fuel and water jugs, sleeping bags and spare clothes, two of Tom's rifles, and more. How it all fit and how the boat actually floated the weight of it amazed me. Tom was concerned most about the amount of freeboard around the top of the motor-well. The transom holding the 'Eighty-Five' was lower than the gunwales and it was easy to see that here would be the first place water would spill into the boat if we over loaded it or were forced to run before a big following sea. But he seemed satisfied when we were finished and had visited the fuel dock to fill the drums. *Elise* was riding low in the water, the band of red bottom-paint could only be seen at the rise of the bow, but there were still over five inches of freeboard in the motor-well. We planned to pull out the next day and prayed for favorable weather.

That evening Janice, Tom, Elise (the girl) and I went to visit the McLinns at their home, a big Geodesic Dome out near Island Lake. A fishing family, Willie and his wife Lois, their two young kids, Lois's dad and her brother, Dave Andrews, made this Tugidak hunt every year and had been as busy as ourselves in preparing but they weren't leaving until the following week. Tom wanted to go over his and Willie's plan to rendezvous at Ugak Island, where *Elise* would anchor for a week-long hunt, then we would travel together to the south end of Kodiak and cross the open water to Tugidak Island. This was good news to me. Willie had a 32 foot fishing boat with a big cabin, named *Rover* which they would live aboard during the hunt. *Elise* was a very tiny and very loaded boat and there were 90 or

100 miles of mostly open water, and notoriously iffy weather between us and our destination. Traveling together whenever possible was the local old-time way of looking out for one another, a proven method of safety. We finally said our good-byes, wished everyone a good trip and returned home to get some sleep. Tom probably slept. I didn't. I kept imagining all sorts of terrible things that might happen to us out there. I knew it was pretty useless to think about calamity, but all I'd ever seemed to hear about were the horror stories, and I had little experience to tell me that 90 percent of the time on the water everything usually goes along beautifully.

I awoke in the morning with Tom looming over me, shaking me gently by the shoulder. "Come on Steve, it's about time to ramble." Tom had the most likeable and gentle way about him and I was most fortunate to have him as my first skipper. He overlooked my inexperience and diminutive size, and somehow engendered self-confidence by giving me tasks to do that were usually just outside my capabilities. We'd long been buddies. Years before; before the earthquake, when he was a Navy Firefighter at the crash-house on Base and going steady with Janice, he had often taken me along when he went hunting or riding his motorcycle, or just driving the old military back-roads that infiltrated the timber of the north coastline. We were buddies alright, but this was work. I didn't expect or desire to be coddled. Tom pretty much knew my capabilities from hunting together, I was awful small and puny, and essentially untried at sea. He was taking a chance that I could do the man's work he would ask of me. On the other hand I was his first crewman and he was an untried skipper, though it never occurred to me at the time.

So I had slept some *after* all, but didn't need to be called twice. The belly-growling savor of a big breakfast pervaded the house from Janice's kitchen, and the daylight coming through my bedroom window made me sneer at my wide-eyed anxieties of the previous night. After breakfast Janice and Elise drove us to the harbor and we said our good-byes, attempting to convince a dubious Janice that we would be careful. Tom and I tried to be solemn about leaving, but I knew that he was just as excited as I was. We went down the ramp to the floats and stepped aboard *Elise*, her gunwale sinking down ponderously under Tom's weight. Tom was anxious to be off and instantly fired up the 'Eighty-Five'. While it was warming up he told me to start the kicker on the skiff, and explained that to save fuel consumption on the *Elise* I would be traveling behind him in the skiff. Then followed much idle dockside conversation with other fishermen, all of whom were busy with their own fishing preparations, and who were passing by on the floats, each wanting to know what we were doing. Tom was already well known and liked in the fishing community and, with his warm Southern greeting he always offered a firm but very gentle handshake. People enjoyed shaking his hand. They couldn't help it. It was fun. Tom's hands dwarfed any I have ever seen. They were large even for *his* size and hung on his thick wrists, sporting fingers like reindeer sausages. It was fascinating for me watching the powerful, tough hands of these fishermen disappear when they shook Tom's hand. I think it always amazed them as well.

Finally around ten-thirty there came a lull in passers-by and we hurried to untie and be on our way. We idled around the outside perimeter of the harbor and finally made our exit between the ends of the huge rock breakwaters into the channel, then into St. Paul Harbor and out around the can-marked rockpiles that lurked off the end of Near Island. The day was gray with clouds and little breezes but the water was fine, being only slightly choppy. Tom finally opened up the 'Eighty-Five' and steered for Cape Chiniak, miles to the Southeast where we would make the turn and start down the East side of Kodiak. When Tom opened up the throttle *Elise* plowed ahead for a short time, her pointed bow rising slowly in the air, gradually picking up speed, then she was up with her load and the bow began to lower again, allowing her to pick up more speed and skim across the light chop, dragging a frothy wake and spurting white spray far out to the sides. It took a lot of power to keep the heavy-laden boat up and traveling on step, much more than Tom had figured. He later told me that *Elise* would burn a lot more fuel than he'd allowed for. We would have the hundred mile trip to the south end and three or four weeks of hunting on the motorcycles, and he was concerned now that we might not have enough fuel to come home on. Well, that was a skipper's worry. My job was all pleasure. By now I was pretty comfortable running the skiff. I filled my lungs repeatedly and deeply with the clean, cold, ocean air, ridding my nose of the stink of town. The fresh views of the little city and its docks and mountains from far out on the water ran shivers of appreciation down my back. I regretted not having my camera. I had never asked Tom if I could, or should, bring a camera. I felt that, since this was work there would be no time for such a frivolous waste of time, not realizing there would be ample moments and opportunities for snapping pictures. I could hardly contain the flood of real exhilaration at leaving town for places I yearned to see. For sure now, we were on our way. Adventure lay near at hand.

I finally turned my back on town and began to focus my attention ahead. It would take almost an hour to reach Cape Chiniak. To conserve fuel, Tom had backed off the throttle as far as he dared, maintaining a speed that would just keep *Elise* up on step, and I ran the skiff almost monotonously slow to stay behind him. I gazed about me, taking in the sights as we skimmed across the chop. On my right were the three bays which lie between the Navy Base and Chiniak; Woman's Bay, Middle Bay and Kalsin Bay. Black rock and tawny, dead vegetation covered the upper slopes of the rugged mountains. The greening lower landscape flowed imperceptibly past, every view made impressive and beautiful by the distance from out on the water. My usual view of Kodiak was from the road system or a local mountainside. This was better! On the other side, to port, out past the end of Long Island, was only the horizon of the Pacific, invisibly vast and empty to the south where now a long lazy swell began to make itself apparent, rolling in beneath the boats, coming more or less broadside. The swells didn't affect our speed though, and we ran on, corkscrewing over the waves and only occasionally falling hard off the bigger ones. This was a new situation to me as a greenhorn skiff operator and I was forced to pay attention to what I was doing, adjusting my strategy in meeting these new demands. It wasn't difficult though, and soon I was again musing on the seascape. Seabirds of all descriptions were in abundance everywhere. They were nestled on the swells in large flocks, wheeling on the wind above and some were flying rapidly a foot over the water, their flight undulating with the seas. We passed far out from a round gumdrop of an island outside of Middle Bay and I could hear the continuous racket from the nesting flocks even over the roar of my outboard. I was in a state of pure and natural bliss.

About halfway across to the Cape my absent-minded rubber-necking was rudely interrupted when I suddenly realized that Tom had cut the throttle back and was slowing down. I was forced to swerve off to the side to avoid a high speed collision with the boat. Fortunately I had reacted properly and cut the throttle at the same time and, since Tom was peering off toward the Cape at that moment he didn't seem to notice my near disaster. When he turned around it probably seemed to him that I had raced up alongside on purpose. "How's it going Steve? You doin' okay?" I smiled back blandly, "Sure, no problem. Why'd we stop?" Tom was getting hungry. Breakfast had been around seven-thirty and it was now approaching noon. "You wanna come aboard and make some sandwiches and heat up the coffee? We'll tow the skiff for awhile so we can eat lunch." This was good news, I was getting hungry too, and a little stiff and cold as well. I made a mental note to be wearing my raingear when we started out again.

I had been cooking since I was about twelve. Mom had made Cliff and me, the two babies of the family, her personal 'bull cooks' two years before that, mostly to give us something creative to do, but teaching us how to work in the kitchen. Bull cook was the term given to the cook's helpers in the logging camps where my dad had worked when he was a logger in Washington before we moved to Alaska. Long before it was acceptable for a man to be messing around in the kitchen, Mom was teaching us her skills. Cliff and I didn't ever want to do anything that seemed unmanly, but since we knew that there were bull cooks in the logging camps, and men cooked on fishing boats, it met with our approval. I had a long way to go to compete with my mother's cooking, but I could certainly slice baloney and tomatoes, and spread mayonnaise on bread. Tom kept the boat moving slowly toward Cape Chiniak while I went about accomplishing my orders. I started on the coffee first so it could heat up while I made the sandwiches. Picking up the huge pot and giving the contents a swirl to judge how much of the cold brew might be left, I found it nearly empty and carried it out on deck, telling Tom that I needed to make a fresh pot as I moved behind him to the gunwale. Lifting the hinged lid, and without checking inside, I dumped the grounds overboard, right along with the big shiny new basket and stem of the percolator. They were already a part of history as they flashed and glinted in the flat light through a rich, brown, cloud of coffee grounds. The critical parts sank quickly, disappearing astern. This blunder Tom *did* see. I looked at him in horror. "What the...!" I didn't think *anyone* would leave the guts in the pot after making coffee. We never did at home. It didn't make sense. When you reheated the brew it would perk again and make the coffee bitter. And Tom himself had made the last pot. "Ohhhhh," He groaned softly, looking hurt, "why'd you dump the *guts* out Steve? I figgered you knew how to make coffee in a percolator." And, after a moment of silence, "Dang Steve, we never even got to break it in." Boy did I feel like a greenhorn, and didn't even have the heart to try defending my actions. Tom gallantly pretended to laugh it off, but I don't think he ever entirely forgave me for that one. Now he had boiled coffee to look forward to all summer long. After a rather subdued lunch on my part, even with Tom clapping a big hand on my shoulder and admitting with a little chuckle that my boiled coffee was "purdy good, but 'shore had a lotta grounds in it", we stowed the half full coffee pot (sans guts) and the stove in my bunk, wedging them in at the foot of the foam mattress, and throttled back up to speed in our respective boats, again making for the Cape. I had a lot to think about. That near collision with the stern of *Elise* had shook me up. I shuddered as I thought about the probable consequences of such a thing, and determined from now on to keep one eye at all times on where I was going. I had managed to luck out so far but knew it was only a matter of time before my luck ran out. I was learning to think for myself and to keep my mind on my work.

Rounding Cape Chiniak, we felt our way through the green and foam turbulence of the rockpile on the inside rather than go way out around. Tom wanted to check for seals in close to the rocks. Sure enough when we got inside the rocks there were a half-dozen adults and some pups riding the surge, their small, water slicked heads being the only part visible as they floated vertically in the confused swell. Their dark round eyes watched us suspiciously. The water here was all a constant and heaving motion, caused by the big swells which thumped against the outside rocks. Partly spent, they came welling and sucking around the black rocks that loomed above us. Great fans of bright spray, blossoming here and there, marked the advance of each swell. Tom had his .22 rifle ready and I kept the skiff out of the way while he managed to shoot three of the pups. They simply went limp in the water as they died. It took some time for Tom to accomplish this. At the first dull SPAT! of the .22, all the seals but one disappeared with a splash. The one lay still. After a couple minutes heads began appearing again near the very same spot. They were startled again at Tom's second shot and the performance was repeated a third time. Three shots and three seals. Tom was pleased with his shooting. It wasn't easy from the rolling boat. He hollered for me to help him retrieve the pups and we managed to wrestle the surprisingly heavy, limp forms into my skiff. We didn't have time to hold any discussions, the boats were wallowing around in the backwash of the breakers, banging together, and coming too close to the rocks, so we made haste to evacuate ourselves to the open water out around the point.

As I started out after Tom I eyed the three dead seals, rolling slightly in the bottom of the skiff. Blood still seeped from the tiny holes in their heads, turning the silver-haired spots red, and spreading back toward me, the dark crimson contrasting brightly with the turquoise blue interior of the boat. Suddenly the seal nearest me made a convulsive arch upward and began to flop around in the boat, splattering its dark blood everywhere. "*Oh shit*!" I yelled and immediately cut the throttle. I leaped forward and grabbed for the only thing available, a six foot oar. As I bent down to untie the oar, the seal lunged up at my face, snarling through bloody teeth. "Kak-ak-ak-kak!" One of its eyes was filled with blood, and bright red bubbles were issuing from its nostrils. I leaped back and began an aggressive campaign, flailing with the oar, to eventually subdue the terrifying creature. I had been attacked by a baby seal! Baby seals don't attack people! It occurred to me later as I relived the ordeal that the poor thing was either trying to defend itself or was in the throes of death, which was more likely. There was no need to forgive the seal. *I* was the aggressor. After I had finished off the seal, and it had taken quite a lot of work as the uncooperative creature just wouldn't die, I looked up expecting Tom to be waiting for me a short distance off, probably doubled over in hysterics. Hell no! *Elise* was a mere speck in the distance, throwing gouts of spray in the air, and already looked to be half-way to the high hump of Ugak Island. "*Dammit* Tom!" I'm having *troubles* here!" I got myself mad again and pushed the tiller hard over and snapped open the throttle, making the skiff squat deeply in the stern with a roar, and veer around in an unintentionally fast, tight, 180 degree spin that turned my guts to jelly. The three seals slid back and piled up at my feet. Jerking the tiller back straight I lined out for the tiny spurts of spray a mile or more away, shoving the pups away with my boots, and sped wildly off to catch up with him. I needn't have bothered. I could have caught him easily at half throttle, *Elise* traveling much slower than I could. Tom acknowledged my arrival but didn't slow down or stop to talk when I caught him and we continued our run toward the hunting grounds. I used the time to work up a tolerably funny way to tell him about my bloody fight with the pup and grinned at myself for my overreaction with the oar. It would have been a comical sight from a little distance away. The skiff had been wallowing around in the chop causing me to skid around in the slippery blood and making it next to impossible to swing the oar with any accuracy or serious effect.

Illustration by Elise Dooley

CHAPTER 5
Ugak Island

The closer we got to Ugak Island, the faster and larger it loomed in our view and we came eventually to a shallow strip of beach on the Kodiak side of the island's rocky perimeter. It was wide open and not at all protected from Northerly winds. It couldn't be called a bay, but there was a small beach indented there and we came idling slowly in, Tom looking for a good place to anchor up. When he was satisfied that we were in the right spot he dumped the anchor overboard then backed off, paying out extra line so it would hold well, then tied it off and reversed the boat, tightening the line to set the hook deep into the bottom and shut off the engine. I eased the skiff up to the stern, killed the kicker and climbed aboard to tie up. We enjoyed for a moment the almost reverent silence of the place. Only the quiet sigh of light surf washing on the beach came to my ears. The water was quite calm here, sheltered from the wind by the island. We noticed a sizable, ingeniously-built Visquine and driftwood shelter on the uppermost part of the beach. I recognized the architecture as that of my brother Dave and figured it must be the camp of him and Red Netupski who was a relative newcomer to Kodiak. Red, originally from around Chicago, had previously worked and hunted with another older brother Mike, up around Fox, just north of Fairbanks, and had moved to Kodiak two summers before. Dave and Red had partnered up for the spring hunt here on Ugak. Their 16 foot Boston Whaler lay high and dry on the beach near their structure, quite safe from all but the worst weather. There was no activity around their camp and we figured they were already engaged in the hunt.

The seals congregated for the most part on the south and eastern beaches of Ugak. This island was almost all rocky bluffs, with only the kelp-covered tidal margins and occasional intervening gravelly beaches offering access to the herds. We would have to make our day-long hunts on foot and carry our hides back around the island in backpacks. The motorcycles were of no use here. We went ashore after first squaring the boat away as much as possible with all the extra gear in the way. It was good to set my feet on this island. I felt like Captain Cook must have, claiming strange, new lands. I had often studied it from across the water at Fossil Beach and Narrow Cape on the Kodiak road system. Tom's intent in going ashore now was to try to find a few seal pups for me to learn on. I had my first (voluntary) kill and skinning job ahead of me. I kept my mind busily focused on proving myself capable of making a good, clean job of it, barring all squeamish feelings into a room somewhere back inside my brain and shut the door. I couldn't think about this, I was just going to have to do it. We searched up and down the short beach and then farther along among the rocks where Tom finally discovered a pup laying next to a drift log, high up on the shoulder of the beach. This seal was about half the size of the ones we had taken at Cape Chiniak, but it had a much more beautiful, dark coat with silvery rings on it. Tom told me that it had been abandoned by its mother and was probably in the last stages of starving to death. It's common for a female seal's first offspring to be orphaned. These mothers don't know what to do with the little pests, and immediately reject its advances to feed on their milk. They will either drive the pup from them or abandon it when it's sleeping. This is one of nature's ways of culling out the weaker genes from the seal population. If their pups don't survive, they can't breed and pass the mother's weakness on to future generations. Other mother seals have only enough milk for their own baby, I have never heard of a seal having twins, and they will not adopt another pup. The orphan pups become lonely outcasts. Without intervention by natural predators or man, they sometimes last for weeks, living off the baby fat they were born with. They remain separate from the herds, alone or sometimes in small groups of three or four, crying weakly all the time until the baby fat is burned up and they finally succumb to starvation and die. My heart felt real pity for this suffering creature, and it helped me to do what needed to be done. My first pup raised its head and watched us approach, our feet clattering in the clean, round gravel of the beach. It gazed up at us myopically with round, liquid eyes, and didn't try escaping when we stopped a few feet away. My first instinct was to help the creature, or comfort it, maybe feed it somehow. "Well Steve, you ready to skin your first seal?" Tom asked, looking dubiously at the puny pup. I looked again at the little critter with its black and silver spotted hair, all soft and dry, having probably never known its true element, the sea. It was obviously weak and in distress. "Just fetch it a good lick on top of the head with your club and go to skinnin' " he offered helpfully. We had brought our clubs along with us, and our knives. Tom's club was a short, heavy-ended, hardwood bludgeon made for subduing halibut. Mine was a little kid's baseball bat about twenty inches long, called a 'Little Slugger'. I seriously doubted its capability, but it would prove to be ideally suited for the job, being just the right length and weight for my puny arms. We were here for a purpose (I told myself again) and that was to take as many pup hides as we could manage. Tom had a boat-load of new bills hanging over him now and, though I didn't realize it at the moment, from this time on we would seldom rest. So I pushed all thoughts of cute, helpless little animals out of my mind and whacked the pup hard on top of the head. It went limp and never quivered.

Then Tom proceeded to direct me as I went about skinning the carcass. First I pulled the seal around so that it lay on its back, with me kneeling astraddle the hind flippers. Then, with my ringing knife I cut through the skin in a ring around the muzzle just behind the eyes and down around the jaw, and again around each front flipper right above the elbow joint. I made a similar cut around the base of the tiny tail and back flippers, my ringing knife slicing through the tender hide like a razor. Next a long, straight slit was made from the tail end to the top ring cut, taking care to keep the angle of the blade to a minimum so the sharp point wouldn't dig in and slice open the gut cavity. Now the skinning could begin. Since I am right-handed I started on the left side at the apex of the long belly cut and the ring cut at the throat. The idea was to carefully skin back a corner to make a hand-hold, then push the curved skinning blade close against the skin separating it from the layer of white fat that lay, sometimes inches thick, between the skin and the meat of the animal. There needn't be much actual slicing with the knife. You pulled up on the hide to stretch it and pressed down with the blade, letting the curved razor edge scrape snugly against the skin to remove as much of the fat as possible. This worked well on the hearty, well fed pups. My first seal was probably the worst possible practice animal. There was zero fat on the little orphan and the skin adhered stubbornly to the purplish meat. I had a very tough time doing what Tom directed me to do. He finally admitted that it was "prob'ly the scrawniest seal pup he ever saw." Eventually I stood up with my first seal skin. I hadn't cut any holes in it or scored the hide, but it wasn't much bigger than a terrycloth dish-towel. I didn't feel I'd accomplished much. At least I hadn't ruined the hide, which had been my greatest concern. We took the pup hide back to the boat and worked on the three other pups, me skinning one and Tom the other two. Tom's hides were very clean, having almost no fat on them. I had been skinning deer since I was a young boy, our dad and brothers teaching Cliff and me, and 'Lord help us' if we ever cut a hole in one. This was even *more* critical and the technique was different. If I cut a hole in one of these hides it would knock the price down, and Tom made sure I realized that. I was so careful that I left too much fat on the hide and we had to flesh it off. Then we washed the hides in a solution of Joy dish soap and salt water. Tom had told me that Joy soap was the only kind that would produce suds in cold salt water. It worked wonders in getting all the oil and blood out of the hair. After one more good rinse in the ocean we wrung them out and Tom showed me how to salt and fold them into quarters. Our first four hides looked pretty lonely in the bottom of the salt barrel but it was a start. The salt would draw nearly all the moisture from the skins, creating a liquid brine that covered the hides as they were added. This kept them from the air and helped preserve them. We kept all our supplies and equipment on the boat while we were at Ugak in case the wind came up hard from the wrong direction and we needed to pull the anchor and get out of there in a hurry.

Later, we went to visit Dave and Red in their spacious, Visquine villa on the beach. Visquine is one of those items like its cousin, duct tape, which Alaskans adopted as soon as they first saw it. For about ten bucks you could buy the equivalent of thirty tents or tarps, or roofs and windows for cabins, fabric repair kit for the airplane and endless other inventive uses, limited only by the imagination. Visquine came in giant rolls, of various lengths, from ten to a hundred feet, all compactly folded together down its length. When you needed a piece all you had to do was roll out the right length and slice it off with your knife. Dave and

Red's humble shelter appeared palatial to me. It had a low, intricate weaving of smaller drift logs and branches for the walls that even a bear couldn't tear apart. Small log purlins ran from the walls and intersected a ridgepole, all lashed in place with parachute cord. The ridgepole was supported by three posts, buried in the sand at the ends and middle, and was guyed fore and aft outside with stouter line tied to heavy logs. There was a partition separating the 'kitchen' from the main room. The floor was the beach. It was a 'comfort inn' compared to our place. They had a half-barrel stove, sitting upright in one corner, its open bottom pushed into the sand and the stack running straight up through a square hole framed in the plastic of the roof. That stove would keep this place real cozy, even on the wettest day. The only thing I disliked about this Visquine palace was the constant, rapid *flaa—flaa—flaa--flaa* of the plastic sheeting being rattled by the wind. Which noise I knew would increase in frequency and volume as the wind blew harder, *FLAA!-FLAA!-FLAA!*.... all night long. I preferred the quiet of the boat. Tom and I helped ourselves at their invitation to coffee and two-week-old doughnuts, taking a sweet toothed advantage of their hospitality, and relaxing in the diffused sunlight, out of the wind. After a fairly lengthy visit with Dave and Red we finally went outside and pushed the skiff back into the water, it having gone dry where the tide left it, and rowed out to the boat for a hot supper. Later we lay in our sleeping bags discussing again about how we planned to hunt the island. The talk tapered off and we eventually drifted pleasantly off to sleep, lulled by the soothing, irregular rocking of the boat and the light lapping of tiny waves slapping at the bow. Before drifting off I re-lived the fresh memory of my first seal. I thought about the deed, feeling a little of the natural guilt rising in me. I avoided the confrontation though, and justified the killing to myself using all my practical reasoning, then put it back inside my mind and rarely allowed it to surface again.

CHAPTER 6
First Hunt

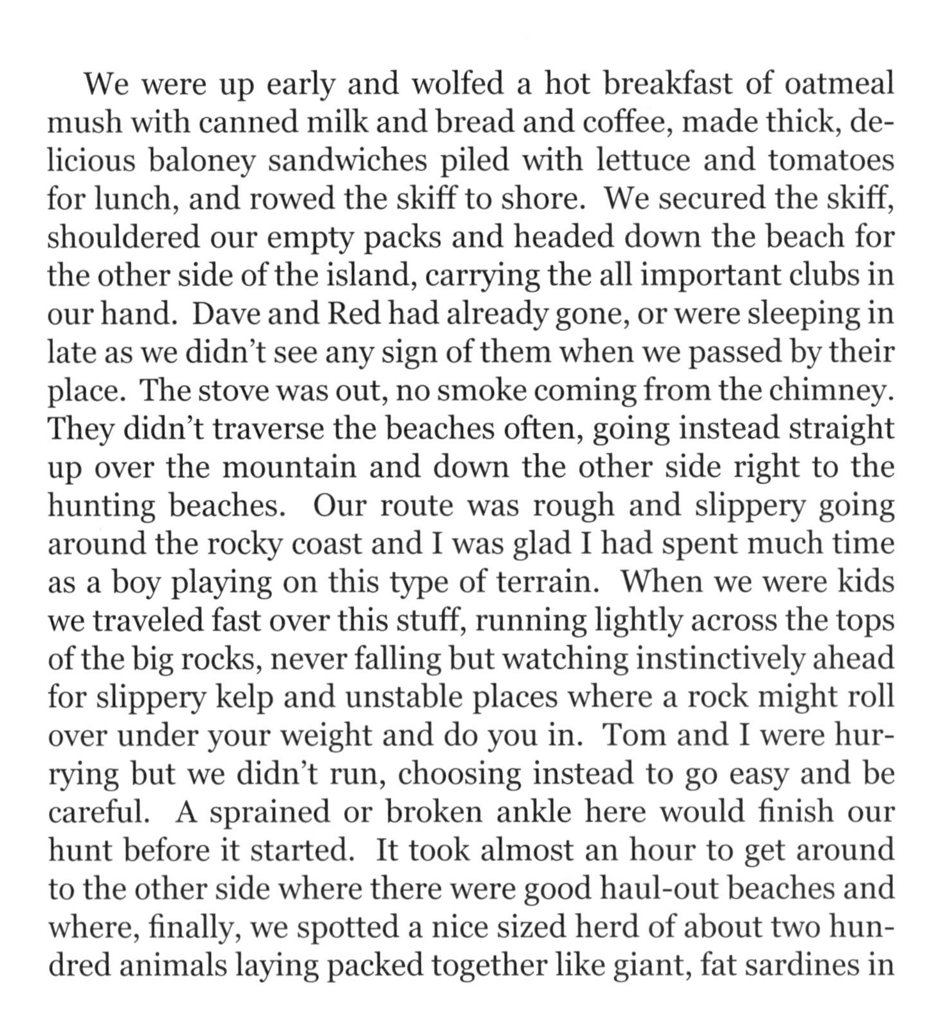

We were up early and wolfed a hot breakfast of oatmeal mush with canned milk and bread and coffee, made thick, delicious baloney sandwiches piled with lettuce and tomatoes for lunch, and rowed the skiff to shore. We secured the skiff, shouldered our empty packs and headed down the beach for the other side of the island, carrying the all important clubs in our hand. Dave and Red had already gone, or were sleeping in late as we didn't see any sign of them when we passed by their place. The stove was out, no smoke coming from the chimney. They didn't traverse the beaches often, going instead straight up over the mountain and down the other side right to the hunting beaches. Our route was rough and slippery going around the rocky coast and I was glad I had spent much time as a boy playing on this type of terrain. When we were kids we traveled fast over this stuff, running lightly across the tops of the big rocks, never falling but watching instinctively ahead for slippery kelp and unstable places where a rock might roll over under your weight and do you in. Tom and I were hurrying but we didn't run, choosing instead to go easy and be careful. A sprained or broken ankle here would finish our hunt before it started. It took almost an hour to get around to the other side where there were good haul-out beaches and where, finally, we spotted a nice sized herd of about two hundred animals laying packed together like giant, fat sardines in the hazy sunlight, completely unaware of our presence. My first herd. We had the wind in our faces and their stink almost sickened me. We backed quietly out of sight and shrugged out of our packs. Tom gave me a few last minute words, which I had heard often before, "Okay Steve, we run flat out toward the herd. You stay down close to the water line, I'll go through the middle, and keep running right through the whole herd 'til they're all in the water. Get as many as you can on the way through and try not to kill any adults, even if they come after you. You ready?" I was ready, and nodded so. "Let's go!" Tom leaped up and was off like a shot, so fast I was hard-put to catch up, which I didn't, but it didn't matter much. He was halfway through the herd when I got to the near edge. The seals were moving long before even he reached them, humping rapidly along, spilling down the beach in full flight, all bellowing and blah-h-h-ing and barking, sounding for all the world like a flock of panicked sheep. I saw Tom's arm plying his club about him on either side like a one-armed drummer in a rock-and-roll band as he charged in among them. Then I had my own gauntlet to run. The seals poured around me, the confused pups often frozen in place, looking around them and bawling. My club seemed to have a mind of its own as it found target after target, a meaty 'splat!' accompanying each swing. My heart was pounding from the wild barbaric excitement of the fray, and several times I was threatened by adult females which bore down on me baring their dog teeth, their fat rolls quivering, growling the same asthmatic, non-vocal "Kak-ak-akk!" which I had first heard from the seal pup in the skiff at Cape Chiniak. Tom had told me not to kill any adults. There was no market for them at this time of year and they were out of season, making them illegal to take. I easily avoided these threats but they sure kept my blood up. I finally ran out of seals before catching up with Tom. He was already busy dragging dead pups from the surf up to the shoulder of the beach, sometimes two in each hand. I joined in and soon we had twelve or fourteen fat carcasses lined up on the clean, round beach pebbles.

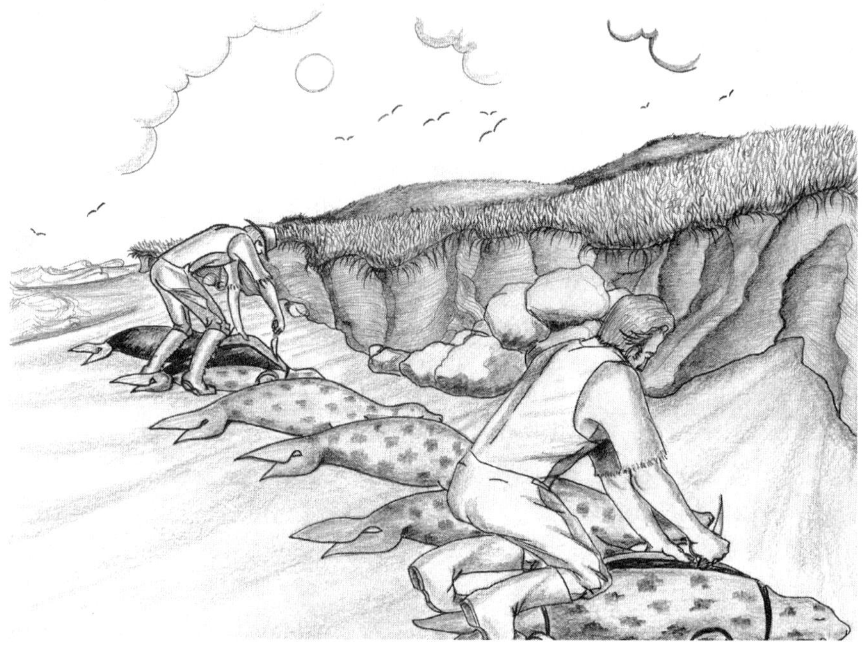

Illustration by Elise Dooley

We took a little break to catch our breath, enjoying a good drink of pure, icy water from a small crick that gurgled off the mountain, and smoking a cigarette apiece, and then started in on the skinning. There in the beginning of our season Tom started on one end of the pups and I the other and worked toward the middle. I felt bad that Tom was doing about two-thirds of the work, but there was no help for it, I was still green. I tried hard to get a good clean hide off each one I skinned, but, being timid about cutting holes in them, I could tell I was still leaving a lot of the fat on them. My hands were slippery from handling the greasy hides, my left arm and shoulder ached from lifting, lifting, lifting on the heavy carcasses, and my back was killing me from bending over the animals one after another after another. Tom was a fast skinner. He skinned about three to my one and when the work was finished we washed the greasy, bloody hides in the surf, wrung them out, and dropped them into our packs. After taking another short break to relieve our aching backs, we climbed inside our pack-straps and started on down the beach to look for another herd.

The only way to hunt this place was to work our way around the island, moving farther and farther from the boat. Once we stormed a herd it would be hours before they would haul out again and they remained pretty spooky for the rest of the day, bolting for the water at the slightest notion of danger. We managed to make a pretty good day of it and by the time we'd run out of beaches had over thirty hides in our packs. We had traveled about two thirds of the way around the island and were much closer to the boat if we'd continued on around in the direction we were going. But there were other hunters out there and we didn't want to disrupt their herds. Two Native Alaskan brothers named Pavlik were also hunting the island. Their camp was a bit farther down from where we had taken the starvation pup the day before. We hadn't seen hide nor hair of Dave and Red or anyone one else on 'our' beaches.

The hike back to the boat was no picnic for me. Tom was a smart teacher and had persuaded me that we should each carry the hides we'd skinned ourselves. I had about a dozen in my pack. He had more but didn't even seem to notice the weight. I sure did. As I trudged along behind him I pondered this agreement and did some math in my head. A close skinned pup hide this early in the season might weigh three pounds, maybe a little more if it was a big one. If Tom had twenty hides on his back he was carrying about sixty pounds. I, on the other hand, carried a dozen or more, and my fat-laden skins probably weighed five or six pounds each. My pack also weighed about sixty, and I wasn't in very good condition. This ocean side of the island had all the best beaches but there were plenty of long stretches of high bluffs where there was only jumbled, angular rocks to walk on. We avoided the tidal margins where the slippery kelp reigned. I had to move very carefully over these rocky stretches, knees wobbling, calves and ankles working overtime. We had decided long before to wear lace-up leather hunting boots instead of rubber ones for the hunt. We knew our feet would be constantly wet, and the boots might be ruined, but our ankles needed the support and that made them worth the sacrifice. Tom strode along like he was on a Sunday walk. He pulled far ahead of me, eventually disappearing around the bend of the island. Well, I didn't expect to be babied. I took my time, resting more often now that the boss wasn't in view. I'd lay back against the rocks on the pack-frame for maybe five minutes, savoring the cool freedom of the wind, watching the surf boil among the rocks and soaking up the increasing warmth of the spring sun. Eventually I made it back around to the boat where Tom was already finishing up with salting his hides. He eyed my handiwork as we unloaded my pack. "Dang Steve, you're gonna have to skin closer than this. We'll have to flesh these out before we salt 'em or they'll spoil. Too much fat will keep the salt from penetrating the skin, the hides will sour and it'll make the hair slip." I knew that already, and it didn't make me feel too good hearing it again now, but told him I would get better with a little practice. He needn't have mentioned it. The extra weight alone was reason enough for me. We worked on my hides and eventually got them in the salt barrel. I told Tom of an owl head which I had once got and how I strung it on a length of twine with some lead weights and hung it from the floats in the harbor. The sand fleas had eaten every scrap of tissue from it in less than twenty-four hours, leaving the skull clean, white and bare. We thought it might work on these fatty hides and so we had saved the least attractive one out to hang over the side of the boat near the bottom overnight. It worked too well. The next morning we pulled up the holey rag of a skin. Sand fleas can't tell where the fat stops and the hide begins. That sure didn't work and it cost us a hide to find out. It appeared there would be no short-cuts to a close-skinned hide.

We hunted Ugak Island for a full week, enjoying unusually dry, if mostly cloudy, cool and breezy weather, and got a fair start on our season. The first few days were long and physically brutal for me, but I worked to get better and faster at close-skinning the hides and eventually toughened up enough to carry my daily burden back to the boat without undue suffering and resting. By the end of our Ugak hunt, I was easily keeping up with my long-legged boss as we made our way around the rocky coast, and had become a pretty good skinner. Now we were skinning half and half, but Tom always had to wait for me to finish. He still out-skinned me by a goodly margin. He finished his half, washed them in the surf, stowed them in his pack, and then took a break while I kept working on mine. At times, when my back was killing me from the constant stooping over, and my left arm was played out from lifting the heavy, slippery bodies while my knife peeled the taut hide from the fat, I yearned silently for him to show a little pity and take a pup or two off my hands. I never verbalized this little fantasy. My pride would never let me ask for help in doing what was supposed to be *my* job. It's always been hard for me to ask anyone for help. Sometimes Tom did skin a couple or three, probably being tired of waiting. Usually he lay back on the sand for awhile to ease his own aching back, sometimes putting a lit cigarette in my lips with reasonably few oil-stains on it, (seal oil tastes terrible smoked through a cigarette) or he would be off up the beach prowling among the drift. He had every right to expect me to keep up. He was paying me for my work and I didn't want to be found lacking in effort. All I could do was grit my teeth and keep working. It may seem that I must have been an awful puny lad, and I'll admit I was, but even a full grown man had a big job, working alongside Tom, who ate up hard work by the boatload and never slowed down. Tom still out-ran me when we made our dash into the herds. An Olympic sprinter couldn't have caught him. For his size, he was extremely fast on his feet, his long legs making strides no one could possibly match. His competitive spirit fired him into such a state that if you happened to get in his way you were apt to be trampled. All in good fun of course, and though he was a gracious loser, Tom hated to be beat at anything.

One day on the way back from the end of the hunt we rounded a point of land and saw a pair of bald eagles up high on the beach near the bluff. Upon drawing near we could see that one of the birds was actually standing on the back of a beautiful, fat pup. The eagle's claws were buried in the hide

Illustration by Elise Dooley

on the back of the pup and the huge bird was busily pecking at its eyes, which were both already streaming blood. The little seal kept arching back, snarling blindly at its antagonist and causing the eagle to flap its wings, pulling awkwardly back to avoid the seal's threats, but never releasing its claw-hold on the beautiful spotted skin. The other eagle walked impatiently about nearby in its clumsy way, flapping airborne to move a few feet now and then. They would eventually kill the seal but would feed on it alive until it succumbed. The pair would carry bellyfuls of the rich, dark meat to their nest and regurgitate it for their young. Tom and I weren't going to stand by and watch the pup suffer. We went right up and interrupted the eagles, which instantly flapped away up the beach then began to circle above us, shrilling obscenities in their piercing whistles. The pup's eyes were gone, leaving gory, blood caked holes where they had been. It remained arched back hearing our approach, its bloody head weaving in the air, mouth slightly parted, waiting the return of its tormentor. Tom quickly conked the pup on the head with his club, ending its suffering. The hide was ruined, the back being shredded by the eagle's talons, so we left the pup where it lay and before we were far down the beach the eagles had returned to the carcass to continue their feast. We had actually helped the eagles as well as the pup. This little scene made me feel better about taking the cute, abandoned pups which would make up nearly a quarter of our kills. At first I felt a little ornery toward eagles, but soon realized that they had more right to the seals than we did, and made better use of them. After all, except for the liver, of which seal is the sweetest and mildest in the world, we didn't even eat the meat of the critters we took. We tried cooking some ribs once but it stunk up the boat so bad we couldn't bring ourselves to eat much of it. Our kills however did provide a great, continuous feast for the crows, magpies and seagulls that thronged the island. I still cringe a little when I think of the awful way thousands of these pups die every spring, being eaten alive or slowly starving, outcast from their kind. It's one of those things about the natural animal environment that seems especially cruel and unfair to baby animals everywhere. They are easy prey for the carnivores of the world. We saw this scenario being played out several times on Ugak. Usually we arrived too late to relieve the suffering of the pup.

CHAPTER 7
The Run To Tugidak

We made our last day on Ugak a short one since we expected the McLinns to rendezvous sometime that day with us on the *Rover*. It didn't take us long to wash and pack our day's hides in the salt barrel and get the boat ready. We went to the beach and had another coffee mug-up with Dave and Red for awhile and caught each other up on the last few days. We had all been so focused on the hunt we never had time to visit. It was still early afternoon when *Rover* idled up close to *Elise*. Tom and I made short work of pulling the anchor and with a wave of good-bye to Dave and Red we headed off down the coast under an overcast sky toward Dangerous Cape. It felt good being in the skiff again instead of hiking everywhere. We had to travel much slower now. *Rover* had more of a displacement hull and could only make about eight or nine knots. We were used to traveling fifteen or twenty. *Elise* plowed along down the wide Ugak Narrows pushing a bow wave, unable to rise up on step at this speed. This stretch of water was an eerie place to me. I'd long heard of the horrible sea conditions and unpredictable tide-rips that were possible here. I was extra alert while we were in the Narrows. I could see Tom talking to Willie on the radio, ducking now and then to avoid a particularly heavy windblown spray caused by the ever present choppiness. He was probably telling Willie about our success (or lack of success-Tom never being quite satisfied that we had taken enough hides) and getting updates on the weather forecast. We poked along down the coastline, riding over the undulating green backs of the following seas. Crossing the wide open water outside the mouth of Ugak Bay I felt suddenly very small and unprotected. There was only water for miles in all directions and I was very glad that this skiff would never sink. It took a long time for Dangerous Cape to loom up close to starboard and when we'd rounded the point outside of Boulder Bay, the sea lump diminished. Our little boats lined out on a new course across the mouth of another wide expanse named Kiluda Bay, toward the entrance to Sitkalidak Strait. We entered gratefully into the lee of these narrow, protected waters which separated Sitkalidak Island from the Kodiak mainland. The Aleut village of Old Harbor is nestled about half-way through this waterway near Barling Bay. Tom and I pulled into Old Harbor and tied up to the dock. He wanted to replenish the fuel we had already burned getting this far. I took the opportunity to stretch the stiffness out of my legs and walked uptown to the village store. Even though my dad and mom knew many of the folks here, and I had friends from high school who were from Old Harbor, I still felt the white-skinned foreigner I was. At the least now I could say I had been here. Curtains moved furtively in a few of the houses I passed, people peering out at the strange kid in town. I must have been a sight, oil-slicked jeans, shirtsleeves off at the elbow, leather laced sheepskin vest and an untamed mop of wind-tangled black hair. There wasn't much sign of life in the village. At the store I talked briefly with the owner, who also knew my folks, while I bought a half-dozen candy bars to share later with Tom. I told him what we had been doing and where were going. His nose, no doubt, had already informed him. The man didn't seem very impressed at our endeavor, responding to my information with an "Ohhh?" or an "Aah, I see". But he wished us a good hunt as I left the store. The chocolate tasted *good.* Tom didn't consider candy to be a priority on the grub list. It wasn't even on the grub list. He only bought the bare essentials, and darn little of that.

We left Old Harbor behind us, and ran to overtake *Rover* which was still motoring along down the island, bucking into an increasing wind, now blowing southwest and kicking up a gray and white, two-foot slop. Having quickly caught up with the McLinns, we lowered our speed again to a seeming crawl. I had plenty of time again to study the unfolding new scenery, now pretty much all the same as we had been passing since leaving Ugak. Here were the very spare, beautiful elements that make up most of Kodiak Island; sea, sky, rocks and brush. The dense green blanket of Spruce forest had thinned out rapidly to ragged edges after Narrow Cape, soon giving way entirely to tall grasses, pushki, fireweed, Salmon-Berry brush and Alder thickets, which were now stealing up the mountain slopes in an intense green cover, softening the steep ravines, climbing higher almost visibly under the extended daylight and warming temperatures. Mysterious new bays and capes advanced slowly, and unfolded as we steamed along, revealing the real details of what I had seen on the charts. Tom and I had followed this course with our fingers many times last winter while planning the trip, and I had paid close attention as he'd told me where the best hidey-holes lay, places where a boat could hide from bad weather, and how to avoid the reefs and rockpiles and tide-rips that lurked where you might least expect. Many of the seemingly unpronounceable names I had heard since childhood. I ticked them off in my head as we passed slowly by and left them astern; Three Saints Bay, Kaiuginak Bay, Cape Kiavak; we passed close between big Two-headed Island and the mouth of Japanese and Kaguyak Bays. We warily skirted an extensive, dangerous looking rockpile off the point near the site of a recently extinct Aleut Village called 'Old Kaguyak', then began the short run to the end of Aliulik Peninsula which led us to the Geese Islands. With night closing down, robbing the color and contrast from things, and the wind picking up even more, we motored through the extensive beds of bull kelp that ebb and flow with the tides in Geese Channel, which lays between the three islands of the same name and the mainland of Kodiak. Bull kelp begins its life as an anchor rooted onto a rock at the bottom of the ocean in the comparatively shallow water near the coastline. It rapidly sends a rope-like tentacle with an air filled bulb at the top toward the surface. The bulb grows long ribbon-like streamers of a dark olive color. Thousands of the kelp plants grow together in large rafts usually around the rock-piles. An outboard motor stutters repeatedly as the propeller chops through the thick strands. During this short passage Tom and Willie got on the radio again and held a short conference. Tom was wisely a little concerned about traveling at night across the open water between the end of Kodiak Island and Tugidak Island. The sea was now rougher and *Elise* was carrying quite a load. He tried to convince Willie to run in with us and anchor up for the night in the shelter of the north side of Sitkinak Island, the last bit of protection before crossing to the hunting grounds. But Willie was getting a late start as it was. He was in a hurry to get to Tugidak so they could begin their hunt as soon as possible. Besides it was only a few miles across, it would be fine. He and Tom couldn't seem to agree, so Tom opted out, telling *Rover* that we would see them next day at the small lagoon on the north end where we both planned to make our camps.

So with night nearly down, we parted company with *Rover* some time after passing under the barren, black hump of Aiaktalik Island. Tom steered off slightly to port, and we pounded our way across a few miles into the lee protection of Sitkinak where the wind fell off and the water became calmer, with only a few cat's-paws ruffling the surface close in. We came in at slow idle, Tom playing the spotlight over the beach and around the boat, double-checking the chart for water depth. He idled around some to get the feel of the place, was finally satisfied he'd found a good spot far enough off the beach, and dumped the anchor. I was stiff and sore and shivering with cold even inside my raingear and the air was delightfully still here close to the island. We lit the Colman lantern inside the cabin, and heated up the coffee and some canned soup on the stove outside. We seldom used both Colemans in the cabin at once, being afraid of carbon monoxide asphyxiation. When the dishes were done, washed out on deck in a tiny plastic basin with Joy soap and cold salt water and rinsed by swishing them in the ocean, we settled in for a much desired rest. I was partly wet, and chilled clean through from the wind and spray I had been taking for the last few hours and the little cabin was quite warm from the hissing lantern, so I made use of the heat to dig a dry tee-shirt and a flannel with full sleeves out of my duffle and change into them. The clean clothes felt like the finest calfskin, all light and loose, and warm and dry. Very soon it had grown *dark*. It being spring, the hours of daylight and darkness were more or less equal. Having a last smoke out on deck, we let our eyes adjust for a long time and we still couldn't make out the skyline or even the shore of the island, though we sensed it there. We retired to our bunks, turned off the lantern and talked quietly for awhile, Tom leaving the radio on as we lay there in the dim light from its channel dial. He had tuned it to an AM broadcast station and we listened to Oldies music from somewhere in California. "A white—sport coat--and a piiink car-nation...." The boat veered around lightly on the anchor-line from an occasional eddying breeze that found its way offshore.

Every twenty minutes or so Tom would reach up and dial it back to the CB channel he and Willie used and we would listen to the static silence for awhile, wondering how they were making out. During one of these quiet interludes we were suddenly brought upright in our bunks exchanging frowns of consternation. On the radio we heard Willie's highly excited voice shouting, "MAYDAY! MAYDAY! MAYDAY! U. S. Coast Guard Kodiak! This is the *Rover. Do you read?* Over!" This raised the hair right up on my head. *Rover* was in trouble! Tom reached up and adjusted the volume knob. He took the microphone in his huge paw and held it up close to his mouth, his big head cocked to one side, but didn't press the transmit button. We listened as Willie made contact with the USCG Rescue Coordination Center and apprised them of *Rover's* situation. They had been bucking into increasingly steeper seas, running on the compass and radar with most of them sleeping, when *Rover* plunged down hard off a swell and buried her bow into the green water of the next wave. A forward, portside window in the cabin shattered from the impact, and frigid green water poured down onto Dave Andrews who was sleeping on the top bunk on that side. Dave immediately leaped out of the sack, shocked awake, and reacting quickly, grabbed his pillow and moved to stuff it into the hole where the window had been. As he made this move the boat dove down into another wave, and the pillow, and Dave's arm, went through the opening as he staggered forward. Jagged glass on the bottom part of the window sliced deeply into Dave's upper arm, severing through the meat of his inner bicep and got an artery and maybe some tendons. Tom and I listened helplessly as Willie, calming down a little, talked on the radio to the Coast Guard, answering the multitude of questions they required of him. "What is your exact position? How many persons on board? Names of every person on board?" The questions went on and on. Willie answered them concisely, phonetically spelling questioned names or words. "Coast Guard Kodiak, the injured man's name is David Andrews, that's David, *Delta-Alpha-Victor-India-Delta*, Andrews, *Alpha-November-Delta-Romeo-Echo......*" We heard him talking frantically away from the microphone to the others. "W! What the hell is W.....?" After a few seconds of silent, mental searching we heard Lois's muffled voice yell the answer at him, *Whiskey*, it's *Whiskey*!" And he finished spelling Dave's name. He was still running the boat and fighting the seas, and we could hear the commotion of voices in the background whenever he keyed the mic as Lois and her dad, following the calm advice of the Coast Guard radioman, tried to stem the flow of blood pumping from Dave's arm and apply first aid. The Coast Guardsman on the radio finally told them that it was not possible to dispatch a helicopter for Dave tonight but a chopper would rendezvous with *Rover* at the little lagoon on Tugidak Island in the morning and Medivac him to Kodiak. They would have to keep him from bleeding to death until then. More radio talk followed between *Rover* and the Coast Guard, and it was nearly an hour before Tom could call Willie and offer what advice he thought might help. We were powerless to offer any real assistance. Even if we pulled the anchor and went after them, they'd be in the lagoon before we were halfway across. When we finally lay back and snuggled safe and warm down into our bags, Tom kept the radio on and we fell asleep to the emptiness of the static. My last thought was one of admiring gratitude for Tom having sense enough to call it quits when he did.

Next morning we were awake early, slurping our first cup of coffee and, while we shoveled down a big bowl of hot mush laced with raisins, milk and brown sugar, Tom raised Willie on the radio and we got the good news that Dave was pretty weak, but doing alright. His arm was a mess though, and he would probably miss the whole sealing season. The Coast Guard was on the way to pick him up. We warmed up the outboards and pulled the anchor and sped off around the island. Today the sky was still cloudy but the wind had backed off during the night and we enjoyed fair traveling weather. About halfway around the west side of Sitkinak Island we saw the big white H-60 with the orange stripe heading our way from Kodiak. This was always a good sight for me. I had been rescued by them a few years before, after the boat I was on grounded hard on a rockpile on Long Island near town. I felt better knowing the Coast Guard was there, listening for boats in trouble and flying out to help. We watched the helicopter roar over our heads and grow small as it flew a bee-line for Tugidak, giving me an idea of where our course lay. Twenty minutes later it again passed overhead on its way back, presumably with the injured Dave aboard.

Tugidak Island has no mountains and is invisible from a small boat heading from Sitkinak. It looked to me like we were aiming for the open ocean, but not long after leaving the last point of land on Sitkinak, it began to show. Just an indefinite, dark line above the sea at first. Then it slowly grew in size until very soon we could see that it was definitely our island. We slowed down pretty far out. We knew that this area was all fairly shallow with a sand bottom, being marked so on the charts, and who knew where a sandbar might be lurking beneath the surface. I was surprised to see that the beaches were white sand, not black as most of the Kodiak beaches are. At length we idled into the small lagoon on the north end of the island and softly coasted the boat up to the beach. We had arrived. We saw *Rover* anchored up on the far side of the flooded lagoon. There was no one moving around on deck and all appeared quiet on the boat. We figured they must be sleeping after putting in the long and hellish night tending to Dave's arm and making the rough crossing.

CHAPTER 8
The Life of a Seal Hunter

The tide was nearly full and I carried our anchor up the short beach and socked it into the fine white sand, glad to be moving on foot again. While Tom went off scouting for a good place to set up the tent, I started packing some of the lighter stuff off the boat and depositing it above the last high tide line. Tom came back to the boat and we continued with the unloading until everything we needed, tent, camp gear, some of the grub, motorcycles and sleeping bags, was on the beach. *Elise* floated higher now that she was empty of nearly all but the fuel drums and salt. Lastly, we perched the anchor on the bow, being tied off to the deck cleat with plenty of scope allowed for it to hold well and with a shore line tied to the ends of the stock. Tom gave the boat a mighty shove, sending her out away from the beach and paying out the shoreline. When *Elise* stopped drifting out Tom gave the shoreline a tug and the anchor plunked overboard into the water. The wind or tide would set the hook in the soft sand. Tom fastened the shoreline to a big log buried in the sand so we could still pull the anchor and boat in at high tide if we needed to and so the boat couldn't get away from us. *Elise* would be idle now that we were moving ashore. Our first task was to haul our gear to the tent site some couple hundred yards from the boat. Tom kicked the foot lever on his three-wheeler and fired it up, indicating to me to start the yellow trail 90. Here again I was a little embarrassed to admit that I had never actually ridden a motorcycle. He grinned at me and cut me no slack, "I guess now is as good a time to learn as any." I knew how to start the bike, just make sure it was in neutral, turn the key on, twist the throttle and kick down on the start lever. It fired up after a few tries and puttered at idle while I struggled a little trying to balance it. "How do you shift it again?" He explained that this bike was about the easiest-shifting model around. There was a toe lever on the left side, which, when pressed down with your foot, shifted the bike into low, then you accelerated for a short distance, backed off the gas, and clicked the lever down again to shift into second and so on through the rest of the gears. There was no clutch involved. To downshift you put your toe under the pad on the lever and clicked it up for each gear you needed. He suggested that I follow him to the campsite and back without a load so I could get the hang of it. My take-off was a little wobbly, and I only managed to get in one shift to second gear, but I managed to follow him without spilling the bike, and by the time we returned to the boat I was riding a motorcycle. This north end of Tugidak was all sand, no real chance of getting hurt if I did lay the bike down. We tied gear onto the ample steel rack on the back of the 90 and Tom took a pile of stuff before him on the seat and under one arm, and we proceeded to move all our stuff up the beach to the camp site, making several trips apiece. We spent most of the morning setting up camp, erecting the big white tent on the sand with guy-lines tied to driftwood logs, unrolled our beds on the ground on each side, and set up a low cooking area up off the sand floor using beachcomed plywood and boards, and stowed our grub-locker ice chest inside. There were no bears on the island, which meant total freedom from worry on that account. Our groceries would be safe and we would have untroubled sleep.

While this was going on the tide had begun to fall, draining quickly from the shallow lagoon, already leaving *Elise* high and dry on the sand. Tom was antsy to check out the beaches down the outside shore to the south where we would be hunting so we hopped on the bikes and I eagerly followed him off down the shore of the lagoon, experimenting with the new sensation of riding the bike. (Look Ma, no pedals!) Tom's huge form reminded me of a clown riding a kid's tricycle but the little three-wheeler didn't seem to mind the weight. We rode past the McLinn's boat which was still floating in the deepest hole of the lagoon. Still no activity, so we continued on around the sandy lagoon beach to cross a narrow strip of sand to the bulk of the island. We spied no seals and hadn't gone far when we were halted at the first point of land where the low bluffs began. The tide had not fallen enough to permit passing around this rocky point. Most of the beaches on this side of Tugidak ran along rough, thirty or forty foot bluffs, the highest elevation on the island being about sixty feet. All of our riding would have to be done while the tide had gone out at least far enough for us to skirt the rocks. This allowed us about ten hours to hunt while the tide receded and started in again. It was a serious matter according to Tom to get caught by the tide halfway down the island. That meant you would have to somehow get your motorcycle up in the rocks as high as possible to keep the tide from submerging it. We fooled around on the beach for awhile, waiting for the tide, and checking out the driftwood piles for useful or interesting objects. Tom found a giant , rubbery fishing buoy with Japanese markings on it. This was the answer to a problem we had been trying to solve; how to carry the seal hides on his bike. We had tied a wooden Blazo box onto the rack on the back of my '90' for this purpose. At that time the square, five gallon cans (Blazo cans) of fuel were shipped in wooden boxes, two cans per box. These boxes were another God-send to bush living and were utilized for every conceivable purpose. The three-wheeler didn't have a rack, just the seat and a low steel guard-bar behind it. Tom was pretty inventive, and soon figured out how to make use of the buoy. He cut a six inch round hole near the eye of the buoy, deflating it so that it looked like a giant tick, and somehow lashed it to the back of his bike creating a huge pouch. The buoy was very flexible and would prove to hold more hides than the bike would ever carry at once.

The tide, meanwhile, had now receded enough for us to get around the pile of rocks and from this point on our progress down the island was unimpeded. I was having a good time with the new experience of riding a motorcycle even though I was feeling crowded by the unyielding Blazo box at my back. With the wind hard in my face and fresh, essentially unexplored beaches stretching away before us upon rounding each rocky point, I felt anew the sense of exhilaration and freedom. Untouched piles of driftwood beckoned me for closer examination. Everybody loves beachcoming. Especially in remote places like Tugidak where the pickings are rich and the pickers are few. But we had no time for play. We were here to hunt seals. As we approached each rocky point we slowed to a crawl and cautiously poked our noses around the rocks to see if the next beach held seals, and eventually were rewarded with the biggest herd we had seen yet. About five hundred animals lay packed tightly together in the middle of the beach. The late comers waited in the water at the foot of the herd for the tide to fall away from them. We excitedly pulled our bikes behind the point and sneaked back on foot to study them from the rocks. Tom quietly explained how we were going to make our charge. We knew from hunting Ugak on foot that the seals would likely start for the water the instant we showed ourselves. Seals employ babysitters, adult and adolescent females, to guard the sleeping pups while the mothers are out feeding in the ocean. These guards lay scattered among the pups and every few seconds one or two of them would raise their head and briefly look around. There was always at least one of them watching. When each guard lay its head back down it uttered a sound much resembling a contented sheep, telling the others that all was well. Tom gave me the game plan. We would ride right at them, jump off the bikes at the edge of the herd and run among them as before, as always taking as many pups as we could manage on the way through. We got back on the bikes which were still putt-putting quietly behind the rocks, and roared around the point, riding right up to the outside of the herd. This was a great advantage and we were upon them before they even realized the danger. I slid my bike to a halt and jumped off, letting it fall over in the sand, and began my charge, swinging my club as I ran for the other side, dodging the occasional adult that came at me snarling, and laying pups out in a trail behind. Tom again outdistanced me, reaching the far edge of the herd by the time I was halfway through. The herd had flowed down the beach and around us like a giant, polarized maggot race, all bellowing their barks and panicked sheep-sounds and raising a racket that bounced back off the bluffs circling the beach. There were always a few pups left behind in the confusion and it was usually easy to catch and dispatch these animals before they could escape.

When the excitement was over, we moved our bikes back up the beach, congratulating ourselves for a good haul on the first day on Tugidak, and dragged our catch up there to begin the work of skinning. It took a long time, several hours, to finish this task. We had taken more pups at once than ever before and the Blazo box on my bike was half full of hides when we were finally ready to move on down the island to find another herd. Tom's tick-buoy was showing a goodly bulge as well. For once Tom seemed satisfied with our progress. If we could keep this up we would have a good season and he could get some of his bills paid. I wasn't thinking too much of the money. The experience alone, doing a man's work in a wild place like this, was a thing I had hungered for as long as I could remember, and I was glad that Tom brought me along. I only hoped that I could continue to meet his expectations and not be a drag on the operation. I was becoming more adept at skinning. Although still pretty slow compared to Tom, my hides were now clean, with hardly any fat left on them.

We continued down the island on the bikes, finding other herds and repeating the process with slightly less success until we had as many hides as we could take care of before the incoming tide forced us to vacate the beaches. Finally we began the ride back to camp, which offered the chance to sit on my butt and more or less rest while the bike did most of the work. My two-wheeled bike was much harder to manage with the extra weight sitting so high on the rack and I dumped it several times before realizing that dry sandy places were the problem, bogging the engine and making it hard to steer, requiring that I monitor my gears and speed accordingly. I rode on the hard-packed wet sand whenever possible. On the return we came upon occasional abandoned pups and managed to get a few more hides, which fit easily into the tick-buoy on Tom's bike. After a long, hard day on the cold, windy beaches I would rather have taken a beating than stop on the nice ride home to skin another seal, but upon seeing one I always stopped anyway and did my job, even if Tom had missed it. The hours had flown past and it was early evening when we arrived back at camp.

There was no time to rest though, we had our catch to wash and salt away and finally, *finally!* supper to prepare. Our diet was pretty monotonous; for breakfast we ate oatmeal mush and thick, meaty pieces of bacon-ends, crisply fried in the skillet. Tom had wisely and economically added three, five pound boxes of these trimmed pieces to our grub list; for a lunch to carry while out hunting we made thickly sliced baloney and mayonnaise sandwiches (the lettuce and tomatoes had long since played out); and for supper we ate canned chili, soup or fried seal liver, followed by such things as pilot bread and peanut butter with Nabob canned jam. Our clothes were saturated with blood and seal oil and we probably smelled quite awful, though we couldn't really tell. Our noses no longer registered the offensive reek of the seal hunter. I do remember that we had the most sulfurous, identical smelling gas, presumably from eating the unaccustomed seal meat. We had fun with this, blaming each other with much hand-fanning and nose-holding, denying culpability. I can still hear Tom's "Gaawd Daa-yam Steve! You better go wipe!" We had long since given up on the rank, oily sleeves of our shirts starting back on Ugak, and simply cut them off at the elbows with our knives. Our forearms and the backs of our hands were as black as any African-American's, probably from the combination of seal oil, sun and wind, leading me to think that seal oil might have a great market as suntan oil. It is the finest natural oil, other than whale, that can be found, and is perfectly odorless and tasteless if rendered properly without heat. Our jeans were slick and practically waterproof from wiping our oily hands on them. When it rained which was often, the water beaded on my thighs and ran right off, soaking the denim in the back. There wasn't any point in changing into fresh clothes.

Our camp life consisted mainly of working on the hides, refueling our bikes, cooking, eating and sleeping. We never took time to bother with building a fire. It wasn't especially cold this time of year, being maybe 45 degrees on average, and we were now well accustomed to spending sixteen or eighteen hours outside in the elements every day and the remaining time sleeping on the sand in the drafty tent. Certainly not the worst bed I've occupied, as I was soon to learn. Besides, there really wasn't any excess energy or time to spare in gathering firewood though it was plentiful everywhere. Right after supper, our work being mostly regulated by the tides, we went to bed even if it was still daylight. We were both fastidious enough that neither of us wanted to foul our sleeping bag with the reek of our clothes. We slept in our skivvies, which meant shivering into our clammy clothes every morning. I was completely wore out at the end of each day, and every day the hunt seemed a long repetition of the previous one. Once the newness and excitement wore off it became a grueling, daily test of endurance for me to keep up with Tom. It was hard. He was almost obsessive about the hunt. He never seemed to lose his ambition for it and never seemed to be overly tired or sleepy, though he surely was. Tom had a family to feed and bills to pay, and he went at it with fresh vigor every morning. I was still a teenager. Sleep. Long, blessed, uninterrupted sleep was what I had begun to desire more than anything. Especially when Tom's gentle paw roused me from cozy slumber in the damp, gray mornings.

CHAPTER 9
Feral Boy

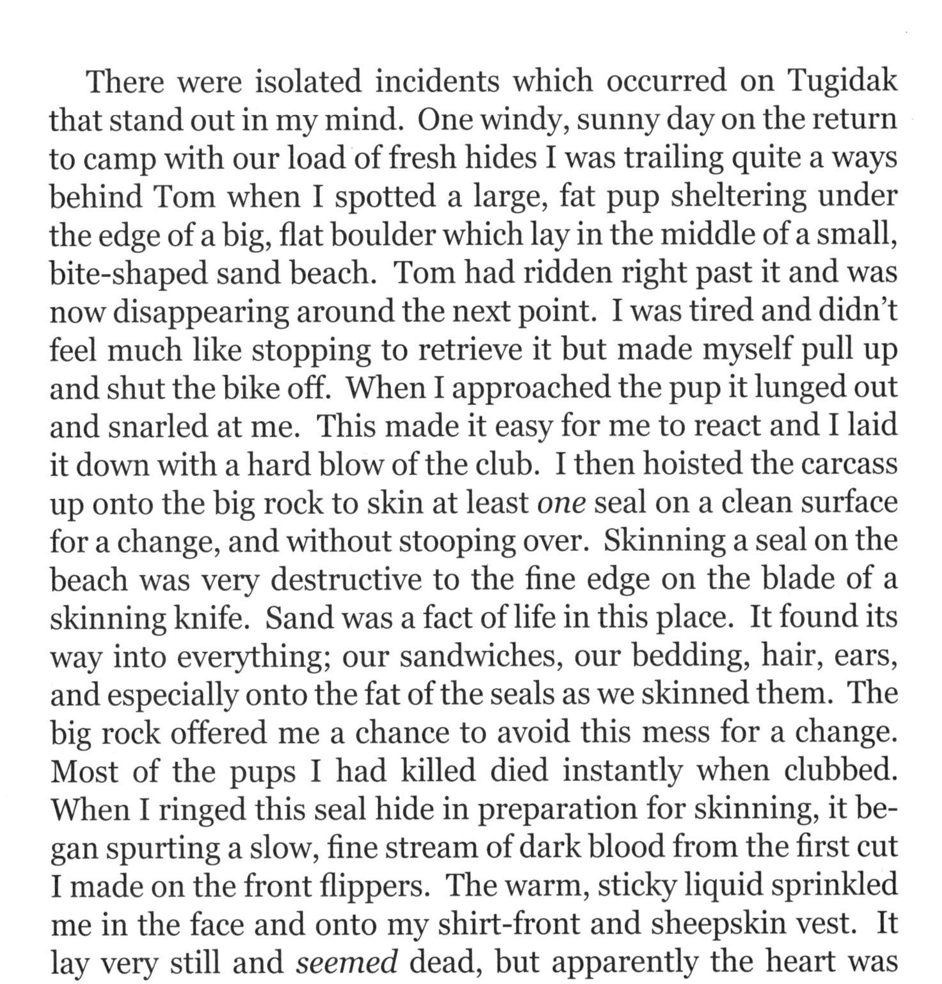

There were isolated incidents which occurred on Tugidak that stand out in my mind. One windy, sunny day on the return to camp with our load of fresh hides I was trailing quite a ways behind Tom when I spotted a large, fat pup sheltering under the edge of a big, flat boulder which lay in the middle of a small, bite-shaped sand beach. Tom had ridden right past it and was now disappearing around the next point. I was tired and didn't feel much like stopping to retrieve it but made myself pull up and shut the bike off. When I approached the pup it lunged out and snarled at me. This made it easy for me to react and I laid it down with a hard blow of the club. I then hoisted the carcass up onto the big rock to skin at least *one* seal on a clean surface for a change, and without stooping over. Skinning a seal on the beach was very destructive to the fine edge on the blade of a skinning knife. Sand was a fact of life in this place. It found its way into everything; our sandwiches, our bedding, hair, ears, and especially onto the fat of the seals as we skinned them. The big rock offered me a chance to avoid this mess for a change. Most of the pups I had killed died instantly when clubbed. When I ringed this seal hide in preparation for skinning, it began spurting a slow, fine stream of dark blood from the first cut I made on the front flippers. The warm, sticky liquid sprinkled me in the face and onto my shirt-front and sheepskin vest. It lay very still and *seemed* dead, but apparently the heart was still feebly pumping. I whacked it again and continued with my work, but now it began to squirm around. This made me feel worse. It was hard enough to kill these little beasts in on the dead run through the herd, never really looking them in the eye, and even then I sometimes had to purposely not think about it. This one seemed to have nine lives. I was forced to club it hard several times before it finally lay still. By the time I had finished skinning it I was liberally sprinkled. My hands and forearms were red. The boulder, the skin and the fat-laden carcass were covered with blood. I imagined the scene as it may have been observed from overhead and saw a bloody sacrificial altar, a dead naked beast, and a wild boy holding the knife. Even though I knew that the pup would have otherwise suffered a much worse death under the sharp beak and talons of the inevitable eagle or faced a long, lonely starvation, this particular seal has since returned frequently in memory and has haunted me more than any other, causing me to question my own *personal* economic necessity of taking the lives of these beautiful, helpless little animals. There were other ways of making money. But sealing was a perfectly acceptable livelihood for trappers, especially in rural Alaska. Acceptable that is to those who chose the wild, independent outdoor life of a trapper and fisherman. There weren't many alternatives. Most Kodiak folks since before the Russians arrived were dependant on the cyclings of the seasonal economy.

Another time we overslept, having ignored or not heard the racket of the Big Ben, wind-up alarm clock. On this day, late in the season, and with all the hunters on the island; ourselves, the McLinns (Dave Andrews had returned a couple weeks ago, pale but determined to finish the hunt), the Pavlik brothers, Andy Nault and his son Andre, and a few other groups, all putting pressure on the herds on the island, Tom and I tried a change of pace. The herds were becoming more scattered and difficult to approach, often fleeing for the safety of the ocean at the mere shadow of a seagull passing overhead. We awoke after a long needed sleep, and found we had missed a good part of the tide. If we followed the other hunters down the coast we'd have been picking up their orphans. But for some time now Tom had been noticing seals hauling out onto a sandbar about a quarter mile off the north end of the island, and announced that we would take the skiff and see how we could do out there. With only a light, gray chop on the water from the incessant wind, and Tom running the skiff, we made a fast dash out to the sandbar. He idled down and thumbed the kicker into neutral and we lay off about two hundred yards from the sleeping herd for short while, contemplating how to make our approach, deciding we would make the usual, full bore beach landing, jump out, and commence taking pups as fast as possible. The sandbar wasn't very big, being entirely covered by water at high tide. There was only a small herd of about fifty seals visible. I crouched in the bow, ready with my club in my right hand, holding onto the bow line for balance with my left, while Tom hunkered as low as possible in the stern as we shot ahead, speeding toward the herd. When we drew near the sandbar the seals started spilling off into the water. We bored in at full throttle, Tom preparing to kill the motor and jerk it up out of the water just before we hit the beach. Quite suddenly the skiff went from skimming along at twenty knots to a dead stop when it ran aground on an invisible shoal beneath the surface, about thirty feet short of the sandbar. I caught a glimpse of my leather boots outlined against the gray sky and found myself mysteriously flying through the air in a somersault right over the bow and landed flat on my back in a foot and a half of icy water still holding the painter in my left fist and the seal club in my right. Tom had sprawled head-long, careening over the tow-post bracing and landing face down in the bottom of the skiff. The sudden shock of this unexpected change in plan didn't even have time to register, so focused were we on our prey. We leaped to our feet and splashed ashore into the fleeing herd and in a few short minutes had nineteen pups to show for our efforts. We laughed long and hard, and a little hysterically, at each other for the frigid dunking I had taken, and the comical folly of our landing. Tom told me he should have realized that there might be a hidden sandbar there. He then declared that since the day's hunt wasn't a total loss, we would haul our catch back to the island and skin them there on the outside beach, and when that had been accomplished and the hides salted away we would take the rest of the day off and lick our wounds. Our work done by early afternoon, we lay around camp drinking coffee with jam and Pilot bread, and used the time to re-sharpen our knives. We strolled down to the boat and checked over the dwindling groceries for spoilage. Our last half stick of bologna was turning green on one end and the remaining box of bacon ends was starting to grow hair. The bread was down to a few loaves but looked okay, and we still had a few cans of beans, soup and vegetables and a little flour and oatmeal left. Our grub was definitely getting low. We enjoyed a leisurely meal for a change that day, taking time to fry up all the remaining bacon to preserve it, after first wiping most of the light, green fuzz off with a wet paper towel. To cap off a perfect and easy day we laid ourselves down for an actual nap.

This short vacation from the grueling routine gave us a well needed break for mind and body, and later that evening I asked if I could take the three-wheeler over to the Nault's camp for a short visit. Andy Nault had invited us down for coffee one day about a week before when we four met and visited awhile on the beach on the way out to hunt. He and Andre usually hunted the Big Lagoon on the other side of the island, but had broken their routine that day to see if the hunting was any better on 'our' outside beaches. Tom consented to my request. We had been one another's sole companions for over five straight weeks, having no time for socializing, and he probably welcomed a little time off from me.

Andy was a real character. He was pretty old and grizzled to be living this kind of torture, but for him it was a second chance at life. He had left Montana decades before, where he'd spent some twenty years tending bar and running a nightclub which he owned there. His doctor told him that if he didn't forsake the smoky, sedentary and unhealthy lifestyle soon he would probably be dead in less than a year. He had all sorts of physical maladies; emphysema, diabetes, arthritis, and a liver that was all but played out, any one of which could kill or at least cripple him before he was much older. So in the late Fifties he quit the bar scene, packed up his belongings and headed for Alaska where he would live a healthy, hardworking, fresh-air life as a trapper and fisherman. The pupping season on Tugidak was one of the first places he'd landed, and here he shed the dross of societal living. His body began to heal itself and by season's end he was in better condition than he'd been in decades. Although he had much to learn about living in the remote and wild places of Alaska, Andy was no greenhorn when he arrived. He had hunted and trapped most of his life in Montana and his new efforts proved successful enough to make him a good living. He attracted friends easily and soon became a very colorful character among the many colorful characters that made Kodiak their home. Andy was a master story-teller, speaking with a French accent and animated expression that added an interesting flair to his tales of the wild. Everyone knew he was no B.S.er, though like any good story-teller he most surely embellished on the truth some. He was out there living his life on the ragged edge of survival, cramming the months and years full with carrying out his dreams, and in the process healing his dying body. Some ten years after I met him on Tugidak he wrote a book which told of some of his escapades in the North. The title had a double meaning; 'Staying Alive in Alaska's Wild'. It makes for fine, entertaining and enlightening reading for anyone interested in the subject of the wilderness bush life.

Since I had never ridden it before, Tom gave me a few pointers on operating the three-wheeler before I left our camp. I knew he preferred to ride with one knee on the seat so he could see farther and control the machine better by using his body to offset the bounciness of the fat tires. It was a very different ride than my familiar Honda 90, seeming at first unstable and tippy but, except for the throttle, the controls were identical and I had no trouble figuring it out. I didn't know precisely where the Nault camp was but Andy had given us some loose directions and after a while I came across the well used track they frequented in riding to and from their place. I was quite pleased with myself when I found their dugout cabin. Had I approached from the opposite direction I would have ridden over the big dune right onto the roof. The shack was buried back in a high sand bank with only the front wall visible. The roof was a camouflaged continuation of the vegetation which flourished in the interior of the island, all grasses and flowers and berry brush. There were poles bracing the front wall against the weight of sand at the back wall. Bright lantern light glowed from the large Visquine windows across the front, the single door being on the right side. When I pulled up in the yard, Andre came out to greet me, wiping his hands on a dishtowel, and seemed pleased that I had come. I was welcomed inside the warm hogan and instantly appreciated the relief from the wind. Andre was a quiet young man about my age, but his dad more than made up for his son's reticent nature. I was treated like royalty, given a seat at their table and served steaming coffee with store-bought cookies (a real treat after *my* monotonous diet) and regaled non-stop with tales of Andy's hunting and trapping escapades, partners he'd had, and bears and wolverines he'd tangled with. Sometimes dead-serious, sometimes comical, his animated face, and twinkling blue eyes added spice and flourish to his tales. Having just met them for the first time on the beach a week before, I was yet made to feel like an old friend. I had no idea until later that Nault was such a celebrity among his peers. He certainly didn't behave like one. Andre was as shy as myself and didn't say a lot, but laughed with me at some of his dad's tales even though I was sure he had heard them all time and again. Mine was a pretty short visit since at that time of year darkness was creeping in even at ten p.m. and I had no desire to be riding around looking for camp in the middle of the night, but I have never forgotten the kind bush-hospitality of Andy and Andre as they repeatedly refilled my cup and pushed the package of sweet cookies across the table to me. The unaccustomed heat from the barrel stove in the corner of the cabin was uncomfortable on my face, having lived essentially outdoors for more than a month with out benefit from so much as a campfire. Our own drafty tent was unheated and always cool, except when we were cooking, billowed by the wind even though we had buried the perimeter in sand. It felt very strange, almost tomb-like, to be closed inside an actual house and sitting on a real chair with a table to rest my cup and my elbow on. They came outside with me when I made my departure and we stood for a few minutes listening to the constant deep-chuckled din made by the hundreds of ptarmigan nesting and feeding out in the vegetation around their shack. What a place this Tugidak was! I had seen so much of the teeming life here, and death for that is nature's way, even when helped along by men. It was a barren, lonely place, beautiful and primitive. To be accepted by these fellow hunters as one of their peers brought out a sense of real satisfaction in myself. I had been tested here and found that I was up to the challenges. One of the things I instinctively knew about behaving like a man was to keep my mouth shut and try to hold up my end of the stick. There was nothing worse than a whiner when things got a little tough. Nothing was spoken of the daily hardships and privation we all endured in pursuit of this livelihood. It was a given. My return to camp was made in the dark after all and, after following a few false trails, I finally spotted the yellow glow of the tent off a ways from the top of a dune, looking rather lonely and isolated in the dark. Tom had kept the light on for me, or more likely was enjoying the rare luxury of reading a book. It was a welcome beacon that guided me in. I felt refreshed in mind from the chance to relax in different company for awhile even though Tom and I always got along just fine.

On another day while on the return trip from the hunt, late in the season, we crossed over to the Big Lagoon to see about adding a few more pups to our mediocre catch. The tide was nearly in and it filled the great, shallow bowl, leaving us only a narrow strip of sand to ride on. The expanse of water stretched away for miles out to the wide entrance to the lagoon. When the tide fell again I knew it would all be dry except for a small basin in the middle. We cruised the beach back toward Nault's camp, looking for a herd or for orphan pups. The place was abandoned, either from the lateness of the pupping season, or from hunting pressure. We saw no other hunters, but as I rode along, following behind Tom, I spied the jewel-like treasure of the largest Japanese net float I have ever seen, half buried in the sand a couple feet from his wheel tracks. These clear, green-glass globes were hand-blown and hand-webbed by ancient methods on the outer islands of Japan. They appeared in all sizes, ranging from a baseball to a beach ball, and were used as floats for fishing nets. Occasionally the web-covered gems came untied from the nets and were lost to drift upon the great Japanese Current, bobbing for months, maybe years, through the gray pacific swells, blowing ashore at high tide somewhere, and coming to rest on foreign sand. The green glass glinted at me in the weak, overcast sunlight. I stopped and leaped off my bike to roll the big ball up out of the deep, wet sand pocket where it lay, half buried, and examined it on all sides. It was perfect in every way, not cracked or damaged in the least, the twisted rope appearing quite new. These glass balls were the 'holy grail' of beachcombers from the Pacific Northwest to the Aleutian Islands and I was ecstatic to have stumbled upon such a most beautiful and coveted find. I grappled it in my arms and heaved it up to set it into the Blazo box. The bottom of the ball barely dipped into the box. It sat like an egg on an ice cube tray, far too big to fit inside. I scratched my head trying to come up with some way to carry it and came up with nothing. I had no rope, my box was three quarters full of hides, and Tom was disappearing from view over the sand hills heading for camp on the other side in the small lagoon. "*Crap.*" I muttered to myself, and reluctantly rolled the big ball back into its socket in the sand, then climbed dejectedly back on my bike, consoling myself with the thought of returning soon to re-claim my prize. Of course it never happened. We were now hunting far and long to get half the hides we'd easily taken every day two weeks ago. We were on the beach for as long as possible, hunting every minute and returning to camp late every evening to wash and salt our few hides, eat, and crawl wearily into the sack.

CHAPTER 10
South-end Cabin

Next morning very early we were getting ready to head out for the hunt and I couldn't find my seal club. I looked everywhere around and in the tent with no result. Tom was impatient to be off and finally I remembered that I had left it on the boat the day before when we salted hides. We rode down to *Elise* and I waded out in knee-deep water to get the club, not taking precious time to pull the boat in. It wasn't leaning against the side where I thought I'd left it so I climbed over the gunwale into the boat to look for it. The club wasn't there. I noticed that the door to the cabin was ajar and told Tom about it. We always closed the boat up tight before leaving it. Now Tom pulled the boat in to shore with the anchor line and climbed aboard over the bow. We checked inside the cabin and found that a loaf of bread, several cans of chili and part of the good half of our last stick of bologna were missing in addition to my club. Someone had made a raid on the boat while we were sleeping. We had no idea who, the tide had muted all tracks in the sand, but this put a serious dent in our remaining provisions. There was a two-legged coyote on the island. Tom thought to check the fuel drums and was satisfied that none was missing. This gave us one more thing to worry about while we were away hunting. Tom told me I'd have to find a driftwood club on the way out.

We rode off from camp long before full daylight, puttering quietly past *Rover*, which showed no sign of life yet, and heading down the coast. Tom didn't want to be following any hunters today. We would have the beaches to ourselves and the first crack at the herds. I scrutinized every pile of drift along the way for a suitable club, not seeing anything that attracted my eye and finally Tom told me I had better find something soon, we were getting close to the hunting grounds. I stopped and urgently cast about me and finally selected a clumsy, beach-washed length of two-by-four about three feet long. The ends were well rounded and, still wet from the surf it was heavy and awkward to swing, occupying both hands. It would have to do. Even with the loss of my little club I was more enthused about the hunt today than I had been lately. Tom had filled me in on his plan last night. We were going to make a clean sweep clear to the south end of the island, spend the night at a cabin down there, and work the next outgoing tide back to camp tomorrow. We had been mostly hunting the north two thirds of the island up until now, either having loaded up to hauling capacity or run out of time when we reached the vicinity of the Fish and Game beach and the tide began chasing us back toward camp. For provisions this day we carried four half-green baloney sandwiches (it didn't really taste as bad as it looked), and the remainder of the moldy, prefried bacon ends, all wrapped securely in double bread sacks, tied in a knot to keep them dry. I always carried the food in my Blazo box and made sure to keep it on the top when adding hides to my load.

Coming up to the beach preceding the beginning of the bluffs, Tom swerved up the beach to ride slowly through the scattered drift-logs near the top of the beach. I followed behind, some fifty feet back. He was peering in among the logs, checking for stray pups. I cast my own eyes around doing the same. Tom putted through a narrow, four-foot opening between a tall, surf-scrubbed root wad and another fat log lying on the sand. I followed his wheel track into the same gap and suddenly the fat log rose up before me on the left, transforming itself into a huge sea lion. I jerked away, leaning far

Illustration by Elise Dooley

over to the side in horrified reflex as I rode past, avoiding the massive, bear-like head. It towered above me, a foot higher than my own head. From three feet away I saw the wrinkled, black lips baring a mouthful of huge, rounded, yellow canine fangs that jutted from mottled pink and black gums. Long, stiff, translucent whiskers laid back like quills along the tawny muzzle, and its eyes bulged wide, showing the red-brown whites encircling large, dark brown pupils. Warm, putrid breath washed over me and a deep, belching noise issued from its throat as if it were loudly gargling a bucketful of Jell-o. "AAU-LU-LU-LU-GHH!" That was all I saw. It flashed by in an instant. The bike wobbled dangerously at my violent recoil but I straightened it out with an instinctive twist on the throttle and shot ahead. Glancing back I saw the huge beast humping madly down the beach for the safety of the water, panic stricken, sand flying from its front flippers. The animal looked as long as the Boston Whaler and its girth as big as a three hundred gallon fuel drum. After the initial scare, which didn't last long now that I was out of 'danger', I began to see it from the sea lion's point of view. Here he was, had probably hauled out here among the driftwood at high tide sometime in the night, sleeping soundly while the tide receded. All of a sudden something snarls past him a foot from his nose, kicking sand in his face (Tom). BEAR! he thinks. He rises up snarling in terror, expecting to fight for his life and another.....*something* comes growling down upon him then runs away growling louder (Me). He panics, and flees for safety. I chuckled to myself, my own heart still thumping pretty good. He was more terrified than I was. I watched him swimming offshore a ways, only his big head showing while he swam parallel to the beach, watching me.

Tom and I had traveled maybe half a mile along the bluffs when we arrived at the first herd. It was fair sized, maybe a hundred-fifty animals. Afraid they'd spook, we lost no time in making our charge. They seemed to have been waiting for us and started for the water the instant we roared into view. I bailed off the '90', sliding the two-by-four out of the Blazo box as the bike fell over, and started my run. My aim was off, and my swing slow, but I was getting some pups. About half-way through I was suddenly confronted by a charging, snarling adult. I dodged out of her way but she kept coming at me. After avoiding her several times, stumbling over fleeing seals, I finally stopped and came over my head with my club in a full-arc, double-handed swing and whacked her hard on the head, the two-by-four stinging my hands and making a loud "BLONK!" and she went still. I ran on getting a few more pups here and there, but the charge was over. Tom and I started dragging the dozen or fifteen carcasses up the beach and I told him about the attacking female. I had hated to kill her but was very glad that I'd had the big two-handed club instead of the little slugger when we met. I went down the beach to retrieve more pups and see about the adult. She was gone. There was her turtle-like trail down the sand to the water. That seal had taken the hardest blow I could deal her and it only knocked her out. Now I was really glad to have the new club even if it *was* clumsy.

The hunting was very spotty from here and we made a pretty fast time down the coast, passing the low green swale above the tide line where Fish and Game had a cabin. It was the only place I had seen on this side where there were no bluffs. The tiny hut squatted in the tall grass next to the small, rusty-looking trickle of a tiny crick, about center on what may be the longest continuous stretch of beach on this end of the island. The two Fish and Game men who stayed in the cabin were stationed here to monitor the hunt, count and study the seals. They were outside the cabin and we didn't stop to talk, but waved congenially as we rode past. I had never been beyond this beach. It became rockier as we continued south. The seals were far less concentrated on this end. Soon it began to rain again and we stopped to pull on our raincoats, and it was a gloomy, wet and windy, late afternoon when we rode the bikes up off the beach at the south end cabin. It was a low roofed one-room affair built above the beach at the high edge of a big field of tall, sparsely clumped bear grass, sand and driftwood. A surprisingly large, clear stream flowed out of the low hills beyond, gullying past the cabin a short distance away. Tom was about as miserable as me when we pulled up to the door and climbed stiffly from our bikes. He must have been somewhat dejected at the poor showing we'd had for our hunt. My Blazo box was only about half-full of hides, his tick-buoy had about the same amount in it. We pushed the door open and stepped inside. It was dim and musty and felt long unused, but it was dry. There was a fairly elaborate barrel stove near the door and dry wood stacked in the corner and that seemed like a good place to start. Tom got the fire going while I scratched around in the weak half-light from the windows to see what might be on the shelves. I came up with about a third of a can of ancient, dried out Folgers coffee and one heavy china mug. We hadn't brought any utensils for cooking, but there was a rusted cast iron skillet hanging on a nail behind the stove. A hot drink really sounded good to both of us so Tom sent me back out in the rain with the skillet to clean it up in the sand of the creek. I scrubbed and rinsed, and rinsed and scrubbed, using the sand and twisted handfuls of the stiff-stemmed bear grass growing nearby, until I figured it must be down to bare metal, then filled it with water and carried carefully it back up to the cabin. We turned ourselves before the stove, letting the snapping, cheerful heat drive the chills away. The water eventually began to boil and Tom dumped the coffee into it, letting it froth for a few minutes. We poured the finished product back into the empty can and gloated over the prospect of a good, steaming, hot cup of Joe, waiting a bit to let the grounds settle then filling the cup and setting the can back on the edge of the stove. The brew we 'enjoyed' wasn't exactly what we had anticipated, tasting more like rusty hot water, but we slurped at it anyway, sharing the cup, and declared it "not that bad". A little extra iron never hurt a body anyway. We had each wolfed one of our sandwiches on the beach about halfway through the day and now were feeling the dull ache of hunger in our bellies again. Tom had me dig out our bacon. We would save the last two sandwiches for tomorrow. After another trip to the crick with the skillet to rinse out the coffee grounds, I dumped the crisply fried pieces into the pan and cooked it a little more to heat it up. We ate over the pan, spearing them on our ringing knives and blowing on the hot morsels, chewing them like hungry dogs, washing it down with the coffee and not commenting on the moldy aftertaste. Our stomachs were too demanding for us to worry about little things like food poisoning. At this point I doubt if rotted seal meat would have done more than give us a worse case of the vapors. We now felt warm and refreshed and a little drowsy from the furnace-like heat radiating from the stove. Outside, the rain had let up and the tide was now coming in. Tom began to feel like maybe we should start working our way back right away, planning to reach the Fish and Game beach where we could get the bikes clear of high water, then wait through the night for the tide to fall again so we could hunt our way back to camp from there. I would have preferred to remain in the warm cabin and feed the fire all night, there were acres of driftwood just outside the door, but it wasn't up to me to decide. Besides, maybe Tom was right, why waste our morning hunt down here on the south end tomorrow when there were so few seals showing. We brought in more wood to replace what we'd burned, rinsed and dried out the skillet and hung it back on the nail. Then we pulled on our clammy raincoats, made sure the fire in the stove was out, closed the place up tight, and rode off down the beach into a diminishing evening light. The coast here on the south end was quite interrupted, with short beaches deeply interspersed between the close-set rocky points. After an hour or two we found ourselves having to ride in the water out around some of the ragged points jutting farthest out from the bluffs. Our progress was retarded by the slow pace, it was difficult to see where we were going, even with our headlights. Eventually at about dark we came to one wall of rock that was impassible. The water was sloshing two or three feet deep around the outside and we were stuck. The tide by now had surely closed in behind us, leaving us caught in the trap that Tom himself had warned me against. We were lucky though. There was a wide and fairly level shelf of rock some six or eight feet high extending out from the bluff above the beach, and after no small amount of ingenuity and physical exertion, we managed to wrestle and heave the bikes and our hides up the sharply sloping rock and parked them back at the base of the bluff. We prayed that the tide wouldn't follow us up here. It was full dark by this time and began to rain again, rattling loudly on my raincoat hood when it came at us on a gust of wind. The steady wind, always a constant on Tugidak, teamed up with its cohorts, night and rain, to torment and demoralize us as much as possible. We were both thoroughly chilled inside our raingear. Our feet had been pretty much soaked since we first came to Tugidak, that was another given. My boss, though as miserable as I, didn't appear overly concerned, only put-out that we hadn't won the race with the tide. It *was* good to be safe from the tide but I wondered what kind of a night we would have. We had been miserable plenty of times together on hunting trips and were both stoic sufferers. But Tom didn't stand around too long before deciding that what we needed was a fire. There was a little driftwood scattered along the base of the bluff and we hunted for sticks with our windproof Zippo lighters, the flames guttering like little blowtorches in the wind but never blowing out. Having run out of lighter fluid, we now burned kicker gas in them. We finally had enough sticks and bigger wood to start the fire on the flattest, smoothest part of our rock haven. It took some real patience and fortitude to coax a flame onto the little wet sticks. All the wood was wet. To sustain the starter flame we used a few strips of rubber-fabric, slit from the cuffs of Tom's rain pants, which he'd dipped into the gas tank on one of the bikes. Tom lay curled on his side on the bare wet rock blocking the wind, and I did the same, facing him and we worked together to nurture the little flames and protect them from the rain and wind. We succeeded only marginally, the fire never really taking off but providing plenty of alternative misery in the way of smoke, which stung our eyes shut and made the snot run from our noses. All in all it was probably one of the least enjoyable camp-outs I ever participated in. We lay fetus-like, facing one another on the hard, wet rock with our knees and heads touching, the pathetic little fire between us emitting more smoke than heat, and windborne rain pattering on our raingear. We actually dozed off occasionally, but mostly lay there making grim jokes and trying hard to laugh at ourselves, sometimes sharing a cigarette, cupping it against the rain as we passed it back and forth, or just bearing the long misery in unthinking silence, listening to the splash and welter of water against the base of our rock and waiting for the tide, or daylight, whichever came first.

A faint, gray lightening in the sky made do for the dawn, begrudgingly releasing the night and revealing the change of the tide. It had been falling for several hours but had a long way to go to where it had been, incoming, when we arrived last night at the impasse. We lay on our rock for awhile longer, shivering and still hugging the soggy illusion of the fire, peering at each other from inside our raincoat hoods, realizing it was getting light, but reluctant to move, so cold and stiff we were. But, as anyone knows, activity brings warmth by way of blood flow, so we picked ourselves up and started bending our limbs and moving around clumsily like storks stalking the marshes for frogs, working out the stiffness and kinks. Next we went to work on getting the bikes back down onto the beach. In the early morning light it became a real mystery how we had gotten them up there. By the time we were back down on the sand, all loaded and ready to go again, we were plenty warm. Tom asked me to dig our last two sandwiches out and we'd have some breakfast while we waited for the tide. I complied immediately, pulling the bread sack out of the Blazo box. I held it up and was almost sickened to see that the bottom corner of the sack had two inches of watery blood in it. The sandwiches were smashed together. Ugh! It must have been mauled in the confusion last night and had been buried in seal hides. Only about half of each sandwich actually was soaked in the blood. There was nothing for it but to ignore the ugly mess and eat the stuff or go hungry. We each took one and began our breakfast without much enthusiasm. It wasn't that bad. Something like eating bread and milk if you closed your eyes. The *thought* of eating the seal blood au-jues on our baloney sandwiches was worse than the actual taste, but I found myself wishing we had a cup of the bland, rusty coffee of the night before to swill with each bite. We slurped some clean rainwater from crevices in the rock instead. Now that we were warmed up and had swallowed our breakfast, we were forced to wait impatiently almost two hours for the tide to fall enough to permit our passage around the point. We paced back and forth, chain smoking our hand-rolled cigarettes. Our store bought-smokes were long gone and we were deep into our single pound of reserve Velvet tobacco. I had been rolling cigarettes since I was a boy. My dad taught me how. He often had me make him one while he was butchering a deer on the kitchen table or working on a boat engine in the garage, his hands being too messy or oily for the task. I always wondered how Tom could manage the delicate job with his huge fingers. Finally, flipping his last butt away, he declared that we would walk the bikes through the foot and a half of water that still lapped the rocks. We'd save a good half-hour. Tom's three-wheeler actually half floated on its fat tires, even with weight of the seal hides. I had to walk mine through the hard way, idling it slowly along in low gear. We were again freshly wet to the knees when we stopped on the other side, but things seemed to be improving. The rain had stopped a little while before, and even the wind seemed to slack off a notch or two. The tide was ours now, and the fresh sand stretched out before us, washed and trackless.

CHAPTER 11
The Biggest Herd

None of the hunters on the island lived on this end. We all hunted from the north end, working our way south and returning with the incoming tide. That meant we had the south end all to ourselves this morning and the herds would be off guard, not expecting hunters here until afternoon. We rode off down the sand, glad to be moving again and in a short time had rounded to the Fish and Game beach. Here, to our great elation we found a very large herd, maybe fifteen hundred animals, packed together on the sand near our end of the beach and stretching away clear past the Fish and Game cabin. All down the crowded sand the heads of a hundred guards were waving in the air at once. The wind was straight onshore and we couldn't smell their stink, nor they ours. I felt a little hesitant about taking seals right on Fish and Game's official doorstep, but Tom had no such inhibition. We were legal. We flew out from behind the point and roared down on the herd, determined to make up for all the bad luck we'd been having. Tom had long since given up stopping his bike at the edge of the herd. He had bailed off one day during our first week, accidentally leaving it in gear. While we raced through the herd, the three-wheeler had idled down the beach into the water. When we stopped taking pups we laughed seeing the bike floating on the water, bobbing against the beach in the light surf, rear tires still turning. Fearful that it might happen someday in an offshore wind that would take the Honda out to sea, from then on Tom rode right through the herd, steering with his right hand, club flailing in the left, and dodging adults, some of which had actually bitten his tires. We ran out of seals before we'd penetrated even a quarter of this herd but in our eagerness took well over forty pups, almost twice what we'd skinned all day the day before. I was getting the hang of using the big, new club, and was glad we had been so successful, but not overly cheered at the prospect of the long hours of skinning ahead of us. It wasn't so bad though. The weather had definitely improved. The sun now warmed our backs weakly from behind a high overcast, the beach was actually beginning to dry out, and best of all was the two Fish and Game men, who came down from their hut to watch us work, marveling at Tom's skinning speed, handling and admiring our hides. They provided a great diversion from our labor as we all talked while we worked. Tom and I, anxious to be off again, continued to skin as fast as we could, taking a little break to stretch our cramped muscles with the completion of each hide by walking down the beach and rinsing it in the surf.

Tom was in a very good frame of mind when we finally loaded our hides and were on our way again. My Blazo box was plumb full, and the tick-buoy was really bulging now, its weight squatting the three-wheeler so that the tires sometimes rubbed the plastic fenders. Our progress was slow as we continued to hunt on the return, checking out every possible place in the rocks and drift that might hide a seal, finding only a few orphans here and there and adding maybe eight hides to what we were carrying. By the time we finally reached the end of the bluff zone and rode out onto the long sand beach that led around to our camp, the bikes had about all they could haul. The '90' was hard to handle with the heavy hides riding high on the rack and I dumped the bike on its side several times here in this loose sand, but Tom's bike seemed to be doing fine. We usually rode down the wet strand of the outside beach then crossed over into the little lagoon, but this evening for some reason Tom turned *up* the beach and headed for a ten foot sand bank leading inland, apparently intending to cross over to the Big Lagoon. I was fifty feet behind him as he down-shifted and goosed the throttle to climb the bank. The tough little bike did what he asked of it and went right up the bank but when it reached the top, the front tire went right on climbing. The bike, and Tom, went over backwards and rolled ass-over-teakettle down the sandy slope. I squirreled to a stop, my '90' falling over on my right leg and pinning me down, the extra weight of my hides making it fair impossible for me to extricate myself, but the loose sand prevented serious injury. I glanced with alarm at Tom, well knowing he must have at least broken his neck, I had seen him land upside down on his head with the heavy laden bike right on top of him. But he was already on his feet, spitting sand and flicking it from his ears and dusting it off his clothes, laughing sheepishly at himself. He wasn't even scratched. I, on the other hand, needed his help in getting out from under my bike, and felt what would soon become a hand sized, purple bruise on the inside of my knee. Later, after counting the hides in his tick-buoy, we calculated the combined weight of the hides, plus himself at nearly five hundred pounds on that little bike, roughly equivalent to a drum of fuel.

We gave up on the Big Lagoon and headed instead for camp. It was late evening, probably about nine or ten p.m. when we pulled up near the boat and shut off the bikes. It was now mid June and though the hour was late, we still had good light to work by. I had barely noticed the rapidly increasing daylight. Summer was just around the corner. Dog tired, I dragged off to the tent to rustle up some real coffee and hot grub while Tom started in on washing and salting our two day take. When we finished up we had sixty-nine fresh hides added to our trash-can salt barrels, almost filling the third one. It was our best haul yet, even if it had taken us two days. I was worn down to the bone as I'm sure Tom was. All I wanted was my bed, knowing full well that we'd be up and at it again in a few hours. We rinsed the hide-salt from our hands in the incoming tide, which had floated *Elise* a quarter-hour before, while we stowed hides in the barrels, then rolled ourselves a smoke and stood silently admiring the blue and orange sky and its lurid, oily reflection on the ocean outside the lagoon. We stood gazing at the quiet scene for several minutes, lost in the numbness of the sleep-deprived, yet drinking in the beauty of it, somehow drawing strength from it. "Hey!" Tom said suddenly, "The wind quit blowin'." It was true. For the first time since landing here, (for the first time since leaving Kodiak) the incessant wind, which never stopped blowing, had suddenly gone quiet. The sea was flat calm. And eerily still. Tom gave a sudden start. "Let's get the hell out of here Steve." I looked at him stupidly, "Huh?" He grinned at me. "No, *really*. We're done. We ain't getting very many hides now. We're out of grub and almost out of salt. We'll pack up and load the boat and cut a trail for town." I knew that we wouldn't get any better traveling weather, we had plenty of light and the boat was already floating. I think that Tom was verbalizing what he'd been thinking about for some days. Back in town we would still have to dry-pack and ship the hides and he still had to get ready for salmon season. We had done about all we could here. I suddenly experienced, to a much lesser degree, the feeling that would later be described to me by my brother Dave, when he had been informed of his Army discharge as he was prowling the jungles of Vietnam, fighting for his life. The misery was over.

Town? I had stopped thinking about town. That seemed far behind and long ago. My life was in the here and now. I had unconsciously gone feral, focused only on hunting the lonely, wild beaches of Tugidak, physically tougher, mentally sharper and far freer than I had ever felt. At the end of each day I gloried in the experience, yet at the same time felt like a slave to a master's bidding. He shook me awake way too early every morning when the alarm clock went off like a fire bell on the cook shelf between our sleeping heads. I never heard a thing. First thing I knew each morning, Tom was shaking me softly by the shoulder, "C'mon Steve, time to ramble." At those moments I hated the sound of his gentle voice, wishing he would just go off to hunt by himself for a day and let me alone to sleep. But he usually already had the coffee heating. The harsh hissing of the Coleman stove and the little heat it dissipated into the tent, plus the thought that he would surely think me a pansy if I started whining about it, convinced me to get up and pull on my grimy pants and lace up my wet boots.

My pride helped me get through most of each day. Unwilling to admit my weakness, I had to push myself hard to follow after Tom. To artificially generate and display some semblance of his intense desire to make our season successful, as though it were as important to me as it was to him. Tom was either fooled into thinking that I was 'up and running' for the hunt and accepted it as a matter of course, or he saw through my game and politely let me feel I was doing a good job. He never said, either way, but I don't remember him ever having to give me any serious pep talks so I figured he was at least satisfied with my work. I had been so focused on the hunt and our daily routine, I now found it difficult to accept that it was over. We were going to town. Rats! A big part of me wanted to stay on and explore the vast, marshy interior, and the Big Lagoon, maybe getting a chance to bring in my giant Japanese glass ball. I didn't know if I would ever be back.

CHAPTER 12
Hallucinations and Killer Whales

We didn't expend great effort in packing neatly. Tom fired up the 'Eighty-Five' and we took in the anchor and shoreline and moved *Elise* up closer to camp. I rolled up our sleeping bags, gathered up all the little stuff and stowed it in the empty ice chest, and began to untie the guy ropes on the tent. Tom showed up and we made short work of striking camp. We loaded the Honda 90 onto *Elise*, and shifted all the heavy stuff around to trim her out so she floated evenly, then crammed everything else in where it would fit, and covered the whole load with the tent. We worked fast now that it had sunk in that we were actually leaving. Tired as we were, having spent the last two days on the beach, hunting hard and sleeping very little, both of us knew that weather like this wouldn't last long, and it would be a good thing to have the open water behind us before it changed. By about midnight we were ready to pull out. We'd loaded the three-wheeler into the Whaler since there was no room on board *Elise* after filling the three big plastic garbage cans with the salted hides. Besides she was still floating a big load. We had burned a lot of fuel and ate most of the grub, losing that bit of weight, but now had added maybe a thousand pounds of sealskins, now mixed with the nearly five hundred pounds of salt. The three-wheeler fit easily in front of the tow-post in the skiff and was tied securely in place fore and aft. The glow from sunset was fading into a

Illustration by Elise Dooley

purplish twilight when we idled out of the lagoon and opened up the outboards, lining out on a course for the high, dark shoulder of Sitkinak Island, bound for home.

All the excitement and the burst of physical activity of loading the boat had kept me too busy to think about my exhaustion, but the effortless operation of the skiff, now that we were on our way, was like some kind of waking dream. I had never in my short experience run the skiff on anything but lumpy or rough water which always took a little, or a lot, of physical effort to maintain a heading. This liquid mirror I was skimming across required only that I rest my hand on the tiller and hold the throttle open. The pearly water near at hand shot past me. Farther out it rolled by at a stately pace. Behind me a glowing, white wake torched from the stern like a rocket flame, disappearing into the gloom of deep twilight. Tugidak was gone. It had slipped over the horizon or was swallowed by night, I couldn't tell which. By the time we had crossed to Sitkinak I began to get quite drowsy. *Elise's* wake stretched before me, straight as a string in the waning light, providing an effortless white path for me to follow and I found myself fighting sleep as the Whaler sped across the glassy water, the steady roar of the motor hypnotizing my senses. I was not especially cold or uncomfortable in any way except for my skinny butt, which was already getting numb from sitting on the hard transom. It never occurred to me that even a real man might have brought along a cushion. I wasn't exactly sure how a real man should behave, except to tough it out. I was exceedingly sleepy and began to hallucinate, seeing things that weren't there. At one point a wide, shiny, steel ladder rose from the ocean just ahead of me, disappearing high up into the void of the sky. I quickly chopped the throttle for fear of colliding with it. Incredibly, it wasn't there. Several times I opened my eyes after drowsing and suddenly saw that *Elise* had stopped dead in the water and I was about to ram her stern. Each time this happened I jerked awake from my doldrums and quickly twisted the throttle down, only to see the boat still flying along far ahead of me, a little black speck with a white tail a quarter mile long. One thing I was very sure of was the killer whale which I had noticed following me from the vicinity of Aiaktalik Island. Every time I checked, and for awhile I checked often, it was still there. It remained a couple hundred yards astern, just outside my wake, pacing my speed, the black, yard-long dorsal fin, bent over a little at the top, cutting the water and making its own small wake through the glassy water. I had no idea why it followed me, perhaps drawn by the stink of seals emanating from my clothes and wafting back astern. It was weird behavior for any wild animal to follow a man, unless it was a bear. But it didn't greatly concern me, having never heard of an orca attacking a boat and besides, I was just too sleepy to deal with it. It took all my focus just to stay in *Elise's* wake. I knew I could never outrun it anyway, but the orca never came closer. The Whaler was a very small skiff and I was riding very low on the water so, as a precaution against dozing off and somehow falling overboard, I tied a rope to the tow-post and wrapped my right hand through the loop. Tom never slowed once. We ran on and on through a universe of twilight, the oily sea as still as a lake. Time itself paused, while I flew through space, disconnected, as in a pantomime dream. Hearing nothing but the stupor-inducing drone of the outboard, the noise becoming like silence itself to my numb senses. The islands and rocks far ahead were floating in the air, whether real or imagined, I couldn't tell.

Somewhere near Kaguyak Bay, with Twoheaded Island looming large, I checked behind me once again for the killer whale and discovered that it had gone, causing me some amount of relief. Soon after that I noted casually that *Elise* appeared to have stopped again in front of me. I had by now realized what had been happening to me and made no move to fall for it again. But suddenly I found myself bearing down on the boat and it was growing in size! *"Oh Shit!"* I again shut the throttle down, now wide awake, and came up along side the boat, back in control. Tom told me to hang the skiff off the stern and come on board, we were going to run up inside Japanese Bay to anchor up and get a few hours sleep. Ahhh! Sleep. This was what I had been wanting to hear ever since we'd rode into camp on the motorcycles back on Tugidak. Was it only a few hours ago? We still had several miles to go so I went in and pumped up the gas tank on the Coleman to heat up the old coffee. We both needed a hot drink and I wasn't worried about caffeine keeping me awake. We slurped the steaming brew as we motored slowly up into the dark, narrow bay and I found myself now alert, and very appreciative of the heavy, sweet scent of new, green alder and cottonwood foliage pervading the air from the steep hills that backed up from the shorelines, and of the quiet stillness of the place. Out on the open sea I had been able to see everything in black silhouette against the water and sky but it was dark up inside these bays, the high hills blocking out the light. We used the spotlight again to find an anchoring place and Tom finally shut off the motor. We had only run some thirty miles from Tugidak but it seemed to me like a hundred and thirty. We relaxed against the gunwales for awhile and absorbed the almost holy silence of the bay as we enjoyed a final smoke outside, talking quietly.

Tom told me we were only going to sack out for a couple hours then be on our way again early. Once he made up his mind to go, Tom went. It was about two-thirty or three a.m. when I crawled gratefully into my bag and settled into the soft foam of the mattress. Tom set the alarm on the Big Ben for six and turned off the lantern. I was asleep before it stopped hissing.

Then I was suddenly awakened rather roughly by Tom's big paw. "Why'd you shut the alarm off Steve?" I sat up befuddled. Bright sunlight glared into the cabin through the open door. "What?" I scratched my head. "I didn't turn it off, I didn't even hear it." I looked at the clock in his hand. It should have been plain to him who had quelled the sudden, five-alarm din of the Big Ben. The plastic face was cracked and busted in. It had probably only made about three loud dings before Tom's big paw had apparently clamped over the clock without him even knowing, and silenced it forever with one hard squeeze. But I could see that he was in no mood to argue about it. It was just past noon and we'd slept like the very dead for more than nine hours. I have no idea what woke him. He had wanted to get moving again early, before the wind came up again, and now we had probably lost our window of good traveling weather. It later turned out that he was right. We heated and wolfed a couple cans of the last of our chili and sluiced it down with lukewarm coffee then re-fueled all our kicker cans, pulled the anchor and roared out of the bay. Tom was grumpy. Well so was I. I was always getting blamed for shit I didn't do. I let myself brood over the unfairness of it all for awhile, but after coming out of the bay my feelings of self pity vanished, seeing the sparkling, royal blue of the sea stretching to infinity, all etched by soft, almost balmy breezes. The cushiony, Irish green of little islands and black shale rockpiles contrasted beautifully with the blue water and sky. The sun so warm on my face and the bright wake of *Elise,* trailing out ahead made me feel rested and alive again, ready for the long run home.

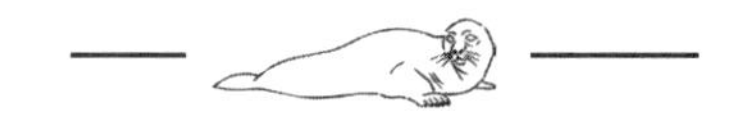

CHAPTER 13
The Weather Breezes Up

We enjoyed good traveling weather all the way from Japanese Bay, past Old Harbor and through Sitkalidak Straits, where we then emerged to a stiff southwest breeze and found that a lively, choppy sea had developed. The blue sky had been gobbled by dark gray clouds that erased the sunshine. By the time we'd breasted Cape Barnabas on Sitkalidak Island a ground-swell had begun to make itself felt, running onshore from the wide open Pacific, and we rode out over the high waves, dashing spray from the fresh wind-chop. After a close-in swing around Dangerous Cape we began crossing outside the miles-wide mouth of Ugak Bay with the island now in full view ahead to the right. I looked fondly at Ugak, now knowing its beaches intimately, wondering if my brother was still there hunting seals. We were bucking the tide, the wind and the seas coming from behind on the starboard quarter. All were fighting us in some way as we plowed along. Tom had to slow way down now to keep from burying *Elise's* tiny bow under green water. *Elise* was carrying such a load that her lowered buoyancy could make it hard for her to recover if the bow went under. But she was a game little boat and it helped having the load aft since that raised the bow a little more. What he was more worried about was the tiny amount of freeboard in the motor-well, mere inches. *Elise's* load was supported by the bow and stern. The voids formed by the seine-well, which straddled the motor-well provided the buoyancy to float the stern. A following sea was the worst he could hope for, especially if they were breaking, which these were. They could rush in and break over the open stern or gush up through the motor-well and dump hundreds of gallons of the sea into the boat in an instant, threatening her ability to recover. The little toy bilge pump was already working overtime, just keeping up with the spray entering the boat and I'm sure that Tom appreciated the wisdom of buying it, probably already planning to stride right up to Sutliff's and upgrade to a bigger size as soon as we hit town. The little hand pump wouldn't do much with a serious amount of water, but the five gallon deck bucket, in the hands of one driven by sheer terror, would far out outperform both the other pumps.

I wasn't having any picnic my own self. I was soon taught to keep my senses alert, eyes *and* ears. I heard the hiss of a swell behind me and almost instantly was inundated by frothy water spilling against my back and pouring over my legs into the skiff. Too late, I gunned the throttle, but learned something as the bow raised and the water all receded back to the stern and began siphoning through the open well of the drain. This little boat was a marvel of engineering. If I had been running a wooden skiff I'd be bailing with one hand and driving the kicker with the other, at a time when either task was a full time job. So I learned to keep my ears open as well as my eyes. Whenever my ears told me a swell was breaking behind me I hit the gas and shot ahead of it.

We corkscrewed along for nearly an hour after entering the outer Ugak Narrows before drawing near Ugak Island. The clouds had lowered, darkening the fading day even more. I wasn't very excited about traveling through these narrows and on around Cape Chiniak. Even though the wind wasn't blowing all that hard, maybe a steady twenty knots and gusting higher, the pall of darkness was closing off my vision and I knew these waters to be spoken of in very respectful terms by the fishermen of Kodiak. This was no place to be in a little skiff in the middle of the night. Hell, big boats had trouble through here in *tough* weather. One thing I knew about Ugak Narrows was that it was notorious for a strong tidal flow, big seas and tide rips. Mountainous swells race unhindered for hundreds of miles to charge in endless procession and pound relentlessly at the shale bluffs of the coastline in thundering, feathery blooms of white spray. When the wind opposes the tide, with a big sea rolling in, the waves stack up higher and get closer together and life can get very hairy. Add darkness, it was coming. I will admit to being a little chicken-livered about this. Tom was several hundred yards out in front, *Elise* grossly wallowing as the seas swept beneath her. I was doing my best to shorten the distance. The combination of breaking swells and the windblown chop, essentially little waves riding big waves, was pretty intimidating. This, I realized, would probably be qualified as *weather*. I remembered my first trip in the skiff from Pasagshak Bay to town, seeming so long ago, when I had been scared by a three-foot chop.

Pasagshak would be ahead to port, just inside Ugak Bay. It would be visible now if it wasn't so dark. If it was one good habit I had formed while playing or hunting or boating around Kodiak Island, it was to be continuously careful about keeping my bearings. We were getting close to Ugak Island, now barely discernable on the right. That meant we were entering the squeeze of the *real* narrows and I felt myself tense with the realization. I was on high alert, watching for a 'queer one', the maverick wave that I'd heard about so often, or the confused, frothy tide rips caused by the shearing of powerful currents against submerged rocks or shoals. The sea conditions remained about the same though, despite my fears, and drawing abreast of the island I was overjoyed to see Tom turn *Elise* and begin to head for our old anchorage. Maybe we were going in to hole up for the night. I sure hoped so. I wasn't particularly chilled, but my back-side was numb. And my now strong left arm, very significantly bulked up as it was from lifting on the seals while skinning them, was aching from the hard work of steering the skiff over the rough mountains of water. My neck muscles were on fire on that side. I was ready for a break alright. A few hundred yards from the beach the waves lessened noticeably, losing momentum and stature as they curved around the south end of Ugak and I noticed the steady flow of water pissing over the side from the electric pump as I idled up to the boat in the comparatively quiet water just off our old beach. There was no sign of a light on shore and we couldn't see in the dark whether Dave and Red's shack was still there. We figured they must have packed it in and went back to town.

I had expected Tom to tell me that we were calling it quits for the night. I almost went limp when he told me otherwise but tried not to show it, pretending instead to study the surf-line as if it didn't matter in the least. Tom's voice had a hard edge to it and he seemed a little tense as he told me we would drift here for awhile and take a little break. We'd keep the motor idling, moving offshore a ways whenever the boat got in too close. I tied the skiff off to *Elise's* tow-post and climbed stiffly over the tent-covered load, which was piled higher than the gunwales. The tent was soaked and I crawled through puddles of water and over the hard edges of our gear, finally reaching the little space at the back of the cabin that Tom had reserved for operating the boat, where I could stand up and stretch. It was a squeeze for me getting into the cabin, I have no idea how Tom would have managed. It was nice to be inside and I took the liberty of drying my hands and rolling and smoking a cigarette right inside the cabin to reward myself for coming through the misery of the last four or five hours.

I had been smoking publicly for about six months. Though I never held it against him, my dad was the one who got me started. Smoking was another one of those things that was simply an ordinary part of life, like eating. Almost everyone I knew smoked or dipped or chewed. I had come in from school one day and found my dad home alone. I could tell he'd had a few snorts, his dark eyes were tracking a little off and his speech quite animated. "Heyyy Kid, how'd it go today? Siddown and tell me some big lies." I could see that I was fairly well trapped so I flopped down in the chair next to his in the living room and prepared for a long session of listening. Dad was a wonderful story-teller and even though I had heard them all, I still enjoyed the re-telling. As he yarned away, he pulled out a pack of Lucky Strikes, shook one free and took it from the pack with his lips. Then, eyeing me for a second, he extended the pack and shook one out for me, raising an eyebrow in question. I was proud to tell him that I didn't smoke. (My friend, Chris Johnson, and I had made a handshake pact not to smoke about six months before and I had thus far adhered stubbornly to my word) Dad sat back with an incredulous look on his face and for the next fifteen minutes or so I got the *'don't you lie to me'* lecture in a friendly sort of way. He just couldn't believe that I wasn't smoking on the sly. "For Christ sake Kid, if you're gonna smoke, smoke in front of me. Don't go sneakin' around about it like a coyote." And so, more to stop the lecturing than to start smoking, I took one of his Lucky Strikes and for the first time, lit up and smoked it right in front of him, nearly making myself sick. I got the impression that Dad was now satisfied that he'd got me straightened out. Naturally enough, once it was approved, I kept right on smoking, much to my mother's dismay. I felt like a coyote for breaking my word to Chris. To start smoking was a natural extension of becoming 'almost-a-grown-up', when you could start making your own decisions. As I see myself then, looking back, I realize that what I wanted more than anything was to be treated as a peer by the adults surrounding me. Just as a teenage boy will grow the insignificant fuzz on his lip, thinking it looks like a mustache, and use mom's or sister's mascara to darken it, or a girl will, in desperation, fill out her bust size with obvious and lumpy socks, so will either sex take up smoking in order to appear more sophisticated and mature. It might work to a degree among your teen peers, but to the world at large it falls flat. Tom, to his great credit was my most staunch advisor against the nasty habit even though he, himself, smoked.

At Ugak Island we rolled about in the small swell that was washing ashore, Tom remaining on his knees just outside the cabin door, keeping and eye on shore, and I in the cabin sitting uncomfortably on the hard edge of my bunk on the deck under the dim glow of the radio dial. He told me that he was a little worried about the weather. I was still green enough not to realize the significance of that statement coming from a skipper. They are generally optimistic and understated about it in front of the crew. The wind might be thrumming sixty through the rigging, heeling the boat around hard against the anchor-line, which is pop-pop-popping tightly in the chock, and a skipper will peer outside over the rim of his coffee cup and absent-mindedly mention that it might be 'laying down a little'.

Tom went on to tell me that this weather was marginally okay for travel right now, but it might really start to blow. If we stayed at Ugak we'd probably be safe enough, but the wind might howl for a week or more. It often does. The weather hadn't been too bad for spring, no big storms anyway. We were overdue for a good blow. There wasn't enough grub to last a day, much less a week. We hadn't eaten since Japanese Bay and were both hollow again from hunger but there were more important things to think about than that. Our only options were to stay or go. Tom told me that if we didn't dally here we could be in town in two or three hours if everything went okay. We were so close, just get around Cape Chiniak and it's a straight run to town, except for the rockpiles off Woody and Near Islands. This news perked me up a little. Only three more hours to endure the endless seas and soaking spray. My shirt front was wet to my belt from spray dousing my hood and running in icy trickles down my neck inside my raincoat but a few more hours didn't seem all that long after what we'd already been through.

I now realize that Tom must have been tumbling this problem around in his head for some hours as we made our way, bobbing over the Pacific swell like fleeing ducks. It was one of those seeming gambles that fishermen must make often for various reasons. And it is not really a gamble so much as a thought-out, calculated risk. Tom being the skipper, no matter the size of his boat, had to make that decision alone. When all the pros and cons had been considered he had decided we would high-tail it for town. We checked our fuel tanks, agreeing that now would be a good time to top off. Climbing back into the skiff, I used a siphon hose to transfer the pre-mixed fuel from its drum on the boat and re-filled the main, eighteen-gallon tank. My reserve six-gallon tank was still full. I held on to *Elise's* gunwale while Tom screwed the bung back onto the barrel and stowed the hose. He gave me a look and a grim smile that told me he felt a little sorry for me. “How's it goin' in the skiff back there Steve?” I gave him my best rendition of a doubtful frown, almost shaking my head. “Pretty shitty.” was all I could think of to say, wanting, but *not* wanting, to whimper. I was hoping that he would see through my brave face and tell me to hang the skiff off the stern and ride with him on *Elise,* but no such luck. He may have seen through me alright, but towing a skiff under these conditions, with the boat already over-loaded, would engender a whole new set of problems neither of us needed. He understood that. I was still pretty green and it never occurred to me that it would be even less safe to tow the skiff.

CHAPTER 14
Engine Problems

I could see that there was no point in dragging my soggy feet, so I cast off from *Elise* and fired up the kicker. As we motored out away from the island, Tom pulled an ample corner of the tent over his head which he'd been using as a shield against the spray that was continually blown at his back from the stern-quarter wind. The flat hull of the boat shot regular sheets of spray out to both sides and the wind blew it right back again from the starboard side. It was really dark by now and all I had to buoy up my courage was a fervent hope in Tom's dead-reckoning compass navigation and knowledge of the waters and the tides. The seas rolled under us not far offshore as once again we lined out on our course and settled in for another unpleasant ride. It seemed that the wind was laying off, not being quite as spiteful as it had before, and hurling less spray. There was no lack of concern on my part. Tom must have nudged the throttle ahead for this leg of the voyage. I found myself playing catch-up right from the start, misjudging his speed and falling behind before I realized it. The ground swell had grown, perhaps due to a shallower bottom along the broad point running from Narrow Cape to Chiniak, or maybe the tide was running stronger now. Whatever the cause, I was now taking much longer rides up and down the swells. It became necessary to focus most of my attention on looking wide-eyed, far forward to catch a sighting of *Elise*.

She was now only visible when both boats occasionally topped a wave at the same time and only then because of the glow from her tiny running lights. I couldn't actually see the port and starboard lights because they are designed to be viewed from the front and sides only, making it easy to tell in the dark whether a boat is coming toward you. The dim lights glowed intermittently on the spray that shot out from under the boat. After long, anxious minutes of watching, my eyes would be rewarded by tiny greenish and reddish flickers bracketing an indistinct dark spot between, lasting only a few seconds before *Elise*, or the skiff, settled back into the trough. I sometimes had to readjust my heading to line up with him, but I had been riding the same swells all the way from Cape Barnabas and by now had an almost instinctive feel about holding my course, quartering across the heaving mountains just so. I really admire the fishermen on the big boats around Alaska. They know what big seas are, and can stand and walk and work on a deck that tilts violently at random, seemingly in all directions at once, like a carnival ride gone wrong. It takes good sea-legs and sometimes a good bit of courage, and once you get used to it provides a sort of macho challenge to keep your feet while you do your work. But I will say that the perspective is much different when you are sitting almost on the water in an open dinghy. Even moderately high seas which these were, being maybe eighteen to twenty feet are pretty intimidating to a young boy. If this was what they call adventure I'd had my fill of it. Enough for *one* day anyway.

I was getting pretty comfortable with my method of staying on course and no longer experienced as great concern if Tom was out of sight for a little while. I couldn't see Narrow Cape which must be a half mile or less to port. The clouds had cancelled all the late twilight we would have enjoyed on a clear night. I still had enough to worry about and was plenty busy steering the skiff and watching for sightings of Tom, when the kicker suddenly coughed, and jerked in my hand. Then again. Then it bogged way down to a shuddering r-r-r-r-r-r-r-r. "*Now* what?" The skiff slowed dramatically, the bow dropping, plowing ahead. I didn't know what to do so I twisted the throttle wide open hoping to keep it running. Nothing happened at first, then r-r-r-R!-r-RR!-r-R-R-R-R-R-R! The skiff took off like a gut-shot cat, leaping over the crest of a wave and plunging down the other side. I quickly backed off the gas enough to regain control and was very relieved when the outboard kept running right. A couple minutes later the outboard repeated the heart stopping r-r-r-r-r-r-r, and then, after a few minutes, shot ahead again. This was not good. I kept watching for my dim, moving beacon, and running blindly on and on. My mind was a blank. Tom was no doubt pulling ahead now. He must be a quarter-mile away or more. I didn't even have a flashlight. The headlight on the three-wheeler only worked when it was running, and I couldn't see myself trying to kick-start it under these conditions. The kicker went into the stutter again, slowing the skiff. I heard a sudden hissing right behind me and instinctively ducked my head as the swell broke green right in over the stern, engulfing the motor, bursting on my back and flowing on with the wave the full length of the skiff. It boiled around the three-wheeler and floated the kicker cans and oars against their tie-downs. The skiff was nearly full of water and the outboard still running like crap, but running. I was now getting pretty worried, but at my young age I knew how to handle fear. I had my first encounter with real mortal fear one night some years before; when the boat I was on wrecked in the rocks of Long Island on a winter night and I had been sure we were all going to die. That fear had lasted hours. This was bad but not *that* bad. I knew this boat wouldn't sink. The next swell lifted the stern, pushing the skiff ahead as it washed underneath, and most of the water ran right out over the bow when the skiff tipped steeply down on the wave. Tom had taught me to *always* tie everything down and now I knew why. When the water poured out it would have carried everything overboard, maybe even the bike if it wasn't secured. Once again I marveled at this little skiff, but I still had troubles confronting me. There was nothing I could do but keep running and try to follow after the only hope I had, the occasional glow of Tom's nav-lights. It went on this way for some time, seemingly forever, the outboard puking out and stuttering along, barely allowing enough power to steer with, then roaring off again for as long as five minutes. It must have been Divine Intervention that saved me from being swamped again. The seas broke close behind and beside me sometimes, but never again into the skiff. Fervent, continuously muttered prayers were a good part of my strategy. My dad always said that the Lord looks out for drunks and fools. I figured I qualified, at least on one count. I needed all the help I could get and wasn't bashful in asking for it. But for every answered prayer there were ten others that weren't, and it seemed I must ride the ragged edge of doubt for a long time to come.

It took too long for me to finally realize a possible solution to the bad miss affecting the kicker. I had been half-watching the eighteen gallon gas can, barely visible in the dark, tied off to the bow cleat. It had stretched its ties and was sliding and banging around from the rough wallowing of the skiff. I decided I'd better tighten it up or it might wear a hole in the fiberglass. Tom wouldn't like that. I backed the kicker down carefully to a fast idle and popped it out of gear, much relieved that it kept running, and crept forward, working my way along the Honda and its tie-downs, to re-secure the big tank. This was no easy job with the Whaler at the mercy of the seas. The skiff went crossways in the swells, tipping and wallowing dangerously. To stay in the boat while I worked, I had to lay on top of the tank and push with my legs to crowd the tank against the bow while I quickly re-tied the line onto the cleat. I tried to see the fuel gauge, picturing the fuel level sloshing around inside and it suddenly dawned on me. Maybe it was water in the tank! Sure! I'd heard of that happening in rough weather. All the pitching and rolling was probably sloshing water around the suction tube of the fuel line. I unplugged the hose from the tank and made a fast crawl back to the stern where I struggled to re-attach it to the reserve tank. I managed to get it snapped on, and quickly pumped up the bulb before the kicker died. There were a few more disappointing stuttering episodes and then the kicker perked up and began to run strong like it was supposed to. This was an enormous relief to me. I no longer even worried about the big seas. With control restored I could play on these swells if I wanted to. I scoffed at them! Spit on them! Now that the 'Eighteen' was healed, I focused my efforts on shortening the distance between me and Tom and I searched for quite awhile before I finally saw the red-green glow flicker weakly out in the dark. It was so dim and illusive I thought maybe I had imagined it, then, just to the right of my heading I saw it again. Okay there he was. I corrected my heading and mentally noted the angle that the skiff was riding over the swells, and began to relax a little bit. Life was good once more. I had confidence now that the skiff could catch *Elise* and wasn't a bit afraid to open it up to not-quite reckless speed and went racing up and down the swells. Sometimes the skiff left the water, launching over the top, and belly-flopped clumsily into the trough. Other times, not on purpose, I shot through breaking seas from behind, barely taking a drop inside and racing the foam down through the next trough. I was careful but no longer scared. I'd got over that back there. This was nothing. Little by little I began to close up on *Elise,* the spray-glow becoming brighter and more frequent and the boat itself taking on shape. The wind had backed off now, and the choppy water began to smooth out. The seas were still high, breaking less now, and the dark was absolute. *Elise's* nav-lights now briefly reflected on the swells between us at each sighting. The reflection provided a three-second glimpse in great detail of an otherwise invisible sea of stacked, moving hills of black water. I could even make out the dim silhouette of Tom's head and shoulders there above the cabin. I felt very much easier in mind now. I even felt safe. We had been at least two hours from Ugak by now and I had no idea how much farther it might be to Cape Chiniak. But my kicker was running right, and I felt comfortable with my ability to handle myself in these easier seas even in the dark. As we rode the swells toward the cape I thought about the water in my gas. Where did it come from? I was always careful to put the cap on the fuel tank right and close the little vent knob to keep moisture out, except while running. Then I remembered fueling up with the siphon hose at Ugak and I knew that I must have had the hose on the bottom of the drum and sucked water into my kicker can. I should have known better, but we were pretty tired and miserable. It struck me that such a small oversight could actually get you killed out here. Or at least in a lot of trouble. Some time later I noticed that Tom seemed to be drifting off to the left a little bit more each time I'd spotted him lately. I hoped he was making the turn far enough around the point and not into the rockpiles there. All I could do was follow the glow as it appeared. The seas started coming more squarely on the stern and I knew we must be rounding the Cape. How he had known when to start the turn I couldn't imagine.

CHAPTER 15
Magical Return

It must have been around eleven p.m. We had been running almost continually since Japanese Bay, at least ten hours. I had no sensation of being sleepy but my backside felt like one big bruise and I was stiff from sitting. And wet. I wasn't especially cold, the temperature was mild and the wind had been at our backs. There had been no time to think of my belly. Suddenly I perked up and looked around me, for the seas were lessening. We quite suddenly became like dolphins, undulating over the water on long, smooth, sensual swells. A strange, bright glow was emanating from the low clouds ahead, silhouetting *Elise* blackly. The eerie, glowing clouds made a wide, subdued band of reflection on the smooth water, filled with oily light-snakes, all appearing and disappearing at once. I was bedazzled. Maybe it was a crab boat approaching with the pick-lights on. I couldn't imagine what else. Tom hadn't increased his speed when the sea had flattened out, since we still couldn't see well, but neither did he slow down now in view of this weird light. If it didn't bother Tom, it must be okay. My concern about avoiding a crabber in the dark all but faded.

The sea continued to diminish until the tri-hull of the Whaler wasn't even *'shushing'* on the water anymore. All I felt was a gentle rise and fall as we watched the glow before us brightening quickly to actual light. Quite suddenly we emerged from a bank of gray cloud, which was lying right over the water, out into a deep blue dome of twilight, with bright stars twinkling overhead. From miles across the smooth black water the intense, scintillating, white light hurt our eyes. It was the city lights of Kodiak! Now Tom idled back and pulled the throttle into neutral, mesmerized like me at the wonder of what just happened. This side of Chiniak was as clear as a bell. No wind. No swell. It would now be a flat-calm run across the few miles of intervening water, riding a band of white light across the blue-black sea. *"Except for the reefs"* I worried, keeping that in the back of my mind and, almost unconsciously began looking for blinking marker buoys even though they were still far ahead. I pulled up to *Elise,* killed the kicker, and stood holding the gunwale of the boat, painfully straightening my legs and rubbing my sore butt. Tom was elated though he tried not to show it. And relieved, I could see it in his manner. His voice had lost the hard edge and was soft and easy again. He was himself again. 'Good ol' Dooley', not, 'Worried Skipper'. We rolled a much earned smoke and talked awhile, enjoying the clear night view and the knowledge that the tough part of this trip was behind us. We eyed the solid wall of fog astern. The lights from town lit the entire face of it, giving it a solidity that made it look like the wide snout of a glacier laying across the water. I told Tom a few of the things that had happened to me off Narrow Cape; running blind, the dying kicker, getting swamped and lagging behind. He pulled a grimace and shook his head apologetically and told me that whenever he had tried to slow down, *Elise* started taking water over the top of the motor-well. He'd wanted to, but was afraid to wait. He couldn't even leave the controls to check on the water accumulation in the boat, much less man the hand pump to help the 'toy' one. The thought of swamping the boat and losing it all rode him like a demon and forced him to crowd the limits of speed. It appeared he had been having his troubles same as me. It hadn't been much fun for either of us. But it was behind us now, who cared? I felt very strong and *alive* in that moment. I filled my lungs repeatedly with the dense, pure, sea air, taking pleasure in the hard coolness of it on my face and neck. I sensed and appreciated all that I could see and smell and feel. I felt closer to God. I looked at the lights of town and felt like some ancient, conquering hero returning to his home harbor. Poking fun at myself by miming my brother Dave, I struck a Napoleonic pose, standing erect, swelling out my chest, pushing out my lower lip and sliding my hand inside my shirt-front. Tom got a chuckle out of that. I knew there would be no bands playing or pretty girls admiring when we tied up to the dock, but I felt strong inside, confident, and much moved by the gut-level experience I'd had in the last six weeks with my first love, Mother Nature. Much thanks to Tom.

We started our engines and Tom gave me his famous grin, pulling his head back a notch, and waggled a big hand toward town. He eased *Elise* gradually up on the step for the first time since Sitkalidak Straits, then opened her up and she dropped her nose and flew ahead. I wasn't slow to follow this time and my elation fairly bubbled over as the little Whaler, by now my *second* love, lifted, laid over and sped after Tom. Once again I could make out the familiar backyard, bays and mountains which I knew well, passing now on the port side as we returned. I was wide awake and entirely at peace with the world. After a restful, skimming passage of about thirty minutes Tom slowed slightly and we began to watch for the buoys marking the entrance channel off Woody Island. They were hard to see against all the light from town, but Tom knew where he was, and where he was going. All I had to do was quit worrying and follow in his wake. A greenhorn could do that. But I didn't feel so green anymore. The rest of the run was fast and easy. We skimmed into St. Paul Harbor, past all the canneries along the far shore. There was Near Island, brightly lit across the channel from town, and the dark black line of the high breakwater, behind which was the harbor and rest. I smelled the familiar stink of town in my nose; the soury cannery odors that hung in the back of your throat and the ever present dust from gravel roads. A few cars moved around, and the street lights lit the night downtown as we came idling into the harbor. We puttered quietly around the outside of the floats, heading for our unloading spot near the ramp below the harbor office where we'd cast off back when I was still an untried boy. Town felt strange. So artificial. All was quiet, and the bright reflections of moored fishing boats scrolled past upside-down in the black, mirror-like water, perfect in every detail until our tiny wake wrinkled the image and set it into motion. I could hardly believe we were finally here. It felt like I was rising from a dream as I held the skiff off and watched Tom pull in and tie up to the floats. I tied up to the rail right behind him, shut the kicker off and stepped stiffly up onto the floats, again going through the stork-like motions of straightening the kinks out. I couldn't wait to get home and take a hot shower and crawl into my own bed at Tom and Janice's place.

But again, Tom had other ideas. He wanted me to stay on the boat tonight and keep an eye on our hides and gear. The wind went out of my sails. As I was later to learn, this sort of thing is just part of being a deck-hand. The boat comes first. He was right I realized. Our whole season lay under the tent. I hated the idea of spending another night on board *Elise* when the real comfort of home was so accessible, and hoped Tom felt guilty about leaving me there while he went home to get all cleaned up and comfortable and fed. But the hard-earned gold of all our efforts was laying here in the open and needed someone to watch over it. He climbed the ramp to the harbor office and used the outside pay-phone to call Janice for a ride home, then came back to wait with me on the boat. We had a smoke and some quiet talk, commenting on how summer had appeared in our absence and such things, and had a few chuckles about some of the events of our trip, like the comical crash landing we'd made with the Whaler on the sand spit off Tugidak, and the bloody, green-baloney sandwiches we'd gagged down that morning on the beach only two days ago, where we'd been caught by the tide. It wasn't long before Janice's little red and white, Chevy II pulled onto the dock above us and we went up the ramp to meet her. Elise was in her arms looking all cute and frowsy, wrapped in a blanket. Her blue eyes came wide awake at sight of her daddy. After a long, happy greeting with Tom, Janice gave me a bear-hug squeeze then leaned back and looked me over, smiling skeptically, "*Well I see you're still alive.*" She seemed surprised by the fact and, somewhat understating all I wanted to say, I assured her that "*We did alright.*"

The boat was lonely after they had gone. The town and the harbor were asleep. I sat on top of the cabin watching for the sky to begin brightening behind the dark loom of Pillar Mountain, the base of which was practically just across the street from the harbor. Once in awhile a cab would drive by quietly on the street above. I walked up and planted my feet on the solid ground of the parking lot above the boat and strolled back and forth for awhile, never out of sight of *Elise.* I was a little unsteady on my feet, having been in almost constant, radical motion in the skiff for so many hours, and now I was hungry. My belly raged at the thought of a big juicy hamburger which could be had for half the ten bucks I still had in my wallet. But there was no place to get a meal at that time of the night except for a few of the bars, and they wouldn't let a kid come in by himself. Besides, I couldn't leave the boat. I went back down and began scratching around in the ice chest to see what I could find and selected the most appetizing thing that was left, a rusty looking can of creamed corn. Perching cross-legged once more on top of the cabin, I wiped the can off with my shirt and used my little army P-38 can opener to get the lid open and dug in with my ringing knife, putting the can to my lips and scooping the cold corn into my mouth. It wasn't very good, no matter how cramped my belly felt and after eating less than half I pitched it over the side in disgust. I didn't want to go to bed, even though I was now more than tired, wanting instead to watch Kodiak come to life as the day broke overhead. It would be a real novelty to see people moving around again. But as the cool dampness of night settled around me, I finally gave it up and resigned myself once more to the warm comfort of my suddenly very smelly sleeping bag in an equally stinking cabin, leaving the door open for air, and very soon fell off into deep sleep.

My mind was sluggishly alerted by the feel of the boat rolling deeply to starboard and I struggled to wake up, but my body refused to move. I forced open my eyes and squinted against brilliant sunlight beaming in through the door around the big head and shoulders of my skipper, setting his curly, freshly shampooed hair afire with a bright blonde halo. He and Jan and Elise had come down to relieve me. It was somewhere around ten-thirty in the morning. Fine watchman I made, I thought. But Tom was in a light-hearted mood. He was clean shaven and was wearing fresh, dry clothes. He wrinkled his nose at the stink of the boat and we all laughed when he told me that when he got home last night Janice had made him strip in the arctic entry and had then taken his reeking clothes outside with the broom-handle and put them in the garbage. He handed me a ten dollar bill and said I 'orta' go uptown and get some breakfast before we unloaded the boat, telling me to take my time, no hurry. He began pulling the tarp from our load to start packing stuff up to the truck. I didn't wait around to be told twice, I thanked him for the ten and flung a "*Be back in a bit*" over my shoulder on the way up the ramp. All I had to do was cross the street to the greasy-spoon cafe on the little mall across from the harbor. A big, black mongrel dog came trotting sideways after me, furtively drawing near, his head low, nose outstretched and a worried look about him. I stopped to call him to me for a pat on the head and he backed off and started barking loudly at me. I knew I probably looked and smelled pretty bad. I hadn't had a bath for over a month and a half. The stink of many dead seals was upon me. The truth be known, my odiferous self and clothing probably rated right up there with a dead, maggot filled dog I had turned over with a stick once as a boy, back in one of Kodiak's pre-earthquake alleys. But I didn't care. I had been waiting a long time for this. I was going to buy myself the big, juicy hamburger and crisp, piping, golden French-fries that had been haunting my guts for weeks. And I did. Walked right into the burger joint and picked a stool in the middle of the counter, selected from the menu and ordered coffee to sip while I waited. I didn't even look around me or I would have seen the wrinkled noses and ghastly looks that the few other diners must have been exchanging. I did see the slight questioning frown and sideways glance the waitress gave me. It didn't matter. I sat there at the counter with uncaring new confidence, taking my time, hunkered over my plate, gorging on the dripping burger and sopping up catsup with the hot fries, swilling it all down with strong, fresh coffee that had no grounds in it for a change.

The End

Steve Descloux – July, 2005

Authors Notes:

(1)The plant locally known as pushki, also known as wild celery, cow parsnip or Heraclean Maximum, grows rampantly over most of southern Alaska. Very easy to identify, the mature plant has tall, tubular stalks sprouting from branching bulbous forks, the stems of which support huge, fuzzy, dark green palmate leaves, and flowers out in a canopy of tiny white flowers called an umbra. The plant produces seeds which are dried with the stalk throughout the fall and winter and scattered about the parent plant by the wind or as the stalk is snapped off by a passing creature.

It may be beneficial to know about this plant because it was an ancient food source and medicinal plant for the original people of the island, but maybe even more beneficial today would be a knowledge of the inherent danger associated with the plant. A great degree of caution would be advised if one plans to overlook the possibility of sap burns and sample some of this wild celery.

As young children living on Kodiak Island we learned from Native friends how and when to select and eat stalks of this plant. It is reported to be quite high in protein. Kodiak Bears gorge on pushki in the spring and I have heard it said that they will roll in clumps of it to soothe a bloody wound, taking unknowing advantage of its healing properties. Pushki establishes itself in the first year as a base-plant, with leaves but no stalks. The obvious stalks of the second year plant which has not flowered yet are the ones to select for eating . You cut only the sections which grow between two branch-attaching bulbs (never the base stalk or the leaf stalk) and with a knife or thumbnail, strip the celery-like strings off and consume it immediately while fresh. The green tube thus prepared is tender, crunchy and has an almost-sweet, mild flavor which, curiously, has very little essence of the strong medicinal odor of the bruised or cut plant. I prefer stalks from ½ to ¾ inch diameter as they are still tender at that size, more filling, and easier to strip than smaller stalks. I do not know how much of this plant one needs to eat to simulate a meal, but as boys, we snacked regularly on pushki and other greens and berries while on daylong hikes or expeditions or while at play around town, and seldom bothered packing a lunch. I discovered that the prepared stalks can be kept fresh for later consumption by placing them in the cold water of a crick. If you eat the wrong part or neglect to skin a stalk cleanly, the taste becomes slightly piquant and leaves a temporary unpleasant taste and mild numbing or tingling sensation in the mouth.

I would not advise anyone to try even tasting it until you learn from a studied and trusted source how to avoid burns, but I will add that if in a survival situation it is probably safest to gather and eat in the cool of morning or evening to avoid the sun. The plant produces a milky, distasteful sap which flows in the outer layer of the stalk which, if smeared or splattered onto the skin, can cause ugly chemical burns. Pushki flourishes almost everywhere and is easily bruised or broken. The sap gets on the skin and is absorbed through the pores, but apparently remains benign unless the sun shines on the affected area. Ultra-violet sun rays trigger the chemicals in the sap and it begins destroying skin tissue. No pain or itch is immediately apparent but, depending on the degree of exposure and individual sensitivity, in a day or two there will be a severe rash or extensive, pus-filled blisters accompanied by mild to severe itching, which can take weeks to heal and often leaves behind a patch of brown, discolored skin that may take a couple years to dissipate. Light skinned people are believed to be more susceptible to burns.

To further educate yourself about this northern variety of the Pushki plant on the web, search for - cow parsnip alaska.

About the Author

After graduating High School, the author served in the U.S. Navy as a jet engine mechanic during Vietnam and was assigned to a fighter training squadron of F-4 Phantoms at Naval Air Station Miramar, California. After serving his term he spent several years as a part time commercial fisherman but has worked mainly in the construction and industrial fields as a laborer, welder/fabricator, mechanic, truck driver, equipment operator and also in aviation as a small plane mechanic, air cargo agent and airline instructor. In his own words he has employed the 'tools of ignorance' in making a living, but has enjoyed the challenge of inventive thinking and physical labor often required to 'get the job done' under less than ideal conditions. Descloux has recently returned to live in Kodiak with Diane, his wife of 32 years and Chinook their Black Lab. He currently works as a maintenance engineer at a Kodiak seafood processing plant. Two Tales of 'Old Kodiak' is his first effort at published writing.

About the Illustrator

Elise Dooley, illustrator for her uncle's book, spent many years during her childhood fishing salmon with her father, Tom Dooley. She also worked early on at her aunt's set-net site on the remote west side of Kodiak Island. She learned to capture 'characters' and draw them from memory. This gave her the insight to sketch people she never knew and create the characters for this book. She is pictured here on the docks of Kodiak in her raingear, fresh from working on her father's boat Rebel, in the immediate background. Elise currently resides in Alabama.